Praise for *Tough Crowd*

'One of the very best television comedy writers of all time delivers a book
which is a must-read for anyone who has ever wondered:
a) how to create a hit sitcom and b) how it feels to lose everything.
It's funny, complicated and utterly compelling'
Jonathan Ross

'One of the most compelling and unflinchingly honest memoirs I've read
in many years. It's also the funniest'
Andrew Doyle

'Graham Linehan has long been one of my favourite writers –
and this book shows that his brilliance in prose is the equal to his brilliance
as a screenwriter. It unfolds with the urgency of a Sam Fuller film:
that of a man who has been through something that few have experienced
but has managed to return, undaunted, to tell us the tale'
Richard Ayoade

'Hilarious, raw and touching. A must-read for anyone who wants to know
the backstory behind **Father Ted** – and why he gave up the life
of a luvvie to fight the threats posed by trans ideology
to women's rights and child safeguarding'
Helen Joyce

'This book is great company, and reminds us that Graham is first and foremost
a writer, and a very funny one indeed. It is a not inconsiderable relief,
in fact, to see that he has not lost the gift'
Simon Evans

'A brilliant account of the evolution of a comedy writer,
but also an extraordinary and chilling portrayal of cancel culture.
I found it unputdownable'
Lissa Evans

TOUGH CROWD

GRAHAM LINEHAN

EYE BOOKS

Published by Eye Books Ltd
www.eye-books.com

Cover design by Ifan Bates
Front cover photo by Simon Edge
Back cover photo by the author
Typeset in Palatino LT Std and Century Gothic

British Library Cataloguing in Publication Data
A catalogue record for this book is available from the British Library

ISBN: 9781785633065

For my daughter

'The people who must never have power
are the humourless'
Christopher Hitchens

'If you're going to tell people the truth,
be funny or they'll kill you'
attributed to Billy Wilder

CONTENTS

PROLOGUE:
THE END

Some time before I lost everything, I heard laughter drifting up to my office at the top of the house, a sound I could never resist. My family were my favourite audience, and if they were already laughing, well then, even better. Normally, I'd gallop down, asking what was so funny, to join in or see if I could steal something to turn into a joke or a sketch or a scene or a show. But this time I just stood at the top of the stairs and listened. This was after the first year of relentless harassment, while I was still dissecting the workings of the trap I had walked into, and the limits of friendship that had allowed it to snap shut on my remaining testicle, the one that the cancer had somehow not stumbled upon during a recent tussle with its immediate neighbour. I didn't yet know how firmly the trap held me, but it certainly held me at the top of those stairs.

It was still early days in my exile from the dinner party circuit; work, opportunities and social engagements had only just ceased to darken my door. Sure, no one was saying anything, no one was helping – my friends were, in fact, giving me odd looks, ghosting and blanking me, not returning calls, giving my wife shit on the phone, writing nasty letters about the importance of kindness, and perhaps worst of all, sympathetically nodding while telling me why they couldn't get involved – but I still believed it was only a matter of time before these friends and colleagues from the entertainment industry would fly to my aid. The satirists, the stars, the progressives, the feminists... Those I'd made famous, and who had made me semi-famous in return. I thought they'd be along any minute.

But no one around me expressed an opinion about the issues I was desperately asking them to address: women losing their words, spaces and sports, and the systematic dismantling of basic principles of safeguarding that protect the most vulnerable. My nerves were shredded, waiting for my friends to turn up and them not turning up. So when I heard my family laughing from downstairs I knew I couldn't go down because it would all be written on my face and I'd do to the atmosphere what the internet did to privacy: kill it stone dead.

It was out of the question. It'd be like Lurch from *The Addams Family* walking into the room. So I sat down at the top of the stairs and listened to them, smiling, glad that there was still at least some happiness in the house. Maybe the dog joined me, or one of the cats. It wasn't so bad.

'A nursing home on one side and a graveyard on the other,' the lettings agent had said, forcing a laugh. 'Not ideal, I know.'

'No, no. What could be more convenient?' I said.

It's early in 2020. My modest flat, which is a few hundred yards down the road from my family, is on a corner of the building and does indeed have a nursing home to one side and a graveyard behind it. When I'm preparing food, I look out of a window at the nursing home; when I'm eating, I look at the graveyard. It's quite the rollercoaster! Every day, I lock eyes with one elderly patient propped up on pillows, staring straight back at me through his window. I waved once and got no response. He's either suffering from dementia or he knows who I am and doesn't have the strength to raise his middle finger.

In the earliest hours of the morning, the nurses at the nursing home (it would be odd to have nurses at a graveyard) gather outside to gossip and smoke. Because I've stopped watching the news, the soft trill of their conversation acts as a sort of virus-progression barometer. If I wake up to the sound of laughter, then all is well and Covid has not yet suffered the journey to Norwich, a journey which, to be fair, is a bit of a bugger, even for so-called worldwide pandemics. Norwich isn't on the way to anywhere, so not many can be bothered to make the trip.

My building is at the ancient, overgrown, neglected end of the graveyard, which is a little too symbolically on the nose for this writer's comfort. At the other end of it, the newbie dead are still rocking their Sunday best, but in my corner, squirrels cavort over the disintegrating remains of the long-gone. In the early evening, junkies dart through the staggered gravestones, like dark fish at the bottom of a rock pool, shouting over distances because one is always faster than the other. I don't know it yet but this flat is where I'll spend the next two years, my TV writing career in tatters, stunned at my inability to make people care about the daylight theft of women's rights, or the greatest safeguarding scandal since Rotherham, or the greatest medical scandal since thalidomide.

When I began talking about the issue, there were still five years to go before the resignation of Nicola Sturgeon and the closure of the Tavistock gender clinic, J.K. Rowling had not yet broken cover to take over as the number one target of trans rights activists, and terms like 'assigned at birth' and 'cervix-haver' had only just begun to turn up in NHS documents. On the rare occasions it was noticed at all, the trans issue was seen as a sideshow.

'Why are you focusing on this tiny minority?' people would say. 'Women are not a tiny minority,' I'd reply.

Kinder people than the friends I lost often say, 'I don't know how you can withstand the abuse,' but the truth is that I don't see it. I got the gist a while back and now I would no more google my name than stick my tongue into a plug socket. Besides, I'd had online abuse before, in various forms and for various reasons. I'd even had it before it went virtual, in the form of physical bullying, a phenomenon that must seem both quaint and terrifying to the emotionally tender youth of the modern middle class.

There's a story that I first heard attached to the actress and model Pia Zadora, a briefly famous starlet who won Worst Actress and Worst New Star at the Golden Raspberry awards in 1982. The legend goes that her performance in a stage production of *The Diary of Anne Frank* was so underwhelming that when the Nazis barge in at the end of play and demand 'Where is she? Where is Anne Frank?' an audience member shouted, 'She's in the attic!' But Zadora was never in a stage version of *Anne Frank* – the story was applied to each fresh female actor who had somehow brought the public's withering gaze upon her head. It's a joke, really, a combination of gossip and joke, with a scorned and discounted woman providing the punchline. And yet, for all that, it's funny. An audience member turning you in; it's the worst possible review, and the best example of the term, often said with a shrug by comedians consoling or warning one another about a difficult gig: 'Tough crowd.'

There was certainly no shortage of people shouting, 'He's in the attic!' I was astonished at the pain of each fresh betrayal. I couldn't seem to get used to the experience. When the internet turns on you, as it had the moment I entered into the debate around women's rights, it isn't pretty, but I thought I had a couple of advantages. I had an audience that I had already won over by co-writing some well-loved sitcoms, *Father Ted* being by far the most famous, but also *The IT Crowd*, *Black Books* and *Count Arthur Strong*, and more importantly I had smart, compassionate, progressive friends within the industry who would soon be swooping in to add their voices to mine.

Unfortunately, the fight against gender ideology wasn't funny, and when I wasn't being funny, the public took the opportunity to tune me out. Sitcom writers are not particularly noticed at the best of times, but I never thought I'd become so imperceptible that friends and even family members failed to notice what I was going through. I was targeted by a convicted criminal who had the police in his pocket, and a media eager to find some dirt on me, and it was at that precise moment that all my showbusiness friends simultaneously lost my phone number. One day, I looked at my sunken eyes in the mirror and realised I was becoming one of those depressing BBC docudramas about comedians catching cancer or falling off the wagon or whatever. The big difference with my story was that over the last five years, cancer of the testicles had been the most positive thing that had happened to me.

There is no definitive moment that I became perceived as toxic. But there's no doubt about the sheer scale of the media machine that made it happen. If anyone edits my Wikipedia page to say 'campaigner for women's rights' rather than 'anti-transgender activist', the edit reverts back within fifteen minutes. Gender-goofy newspapers like *The Guardian* and *The Independent* only interview colleagues of mine in the hope they can get them to condemn me, which many are delighted to do. The LGBTQ+ website *Pink News* has to date written more than seventy-five hit pieces on me, all of them designed to paint my perfectly commonplace beliefs as evidence of bigotry and madness.

But that's *Pink News*. I expected a little more digging, a little more discernment from those who knew me well. Unfortunately, friends, colleagues and family members alike decided to treat malicious gossip as gospel. In those early days, I didn't yet know what a ringing disappointment people would turn out to be. There was a spring in my step, and not just because I was lighter by a testicle that had, overnight, grown until it weighed as much as a Rolex. I thought I could offer something to the endlessly febrile debate, perhaps bring some clarity and humour to the increasingly angry exchanges. The beliefs of the other side were so insane that I thought my friends would quickly realise how crazy it all was and start lending a hand.

My first writing partner, Arthur Mathews, and I once wrote a sketch that neatly sums up my situation at this time. An English Civil War captain, played by Simon Pegg, is leading his men into battle. He tells them: 'Beyond those trees lies our enemy, five thousand men, maybe more! But it is important we keep our heads. Now listen carefully, for this is the most important thing I will ever tell you, and I shall not say it again!'

At this point he mumbles something unintelligible and yells: 'CHARGE!'

Having had no time to absorb either his speech or the situation, the soldiers watch him run towards the enemy lines, where he is instantly shot and killed.

The End.

1
WAITING FOR THE INTERNET

DURING THE DECADES in which I grew up, the internet was dispersed among a great number of physical locations and then further dispersed among the items one browsed in these specialist sites. For instance, if you wanted to read something, you visited a 'bookshop', if you wanted to listen to music, you visited a 'record shop', and so on. The world was not delivered to our doorstep, was not yet compressible into a space smaller than a fingernail. We had to schlep everywhere to enter the distracted bliss that now charges by the side of our beds.

I spent my childhood exploring minutely every record, book and comic shop on my way home from school – anything that might alleviate the grinding boredom that came with being alive in Ireland before broadband. So unconsciously impatient was I for laptops and game consoles and social media and all the rest of it that I remember standing at a Speak & Spell in an early electronics shop, refusing to accept defeat as I pounded a series of unsuccessful answers into it. Something in me sensed it was the future, even as it repeated words through a voice synthesiser seemingly made of rubber bands.

Spell 'orange'.

O-R-A-N-G-E.

That is incorrect. Spell 'orange'.

O-R-A-N-G-E.

That is incorrect. Spell 'orange'.

I thought, hang on a sec. Is it saying 'porridge'?

P-O-R-R-I-D-G-E.

That is incorrect. Spell 'orange'.

O-R-A-N-G-E.

No. The correct answer is D-R-A-W-B-R-I-D-G-E.

After this, endless hours flipping through books in Easons, comics in The Alchemist's Head and albums in Freedbird, Comet and Golden Discs, always pausing for maybe a little bit too long at the Scorpions cover that showed a woman with chewing gum stuck to her boob. That was the 'internet'.

When I wasn't scouring the pre-internet internet for distraction, I observed and stored for later use how adults made their own entertainment. One day, my mum's sisters came over and got roaringly drunk on vodka and tonic, a lanky bottle of Smirnoff demolished over the course of an hour, with ensuing rowdy gossip, heated accusations and screaming laughter. My dad couldn't believe the family he'd married into. 'They've drunk the whole thing,' he said, sneaking up to Mum during a pause in the mayhem and marvelling at the bottle's sudden weightlessness. My aunts finally staggered from the house like puppies released from a greyhound trap, 'talking absolute nonsense', as my mum put it. Later, my parents discovered that, weeks before the invasion of sozzled aunts, my younger brother John and his teenage friends had themselves drunk the vodka and replaced its contents in a panic. So my mum's sisters had managed somehow to get hammered by pounding down multiple glasses of tonic and tap water.

Excess forms the basis of my earliest memory: me and a gang of toddler hooligans devouring every last scrap of jam from the jar at some sort of home nursery. The childminder had taken the fatal decision to leave us alone for half a second, so we stomped into the kitchen like the Seven Dwarves and had our pre-school way with the contents of her fridge. A better-behaved child screamed at us in pure terror: 'You're not supposed to eat the jam from the jar!' Every toddler fears getting in trouble more than they fear death, and the trouble that ensued made such an impression on me that decades later I gave that line to Dougal, the childishly innocent junior priest in *Father Ted*. The only other clear memory from my early childhood is seeing The Wombles live. The Wombles were a gang of pre-internet furries who cleaned up litter. 'Remember you're a Womble,' they sang, as if anyone could forget such a condition.

I soon found myself in a boys' school run by priests from the Society of Mary, otherwise known as the Marist Fathers. Nothing untoward to report; they weren't that sort of priest. I was far more frightened of my fellow pupils. The friends I found, fellow wimps, nerds and awkward types, had all come to settle in each other's company like marbles in a wine glass, together partly because no one else would have us. Grateful not to be the target for once, I even took part in the derision aimed at one boy who would later become my best friend. The call of the herd was never easy to resist, even before the internet boosted its signal.

I was bullied because I was tall and too frightened of my own anger to fight back. After a motorbike accident, my cousin Jim spent the rest of his short life being cared for by my aunt Stella and my cousins – his sisters, Ann and Mary. It was the family's great tragedy and also affected my mother, who had given birth to my brother John six weeks before the accident. She suddenly saw life-altering violence as something that could appear unexpectedly and out of nowhere, as it had for Jim. I absorbed her fear and this left me wide open to bullies who, unlike me, didn't see every thrown punch as having the potential to send someone on a one-way trip to an industrial-grey wheelchair in their sitting room.

To escape reality, I entered into various fantasy worlds like a million other bullied kids who saw *Star Wars* at the right age. I won't go on too long about *Star Wars* except to say 'dirty spaceships'. That's what did it for me. I'd never seen scratched and dirty spaceships before then. None of us had. At one point Dad casually pointed out Tatooine's twin moons and I gasped. *Oh, yes!* I remembered. *It's set in space!* Another example of world-building I've always loved was the Sandmen riding in single file 'to hide their numbers'. These brush strokes were the real reason we loved it so. Tropes from Westerns and war movies ingeniously repurposed, with *The Empire Strikes Back* inserting Wagnerian fire and awe into the formula. To a child who thought that *Scooby Doo* was as good as things got, it was immersive on a near-psychedelic level, the nine-year-old's equivalent of taking dimethyltryptamine. When my father asked for my thoughts as we left the cinema, I said, quite earnestly, 'It changed my life.' My dad roared with laughter.

If I'd realised then that hyperbole often left one with nowhere to go, I might have made a better critic. And yet it was true. Instantly, I became a science fiction fan. The books from SF's first and second golden ages imagined futures that would never arrive and their authors wrote them in a world that still contained beatniks and the Ku Klux Klan. Some of them were completely impenetrable as a result. You kiss a lot of frogs as a science fiction fan, but I found a few favourites, often those who put character and humour first. Kurt Vonnegut, Alfred Bester, Philip K. Dick, John Sladek, Harry Harrison... I gravitated towards pyrotechnics of some sort, humorous, imaginative or violent.

The British weekly comic *2000 AD* was a dizzying combination of all three and its arrival came as an unwelcome shock to my poor dad, who had successfully banned from our household its ultra-violent predecessor *Action* a few years earlier. He was delighted when the controversy around the title forced it out of the market. (The tabloids called it 'the sevenpenny nightmare' – which makes me feel a hundred years old.) But the team merely rebranded as *2000 AD*, killer robots taking the place of football hooligans, and continued as if nothing had happened. Both comics were a blast. Not a Paddy joke to be seen in the letters pages, and the creators were obviously telling the stories they longed to read themselves. Part of its genius was its title, a date which seemed to me impossibly far away, and does again, now.

In Dublin in the eighties, the pornography section of the internet was located in the top rack of magazines in Easons. *Playboy* and its

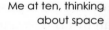

Me at ten, thinking about space

competitors were banned, but some loophole allowed magazines about 'glamour photography' and a naturist magazine called *Health and Efficiency*, or *H&E*. This latter title played the nasty trick of always having a very pretty nude woman on the cover, while inside it was actually about naturism. I found this out to my horror when once I slotted myself in between a pair of glamour photographers and leveraged a suddenly useful height advantage to snatch a copy of the magazine into my trembling hands. Finally, I would see What It Was All About.

To my dismay, the first and only thing I saw within was an old man holding hands with his grandson, both naked. They were both looking straight at the camera. The grandad had a white beard and white hair, and his penis was also surrounded by white hair, so for a moment it looked like there were three people looking at me: one bearded man, one child, and one very small, bearded child. To go from thinking myself unobserved to having three people looking at me was such a terrible shock that I never opened the magazine again. I can still see them sometimes. Their faces are burned into my retina like I killed them in Vietnam.

The hardcore pornography section of the pre-internet internet was beneath a loose floorboard in a small abandoned house at the end of our road. I realise this sounds a little too neat to be true but what can I tell you? That's where it was. A small, thick booklet, written in German, illustrated with photos of men and women presumably up to no good. I say 'presumably' because although we knew it was somehow sexual – why else had the book been hidden? – we weren't sure exactly how. People in crowded rooms, some in masks or bound in ropes, others on their hands and knees as if looking for a contact lens... It was like an escapologists' convention after a free bar. Also missing were any boobs. It was all faintly unpleasant and didn't converge with our developing sexualities. Perhaps I'm wrong and some of my friends went on to become aroused at knots. Little did we know that hole under the floorboards would become one of the few places where you *can't* find grimly alienating pornography. These days, the porn finds you.

My absorption in fantasy worlds and their makers was total. I became fascinated by author Harlan Ellison especially. A legendary figure among SF fans, Ellison was a pugnacious brawler in the Norman Mailer style, scandal and gossip following him like tiny dogs follow romance authors. But he was a humanist above all and his outrage at the murder of a barmaid called Kitty Genovese made a great impression on me. On 13 March 1964, Genovese, who was twenty-eight, was stabbed to death in the courtyard of a New York apartment building, reportedly within earshot of three dozen witnesses who did nothing to help. Ellison famously called these witnesses 'thirty-six motherfuckers' and railed about their cowardice in an essay. When I caught up with it sixteen years or so later in a collection of his journalism, I raged along with him. But the truth of the matter was not as clear as Ellison made out – some people did indeed try to help Genovese – and his intervention could be read as an early example of a celebrity jumping to conclusions before all the facts were in. But I admired the clarity of his moral vision, and how he had zeroed in on a single point which seemed like simple common sense to me, especially as it seemed no different from what my dad had always taught me: when a woman cries for help, you help.

Ellison's fiction was as dark as the space between stars, but I rejected science fiction's endless dystopias except as entertainment. For me, the future was bright. After all, technology – in the form of computer games, my record player, and even the technology required to hold together the pages of a book – was the only thing plucking me out of regular old 'meatspace', as esoteric nerds sometimes call that part of existence that persists outside our screens.

I was staring at screens before it became fashionable. While still in school shorts, I would save money by skipping the first bus – the one that ferried me from my school slightly further into town before another took me on the nightmare journey out of it to my home in suburban Castleknock – and I'd use the spare coins to jolt awake a few games in an arcade. An entire cabinet housed each title – *Defender*, *Galaxian*, *Space Invaders*, *APB*, *Narc*, *Joust*. Compared to today's games, these titles were laughably basic. But I'd have continued feeding them coins had they just been wooden boxes illuminated by lightbulbs, which I guess is exactly what they were.

While still a good Catholic boy, I would see books in Easons with titles like *The Exorcist* and *Rosemary's Baby* and *Let's Go Play at the Adams'* and think of their authors, 'All these people are going to hell.' I suspected the success of these evil books indicated

'Bishops love sci-fi, Ted!' My confirmation, with Mum and Dad

some sort of deal with the devil, perhaps only undertaken at an unconscious level. You did evil things, like write an evil book, and you were rewarded. Maybe you didn't even start with evil books. Maybe you started smaller, so to speak, and things got out of hand. Masturbation was bait, resting on Satan's mousetrap. If I didn't stop doing it, I was going to become a bad person, write evil things, make a lot of money, and end up in hell. What kind of demonic freak was I, that I could enjoy thoughts of SEX? Every time I fell to the temptation of treating my genitals as if I was trying to get a tune out of them, I'd spend a good half hour apologising to Our Lord afterwards.

But that ended the day the more respectable pre-internet internet arrived at my home. It took the form of an actual, real-life encyclopedia salesman. My mum still has the proof in the form of a set of the *World Book Encyclopedia* in brown not-leather in a little cabinet into which the volumes fit snugly. (I wonder what great deal he gave them on that item.) The *World Book* was our family's Wikipedia. Except, unlike Wikipedia, its authors had to get it right, because it was a book.

My dad once told me that his friends at school considered him a bit of a 'holy Joe' and it says much about that lovely, gentle man that his contemporaries felt this way about him in 1950s Ireland. I joined him in his fear and awe at the majesty of God's love. He used to take me on long, aimless drives in which I suspect he had every intention of telling me the facts of life, but he just couldn't bring himself to spill the beans. The only thing I remember was when he pulled the car over after twenty minutes of frustrated silence and said: 'Look...you know James Bond?'

'Yeah?'

Long, long pause.

'Don't be like him.'

We stared at each other for a few moments.

'OK,' I finally said. It was at best a hypothetical scenario.

And yet, my devout dad, who thought there was a danger that I with my lopsided head would one day go on to conquer the beaches of Monte Carlo, shook hands with the encyclopaedia salesman and paid him to plant the tree of knowledge in our house. One day, trembling with Catholic terror and tormented by persistent thoughts of becoming a glamour photographer, inspiration struck me and I looked up 'masturbation' in the *World Book Parents Guide*, which accompanied the set. The entry read 'Masturbation: Perfectly normal. Nothing to worry about,' and in that instant I stopped believing in God.

I had bitten the apple, and realised I was 'completely normal' and 'nothing to worry about'. Along with the relief came resentment at everything religious faith had put me through. I felt as if I had been the victim of a hoax that was centuries in the making. There was no point, it seemed to me, in waiting for a reward that might never come. What a confidence trick to spend your life on your knees for non-sexual reasons, perhaps never realising that it was the only life you had! Impossible, absurd, I wasn't going to stand for it. I met the Devil on the crossroads and he gave me a typewriter (Dad in his innocence, grabbed it from work for my birthday). I used it to start writing short stories. I was going to become a bad person, write evil things, make a lot of money and maybe end up in hell, but definitely continue masturbating.

2

IN PRAISE OF OLDER MEN

THE CELLAR AT THE International Bar in 1989 was a dive in the truest sense of the word. We were subterranean creatures: writers and staff of Ireland's only music magazine, *Hot Press*, in the corner booth, a handful of committed regulars hunched over the bar. I'm sure the women who joined us would rather have been upstairs, perhaps enjoying the last bit of light of a summer's day, rather than downstairs with all the cigarette smoke that, unlike us, had nowhere else to go.

When the smoking ban came into force ten or so years later, everyone suddenly realised that for decades the curtains of cigarette smoke hanging heavily in every pub had been camouflaging the stench of urinal cake and of the things the urinal cake was camouflaging. In the cellar of the International, smoking was partly a form of olfactory ju-jitsu. The men's toilets were right there, behind a thin door. Every time it opened and shut, it was like an old lion coughing in your face. I didn't notice. I was puffing away like everyone else and too enraptured with the entirely novel experience of intelligent, funny adults listening to me and enjoying my company.

A big fortnightly broadsheet, *Hot Press* was Ireland's answer to the UK's *New Musical Express* and *Melody Maker*. I say 'was', but any remaining British music weekly 'inkies' (named after the cheap newsprint that left dark grey smears on your fingertips) are shadows of their former selves, while *Hot Press* is still going strong. I was twenty-one years old and the writers and staff at *Hot Press* were mostly about ten years my senior. They liked my work, and would quote funny lines of mine back to me. This was so dizzying that I would take the 39 bus into town every time I thought I might catch some of them in the office, or hitch a ride with my tortured, generous and loyal best friend, Ken.

Only a year or two before this, while I was still at school, the PE teacher had noticed I was dodging rugby through the operation of various ingenious, P.G. Wodehouse-style schemes. Somehow, at a school where it was mandatory to play rugby for my entire childhood, I managed to make it to my later teens without ever so much as learning the rules. Nonetheless, I soon found myself forced into playing an actual match with real opponents from another school. At one point the referee bumped into me and apologised. This small yet unprecedented show of courtesy from an adult was so intoxicating to me as a lonely teenager that I tried to hover near him for the whole match so he'd do it again. Basic politeness at that stage of my life was hard to come by, so I followed it all over the pitch.

Suddenly, I didn't have to follow rugby referees around for companionship because I was now surrounded by writers like Damian Corless, Declan Lynch, Bill Graham, Cathy Dillon, Liam Mackey and George Byrne, none of whom ever made me feel small or unwelcome. They cleaned it up for the page (Ireland's defamation laws are some of the toughest in the world) but in person they were scabrous and gossipy. Waves of laughter lapped up the cellar stairs with the smoke. There was never anything too serious going on, apart from a thwarted attempt to form an office union. I was told later the words 'But we're a family!' were used, perhaps for the first time in history, but certainly not the last.

We particularly enjoyed meeting anyone coming back from the shattering experience of interviewing Van Morrison. Niall Stokes, the editor, an affable Irish version of the classic hippy entrepreneur, right down to the brown-tinted shades and ponytail, would send unfortunate journalists to do the occasional profile of the great man and it never turned out well. Van's temper and irascibility were legendary. A story goes that he was once midway through a celestial guitar solo in front of a spellbound stadium crowd when a long-suffering roadie noticed something wrong with the drum riser. The roadie attended to it, ninja-like, but on his return, his foot caught in Van's guitar lead and it popped out of the amp. Van the Man was suddenly playing a silent guitar to a puzzled stadium crowd. Legend has it that the roadie saw that this had happened, continued running, hopped down off the stage, and just went home.

A series of lucky accidents had brought me into contact with *Hot Press*, the International pub and the man who altered the course of my life, Arthur Mathews. After school was done with me, I was ineligible for admission to the leading universities since Stephen King novels were not yet on the syllabus, so I applied for a communications course in an 'off-Broadway' college. As I was waiting for my interview with my file of terrible short stories and what I hoped was a clear commitment to becoming either a writer or a glamour photographer, another young man sitting next to me leaned over and said, 'Can I ask you a question?'

'Yes?' I said.

'What's communications?'

I told him. And we both got in.

A few months into the first term, I learned that a member of the *Hot Press* team, the aforementioned Damian Corless, did weekly classes for the journalism students in the same building. I collared him one day and lied by telling him I had a number of film and music reviews written up. He encouraged me to bring them in, so I raced home and wrote them. I think I wrote three and they published two of them later that week. Seeing my name in print was intoxicating – so much so that I immediately left the communications course, thinking I'd hit the big time. From that day on, I found it difficult to write anything I wasn't being paid to write. No more short stories from me! I had written about five at this point, carefully crafting each of them so they would be far harder to read than they were to write.

Soon I became *Hot Press*'s regular film critic, seeing new releases every few mornings in deserted Dublin cinemas. Film criticism was my dream job until I had it. Before long, I realised that ninety-five percent of films were dreadful, and I was reviewing them at a time when Hollywood was not in the rudest of health. It was the late eighties and films about rivalries between fighter pilots did not set me alight as did *Taxi Driver* and *The Deer Hunter* from the previous decade. It's such an odd thing, but movies of the seventies don't seem to age, whereas movies from every decade since seem to date faster than bananas.

Whenever I watch films from the seventies I feel like I'm still standing on the cusp of adulthood. Those films were what made me fall in love with the cinema. There are few moments more powerful than the tiny drops of red wine falling onto the bridal gown in *Deer Hunter* – unseen by the wedding guests, but not by the audience – condemning the young, happy couple to almost unimaginable bad luck. By the late eighties, when I was trying to write about them, such moments were vanishingly rare. Have you seen *Weekend at Bernie's*? I have. And *Weekend at Bernie's II*. My exhaustion was apparent in my shortest review, which was just the single word: 'Shit.'

On the plus side, at far too young an age to be taken seriously, I interviewed some of my heroes: Peter Greenaway, John Cleese, Paul Schrader… Only Schrader treated me with the contempt we both felt I deserved. Everyone else was lovely. Maybe sometimes too lovely. At eighteen, I was still fairly innocent, so I thought nothing of it when one interviewee asked me to his hotel room, left the room to take a shower and then returned casually towelling his Christmas decorations. 'I know you're cool with stuff like this,' he said.

I guess I was being 'me-tooed'. It was like *H&E* magazine all over again!

At this time, U2 were right at the apex of their fame – this was their Joshua Tree era – and they triggered a gold rush in Ireland's music scene, producing countless Next Big Things who announced their arrival on the scene with a free bar. There were only a handful of worthwhile bands about the place. The Would Be's and A House were my favourites, the latter one of the most exciting live acts around, singer Dave Couse the only person I knew who could make you pogo by playing an acoustic guitar. Guernica sounded like a slower, glummer Joy Division – they were, after all, called Guernica – and their lead singer, Joe Rooney, would later go on to stand-up comedy and a part in *Ted* as Father Damo, Father Dougal's rebellious friend who prefers Oasis to Blur. There was also a band who had the genius idea of calling themselves Free Beer because it meant people would always turn up to their gigs.

Arthur Mathews was one half of the *Hot Press* art department with Paul Woodfull, or as we knew him, Paul Wonderful. If there was a typo in the magazine that needed correcting, they had to retype that word, print it out, cut around it with scissors and then stick the tiny piece of paper to the magazine with their actual hands. Can you imagine such a thing? As a result, the weekend before publication was a grindingly laborious nightmare for anyone unlucky enough to be pulling the shift. I was the only one there by choice, because Paul and Arthur would carry on a sort of running comedy routine all night. The *Hot Press* writers were all genuinely witty people, but Paul and Arthur were on another level.

Their Taekwondo sketch was my favourite. Two rough Dublin blokes in charge of a self-defence class, nailing a type of martial arts mysticism that Danny McBride zoned in on decades later in his brilliant low-budget comedy *The Foot Fist Way*.

'*Taekwondo* comes from two words,' Paul would explain pompously in his tough-as-nails Dublin accent. '*Tae* meaning "head" or "intellect" and *kwondo* meaning "to batter".'

A traditional *Hot Press* Christmas treat was 'The Border Fascist', a fake rural newspaper over a two-page spread, written almost entirely by Arthur, full of brilliant made-up news stories and ads. A headline like 'Local Man Declares War On China' would cover the clearly pointless and futile expedition – the man sets out, in my memory, by bus – with great sympathy and enthusiasm, ending with the words 'We at the Border Fascist wish him the best of luck in his exciting venture'.

'His exciting venture.' A comedy of understatement but given further character and charm through Arthur's deep affinity with the voices of his childhood. Arthur was a Louth boy with a funny bone located somewhere between the flat, surreal hilarity of the *Viz* letters pages and the withering contempt of a John Lydon interview. His comic personality was forged in the punk wars, so he had a deadly eye for human weakness to go along with the tea and biscuits. Arthur never said a thing out loud that wasn't funny. He chose his words carefully when speaking but writing a comic idea, he'd rattle out three pages while I was still taking off my coat. I realised quickly that he had the spark of the divine in him. I know I treated him like he was sent from God, which must have been annoying.

He had an ease with his creative side that was inspiring and somewhat frightening. He had no fear of the empty page, because he could fill it up so quickly. On the other hand, I had just spent three years reverse-engineering every film and comedy show I had seen and delivering judgement on them like a twenty-one-year-old tyrant, so I was more self-conscious as a result, seeing the creative process from the other end of the telescope, as a member of the audience. I knew it had to be perfect and I knew that ninety-nine percent perfect wasn't good enough. If something is very good, or very funny, or very nearly makes sense, I know what to do to bring it over the line and make it ring, so it was rewriting that gave me most pleasure. But to rewrite, something had to be written in the first place, and it was that part of the process I hated. Arthur had the good fortune to be inspired by the empty page, and I was inspired by Arthur.

Creatively, I've always been a magpie. My creative process is like my dad's golf swing, which was composed of a number of stages as he applied every tip he had picked up from the great golf coach Harvey Penick's *Little Red Book* in sequence. Dad had a swing like a clockwork toy as a result, a thousand things coming together in one halting yet fluid movement that over and over again put a tiny dimpled ball near the quiet spot he wanted it to go. I too am a creature of my influences. I saw in Arthur's instinctive understanding of Irish manners a way I could also indulge my love of innovative comedy like *The Simpsons* (younger readers may not believe it but for many years, *The Simpsons* was unmissable) and it was a successful partnership partly for that reason. I was made of *Mad Magazine*, Matt Groening's *Life in Hell*, *The Young Ones*, Woody Allen, Gary Larson's *Far Side* cartoons and a million other influences, none of them Irish. Arthur's comic sense was forged in the punk wars; I found mine by picking through the postmodern rubble they left behind.

Woody Allen said the only kind of love that lasts is unrequited love and it always makes me think of Arthur. It is not an exaggeration to say that I worshipped the man. Once, a gang of us were going out for lunch and he deliberately fell down the stairs to make us laugh. The thing that killed me was the confused look on his face as he fell. He pretended to be annoyed and disoriented at something we had all seen him decide to do. It was punk rock in that gonzo New York Ramones style. Blank generation, Richard Hell and the Voidoids. In comedy, I'd only previously seen that kind of purposeful chaos from Steve Martin, and now here was someone I actually knew who could make me laugh like I was at the movies.

Hot Press let me write the way I wanted, and as a result I was becoming a minor celebrity in Dublin. I even started meeting women, which I guess counts as this book's first major 'twist'. I think enough time has passed for me to say this now without getting anyone in any trouble, but when I started to make a name for myself at *Hot Press*, I had sex on the floor of the Dublin branch of Forbidden Planet. That's right, I had sex with an actual woman in a comics shop – something that would get me crowned King of the Nerds if it also didn't also disqualify me from the demographic. Sadly, it wasn't as romantic as it sounds, as the floor was covered in some sort of angry corrugated fibre made for foot traffic. It was anti-sex carpeting. Anti-sex carpeting in a comics shop! The least likely place for anyone to have sex *in the world*!

Despite my sudden and unexpected popularity among a category of human I hadn't spoken to throughout my teenage years, my heart belonged to Arthur. Most of my time was spent trying to elicit laughter from him, which was fast becoming my favourite sound. Arthur and Paul formed a U2 parody act called the Joshua Trio, with me stepping in as a sort of comedy roadie. I helped write sketches that recreated key moments from U2's career, such as drummer Larry Mullen's arrest for possession and God's appearance to Bono in the desert (we took some liberties with the real story).

Paul Wonderful was quiet-voiced and shy in person but in front of an audience he lost his inhibitions and forever contrived of ways to take off the little clothing in which he had arrived on stage. Playing Bono as Jesus after the forty days, with a ragged, dirty shawl thrown about him, he once arrived on a small pub stage riding a donkey that he hadn't told the proprietor would be part of the act. He also brought us to see the Christian Rock outing Up With People while dressed in his stage clothes, so to anyone who didn't know he was Bono, which was everyone, he just looked like he was dressed as Jesus.

Up with People was essentially an evening of American Evangelical propaganda/messaging/celebrating, depending on how far from us you were seated. Paul's appearance scandalised the audience of parents and teachers who, dragging their bemused children behind them, parted before us like the Red Sea to reveal our seats. I don't remember much about the gig except one song was called 'What Colour Is God's Skin?', a question answered in the chorus by 'It's black, brown, it's yellow, and it's red and it's white. Everyone's the same in the Good Lord's sight!' Yellow? Red? Who's that then!?

Paul was one of the first to take rock songs and give them jazz or folk arrangements as a way of taking them down a peg or two. This was partly out of frustration at U2's ubiquity in Ireland and Bono's quasi-religious between-song patter. 'Three chords and the truth' was an example of one of the great man's aphorisms that Paul delighted in mocking. It was affectionate, though, and there was a rumour Larry was seen at one of the Trio's gigs.

This weekly gig at the Baggot Inn was where I began to learn how to craft comedy for an audience. I even gave stand-up comedy a go, but I was no prodigy, and felt much more comfortable handing the jokes over to someone else. I may have intuited early on that stand-up is not a job for sensitive types with a lot of stored-up anger from being bullied at school. Even if you're only doing jokes about how cats are like women and dogs are like men, you reveal a lot about yourself when you take a stage. You can't help it. The very decision to do it says something about you, and that might not be something you're ready to know. But I loved writing jokes. There are so many impediments to a joke landing that every laugh feels like a triumph. When I would later ask Arthur to join me in London to write comedy, my confidence was still riding high from the memory of those nights with the Trio. Without even realising it, I was already moving away from music journalism. I'd become dangerously accustomed to the music people make when they find something funny.

3

THE GOLDEN ASS

I'M A POKER PLAYER and a vital part of the poker skillset is to stay alert to the whims of Lady Luck. I've always lived by advice on the game I read in a David Mamet essay: 'Opportunity knocks, but it doesn't pester.' When I got the offer to write for a new music magazine in London, I leapt at it, feeling that, having achieved a kind of microfame among about a thousand people as *Hot Press*'s boy wonder, I could set my sights on a bigger game. I was filled with the kind of bravado I would come to recognise as that which precedes a truly terrible bluff.

In the old days, all the stuff that's now on the internet, there was nowhere for it to go, so it used to end up in what we called 'magazines'. You can still see them in shops at the airport. Magazines were the only way you could see colour photographs of famous people; they were the only way you could read reviews of very expensive CDs (because it was nearly 1990) on which you had to be certain you wanted to spend money. My time as a journalist coincided with the birth of the loathsome practice of awarding works of art marks out of five or ten or whatever, an early surrender to the demands of the attention economy. If they hadn't turned their review sections into something more like consumer guides for washing machines, people might still be reading the music weeklies now.

It was always nice to get the singles review page in *Hot Press*. Tiny capsule reviews filled with snark and certainty; it was like having your own little fanzine in the middle of the issue. It allowed me or forced me to have strong opinions, and expound on a number of themes while developing a comic voice. Writing the singles review page probably more than anything prepared me for the demands of social media.

Unfortunately, it didn't prepare me for writing for *Select*. My journalism career in the UK sort of began and ended at the same moment. David Cavanagh, *Select* magazine's affable and cantankerous Irish deputy editor, knew my writing in *Hot Press* and wanted me to be part of the magazine's launch. On that first day at the very end of the eighties, we freelancers were each handed a memo that described *Select*'s 'house style'. London was still the city of low-ish rent and high opportunity, which would lead to something of a creative boom, and *Select* went on to be a small part of the machinery behind what people started calling 'Britpop'. That launch day, I stared at the memo for quite a while, unable to get past one rule in particular.

NO USE OF THE WORD 'I'.

And that, I felt, was that.

Like some kind of oldey-days good-time Susie, my arse is my fortune. In a chair, I tend to thrive. It's another reason I like poker. Poker requires of the player a unique set of skills that include: managing one's irritability and annoyance, which is not my strong point; quieting one's mind and ego to make rational decisions, which I'm working on; an understanding of the maths behind pot odds and hand ranges, which I don't actually hold out any hope of ever acquiring; and finally an ability to sit for hours and hours on my big fat behind. At this, I excel, and it's something I can often perform upon demand.

When I was seventeen, I got a two-week warehouse job that was like a task in a Greek myth. My dad thought it would toughen me up, but it only succeeded in hardening me fatally against manual labour. I had nothing to say to my workmates, whose idea of fun was to drive at top speed with one of them sitting on the car's bonnet, looking back at us through the windscreen and laughing like the breakout performance in a Shane Meadows film. Once they locked me in the back of a truck with one of the women who worked in the nearby prefab office, presumably expecting us to mate. We declined as, apart from anything else, there was really no guarantee how long the door would remain closed.

All this was more evidence, pre-*Hot Press*, that the adult world was not going to be much of an improvement on school. The sole unexpected perk was bombing the forklift truck around the warehouse, out into the car park and back inside again. I would careen about, having a whale of a time. If I happened unexpectedly upon a colleague I would scowl with purpose until I was again out of sight and able to resume an expression of pure abandon.

These moments of being seated were fleeting, however. Everything else about the job was hellish, unrewarding, arduous and dirty. I remember particularly an occasion where I had to lift about two hundred thousand billion tins of paint. It was an appalling breach of my human rights. I lay in the bath afterwards and the filth from the dust on the tins separated from my body and drifted to the surface of the water in one piece like a shroud. Before I could leave the bath, I had to gently push it out of the way in case I got dirty again just by standing up. I had to get up so early it was like the scene in *Father Ted* when Ted turns the light on and off and

Dougal starts getting dressed because he thinks he's been to sleep.

The crime writer George V. Higgins has a character say of a dislikable fellow, 'I met him once, I was completely satisfied.' That's how I feel about manual labour; I met it once, I was completely satisfied. This satisfaction extends to many other physical activities enjoyed by our species, which, as you can imagine, makes me a joy to be around. I pretend to understand why people like to 'do things', such as climbing hills or manning a yacht or going for a 'nice walk', but I've never entirely grasped it. One of the great things about being a music critic was having the ability to say, 'Ohhhh, a walk sounds great, but I have to stay home, sit around on my big fat arse and listen to music.'

The first music review I ever read was of the June Brides in the *NME* when I was about sixteen years old. I was seduced, not by the music itself, which I hadn't yet heard, but with a style of journalism that seemed to burn through the page, or fly off it. As all art aspires to the condition of music, all young men aspire to the condition of musicians, but those of us who couldn't carry a tune had to try to hammer something out in prose instead. I was dazzled by the firework displays in the inkies and wanted to explode alongside them.

I realised much later – in fact, just now, as I write this chapter – that the fireworks were simply the product of an intensely competitive journalism scene, where everyone was doing their best to stand out from their peers. If you were extravagant about a band, the hype you yourself created could earn you a front cover. That sounds cynical, but it was in fact a good system because financial necessity forced writers to search out what made them special. Some were acidly funny, some showed off their English degrees, or their working-class credentials, or their joy at using exclamation marks. It was a lively mix as a result. But I learned a few habits from the inkies that wouldn't be any help in *Select*.

Hyperbole needs to be kept in check or people won't believe it when you do happen upon a gem. When I saw the late Jeff Buckley perform a bone-chillingly beautiful set at Glastonbury, the *Select* editor docked a star from my review because, well, who the hell was Jeff Buckley? I couldn't answer with, 'well, he's a godlike musical genius', because that's what I always said.

But I certainly knew I couldn't write without using the word 'I'. Since the age of fifteen, I'd loved writers and journalists who put themselves at the centre of their work – from Woody Allen to Robert Benchley, from P.J. O'Rourke to the legendary rock critic Lester Bangs – and my humour depended on being able to make fun of myself. Without the word 'I', I had nothing. It was the central plank of what I might reasonably have been allowed to call my 'style'.

For me, music writing was only interesting when it felt like the music being written about, and that meant putting your subjective experience centre-stage. I also thought it was more honest than pretending music had some sort of standardised value that we were all able to objectively quantify. I could only go by what the music meant to me. Dave Cavanagh hadn't told me that he actually wanted me to be a *journalist* journalist. I realise now he was paying me a huge compliment in thinking I could adapt, but at the time the *Select* style felt like a saddle and I was never comfortable wearing it.

Another problem was that I was suddenly surrounded by people who liked The Pixies as much as I did. There was a jockeying to review albums that would have languished on the *Hot Press* office shelves for years had I not moseyed in. Consequently, I was often writing about bands in which I had no interest, and it showed. The young gunslinger at *Hot Press* didn't quite make it over to the UK. In his place, someone gaining a small degree of aptitude in 'real' journalism, while losing the qualities that had brought him to London in the first place. I tried to sneak in jokes where I could and eventually I was able to carve out a space for myself, but something felt off.

I supplemented my meagre pay by selling the free albums we received by the dozen every week, keeping the ones I liked, obviously. Once I had to sell an electric typewriter that I had stupidly bought without testing. The keyboard was so sensitive that a cough could produce a hundred words. I was accustomed to writing on the mechanical typewriter – grey as a battleship, its dreadnought weight pinning it to the table – that my dad lifted from work and gave me for my sixteenth birthday. (Even now, because of it, I'm hammering the keys on this wafer-thin laptop as if trying to extract the last traces of ink from a disintegrating typewriter ribbon.) I couldn't be doing with a keyboard that typed 'AGGH!' if you didn't shut a door quietly. Finally, I took it to hell's pawn shop – the Notting Hill Record and Tape Exchange – whose dead-eyed custodians, exhausted from dealing with junkies most of the day, offered me fifty quid for it.

'Fifty!' I was aghast. 'Can I have just a little bit more? It cost over a hundred!'

'No, not fifty,' the guy said. 'Fifteen.'

Outraged and suddenly incapable of speech, I snapped the typewriter from the counter and chuntered out in a huff. It wasn't long before I realised that having fifteen pounds in my pocket was indeed a much better deal than having to carry an electric typewriter around London. Those Notting Hill guys sure knew their stuff.

I didn't need much to live on: I would have spent all my money on movies, comics and music and I was getting all of them for free. At that time in history – and my life – if you had a mattress, a CD player, and photos of Béatrice Dalle, Iggy Pop and Raymond Carver on the wall then you were living large. The low expectations of being young. It's what powered the music industry for many years, as band after band made the same hellish pact with the record companies. 'Oh, you're happy to live arse-to-face in a van for years just to play your music? And at the end of it, you'll owe us money? Your wish is granted!'

Once I read an interview with American Music Club, one of my favourite bands, and they slagged off a pretentious review which I realised with a sick feeling was one of mine. A rave review that the artist hated. That actually takes some doing. Still, there was something neat about a critic getting lacerated by an artist – a payoff to a gag I had spent years setting up.

Something that began to frustrate me about the de-personalised journalism I was being forced to write was sub-editors changing my copy and sometimes torpedoing a joke. Without my beloved preferred pronoun, it took even more work to land a gag, and required much more precision with language. Raymond Carver was fond of a quote by the great Russian writer Isaac Babel: 'No iron can pierce the heart with such force as a period put just at the right place.' Similarly, there is a just-so quality to comedy which has only one correct response and that is an audible laugh. A comma in the wrong place and the laugh disappears like that terrible thing, a necessary yawn that doesn't get there, or a sneeze that turns into a pain in your groin. But again, I was competing for space with a few dozen other journalists, and sometimes funny words would be replaced, for reasons of space, with words that were not so funny. Sometimes even I couldn't figure out what had been done to destroy the comedy in a piece. But the sentences remained, pointless, orphaned from their meaning, the ghosts of jokes. Humourless editors could massacre a piece, which is why I'll always be thankful for the small gang of colleagues at various publications who liked me and were tender with my stuff.

Still, it was leaving too much to chance. I couldn't bear it.

I was enjoying London, though. The anonymity of a big city came as a relief after Dublin's close quarters. Not that I was such a big shot in Dublin, but it's smaller, and I can't remember names at all. So I was permanently on the back foot because people knew me but I didn't know how I knew them. It just made me look permanently rude, or at least it made me feel as if I looked that way. Years later, when I appeared on the quiz show *QI*, I joked that when I didn't remember a name at a party, my tactic was to say 'Excuse me one moment' and then leave. This wasn't far from the truth. Dublin had become a party that was making me more and more stressed, and my stress levels were never low. In London, I could disappear and still feel present.

As always, I was excited by every shiny new thing that passed across my field of vision. Robin Gibson, the sardonic Scottish editor of *Volume* magazine – which came with a free CD, if you can imagine such luxury – once read a review of mine out loud, not unkindly, in his languorous Paisley accent: '"This album blazes across the sky..." Lot of things blazing across the sky in your world, aren't there, Graham? Albums, bands, films....'

There's a solid reason no one ever collected my journalism, but I had a blast, and half-learned a craft. I still really like the people from that scene. Good people. Some of the kindest I've known. Two butch lesbian sisters took me under their wing for a while. Liz and Pat Naylor, who worked for One Little Indian, the record company for the Sugarcubes and Kitchens of Distinction. Liz and Pat took care of me when I had my first E, a gift from the psychedelic troubadours, The Shamen, a band who literally had a hit with a guy just shouting over and over again 'E's are good'. I made such an arse of myself at their gig in Amsterdam that The Shamen – *The Shamen,* mind you – said of me afterwards, 'Well, at least he had a good time.' But it was all proper life-changing stuff, and it was another piece of luck that Liz and Pat were the ones who held my hand while it was going on.

The music press is all but dead now. The internet dropped a big old nuke on music as transformative youth culture. Jarvis Cocker of Pulp put it best when he said that music suddenly had the same utility as a scented candle. The tribal element of pop has also largely gone, which is a great shame, because historically it's one of the human race's more successful experiments with tribalism. Fans of The Cure weren't sacking Rome or sending violent abuse to beloved children's authors. They just liked wearing black in blazing sunshine and listening to music that sounded like it had been recorded in a prison shower.

Music has always been there for me, a golden thread I can follow right back to my seat at the Wombles gig. After The Wombles, it was Abba; after Abba, The Police; after The Police, Springsteen; after Springsteen, Talking Heads; after Talking Heads, The Pixies; and after The Pixies, perhaps my favourite of all, Guided By Voices. Between all those, countless acts I've loved whose blood would run cold if I gave them a name-check in these pages. One of the most painful aspects of my eventual exile from polite society was not being able to share things any more. I could no longer recommend a band or a comic or a game or any piece of art – which is essentially sixty percent of what I used Twitter for, to share the things I found exciting and valuable and life-enhancing, to continue doing even in a tiny way the thing I loved doing, most of all, in my years as a critic – without trans activists immediately contacting the artists, who were also on Twitter, and demanding their official position on my legendary bigotry.

After a very short time, I just stopped sharing things. I didn't want to embarrass the artists I so admired, watch them recoil from my praise, pretend not to know me. But I still loved the music, privately. Crack Cloud are the most exciting band in the UK today, but I'd only feel safe at one of their gigs if I was disguised as a sound monitor.

I forgive musicians for mob-pleasing behaviour easier than I can forgive comedy people. Musicians are the descendants of people who wandered the land singing songs of heroes and keeping the culture alive, and the whimsies of the mob affect their fortunes more than most. But comedians are different. Comedians are the descendants of jesters. Comedians are supposed to speak truth to power. Them, I can't forgive.

4
TAKING OUR SHOT

GEORGE V. HIGGINS IS – or was, he died in 1999 – one of the most influential authors of the last forty years. Elmore Leonard was a fan. Quentin Tarantino loved and was heavily influenced by Leonard (and probably Higgins too), and a hundred thousand screenwriters were influenced by Tarantino. The Higgins novels are ninety-five percent dialogue and concern themselves with the crime economy in Boston, the philosophical and practical engines driving it. 'He made two mistakes,' one character says of another. 'The second mistake was making the first mistake.'

Some people hate Higgins because he doesn't hold your hand at all. Every chapter is just one guy meeting another guy. His characters go off on digressions that can take up pages. He poured as much ink into how to cook a good steak as he did into the steps needed to rob an illegal poker game, but the books never flag because his ear for dialogue is so true. *I didn't hear him say nothing about that. He just decided he wanted to get all pissed off because somebody might've used something or maybe was doing something or something.* That kind of dialogue sets off the pleasure circuits in my head like a pinball machine. I love the way spoken language works and I love people who can put that on the page or in an actor's memory.

So you can count me among the people he influenced. I knew dialogue had to feel true but also make sense, and make the character pop into your head with every line. It was another Higgins disciple, David Mamet, repurposing an Ernest Shackleton quote in the survival movie *The Edge*, that made me phone Arthur and ask him to come to London to give comedy writing a try. 'What one man can do, another can do.' We both knew how to do it; we just needed to get on with it. To my eternal astonishment, he agreed to the proposal. Arthur, one of the biggest romantics Termonfeckin* had ever produced, was finding Dublin painful after a break-up, so he was eager to escape. Intending to stay a few months in the UK, he ended up living there for ten years because we absentmindedly created one of the most beloved sitcoms of all time.

After having to share Arthur with the *Hot Press* staff, I now had him all to myself. We rented a cheap flat in Bounds Green and started writing material. It was universally accepted that radio was the correct entry point to the business they call show, but that largely meant becoming comfortable with political satire. Arthur and I were wary of satirical comedy as so much of it arose from liberal groupthink – a winky, middle-class, everyone's-reading-*The Guardian* secret handshake. Always the same targets too. There was one particular award-winning TV show that we literally couldn't watch, it was so grimly politically correct; all the right opinions, all the right targets.

---

* If you're not from Ireland, you may struggle to believe this is a real place, but it's honestly the name of Arthur's home village in County Louth.

When people say 'comedy should punch up', they actually mean that it should operate along tribal lines, and they specifically mean along the lines that their tribe decrees. But comedy isn't tribal. Comedy is a mirror in which the whole of humanity is supposed to see itself. If you remove certain groups from comedy and criticism, you remove their humanity. Cosy political satire only served a single purpose for a single group; to flatter the Richard Curtis characters who were writing and producing it. We were suspicious of it. It felt distantly like the work of the hippies, a group whose name Arthur couldn't mention without his upper lip curling to reveal some teeth.

On the other hand, there was *Vic and Bob's Big Night Out*, which ignited in both of us a fierce devotion and understanding. Vic Reeves and Bob Mortimer were punk through and through. *Big Night Out* was amateurish and under-rehearsed, but it had great gags and concepts and there was a simplicity and humanity to it that was inspiring. It treated its audience with respect; there is nothing more punk than providing a crowd with a catchphrase they can use against you if a joke doesn't land: *very pooer*.

But even this comedy made with staplers and glue was beyond our reach. We got one sketch onto a Lenny Henry radio pilot. It was about one of those guys who haunt toilets dressed as theatre ushers from the last century and hand out sweets and aftershave. The phenomenon had taken us both by surprise when we arrived in London so we had some material ready to go. I remember lying on the floor in that terrible Bounds Green flat with my ear to a radio, trying to hear if our jokes landed. The audience sounded very far away, in every sense. We also wrote a radio sitcom, *You're Our Special Friend Now*, about a psychologist who moves into a rural area full of lunatics. Like you, I'm only realising now that it was a proto-*Father Ted*. After all, what is a priest but a psychologist for the poor? The only lines from it I can remember are:

'Look! It's the psychologist!'

'Watch out! He'll try to analyse you!'

God knows how Arthur put up with me in my early twenties. Although he was only nine years older, his time in the punk wars had added a few in temperament. But we somehow made it work, not just the job itself but the friendship. We were in each other's pockets for four years. We had a couple of flare-ups but never anything serious. Some of my fondest memories are of watching TV with Arthur and crying with laughter at his sporadic commentary. Because he was quiet, his hit rate was higher when he did speak. Meanwhile I was saying everything that came into my head, a one-man band with cymbals tied to my elbows and knees, stamping my feet and nodding my head and blowing a kazoo to make him laugh.

In repose, Arthur's features could acquire a cold, forbidding air, and my insecurity always led me to think it was because of something I'd done. Once, during what I felt was an awkward silence, I said 'You're very quiet' and he exploded, with an exasperation that had been simmering for years, 'I KNOW I'M QUIET. PEOPLE ARE ALWAYS TELLING ME I'M QUIET! I KNOW!' Now I'm older and wiser, I realise that Arthur had no idea that he was giving off these vibes. When my face is in repose, I look like a pirate with a secret, but Arthur wasn't constantly following me around with a map and asking for clues.

But the flip side to this (occasionally) (somewhat) unapproachable air that Arthur had about him was his laugh, which was high and girlish and contained no hint of derision or unkindness. He didn't give it out cheaply, but when you made him laugh, it was like getting your own little surprise party. Another part of our artistic manifesto – an internal one that we never had to write down – was a revulsion at cheap humour. Jokes about sex had to be top tier, for example, which is why Father Ted only mentioned the Catholic Church's gravest sin, the child sex-abuse scandals of the nineties, once: 'Well, Niamh, we're not all like that. Say if there's two hundred million priests in the world and five percent are pedophiles, that's still only ten million.' I can hear Arthur's laugh at that even now.

There's a good rule that's helped me many a time: if you're in a dark area, try and find the light. Try and create delight. Arthur once told me of the time he and his sister Ria met Sex Pistols frontman John Lydon at a rock festival. Mindful of Lydon's time and privacy, Arthur and Ria stepped up to him, not without trepidation, and Arthur said, 'Look, just wanted to say, thank you for everything, love everything you've done. Brilliant to meet you.' They went to move away but Lydon collared them and said (and here Arthur would turn in his impeccable Lydon impression, that lethal, sing-song cockney gunslinger): 'Hang on a second, you know everything abaht me...but I don't know anything abaht you,' and he spoke with them and asked them about themselves and they hung out for a while.

Isn't that nice? That's what I always think of when I think of Arthur. The punk façade falling away and revealing a gent. I called my first blog 'Why, That's Delightful', probably thinking of Arthur, and later I formed a production company called Delightful Industries. Arthur needed to be delighted by a joke, and when he was, he rewarded you with that laugh, a hit of dopamine for someone who admired him as I did. I loved writing something and going away and watching him read it. When he laughed, I'd ask 'Which bit?' and luxuriate in pleasure as he responded to what were, after all, hunches on my part. Every time you write a joke, you're essentially working off a hunch that something might be funny. Arthur's taste was impeccable. If he laughed, you knew an audience would too. We were trying to impress each other, and beat each other's gags...not in a competitive sense, just for the love of the thing, for the pleasure of endlessly tending to an idea until we both could step away and declare it perfect.

One day, we were watching *Smith and Jones*, the long-running sketch show starring Mel Smith and Griff Rhys Jones that developed as a spin-off from *Not the Nine O'Clock News*, and during the end credits I noticed how long it took for the list of writers to travel up the screen. Of course! 'They probably take submissions!' I think I said, because I can't imagine Arthur saying any sentence with an exclamation mark at the end of it.

We took a note of a producer's name – Jim Pullin – and sent a few sketches to him, using the address of the production company, Talkback. There's a bit of advice for you. Write to producers. They won't steal your ideas, if that's what you're worried about. Good producers are looking for people, not ideas. They know that even the greatest premise is, as they say, 'execution dependent', so it's good for them to start building relationships with the people doing the executing. Write them a letter, send them some material, and see what happens.

What happened to us was we found ourselves sitting in the Talkback offices in Fitzrovia, having been invited to meet Mel and Griff by Mr Pullin. I noticed some photocopies of our sketches on a table with great big tick marks on many of them. Some of them had two ticks, or even three. I asked the receptionist what it all meant. I sort of knew already, but I wanted to hear someone say it out loud, and she enjoyed playing her part as the herald of good news.

'Oh when Griff likes something, he gives it a tick mark. When he loves something, he gives it three.' During the meeting, Griff asked if we had an agent. We said no. Griff said, 'We'll get you an agent,' brought us downstairs to Talkback's in-house agency, and they signed us up. And that was that. We were in.

I loved hanging around at the writing meetings with Mel and Griff and they enjoyed our enthusiasm. Mel was the Oliver Hardy of the couple, effortlessly turning in comic performances, whereas Griff was Stan Laurel, always trying to make the show better, to hit the bullseye more frequently. Griff would also regale us with his theories of sitcom, and I suspect he hoped we might have written one for him. 'Every sitcom needs to have a trap,' he told us. 'Some reason that these incompatible characters don't just stay as far away from each other as possible.' I soaked it up.

Our sitcom pitch for Talkback was called 'Wheels of Speed', about a Formula One racing driver and his manager. I can't recall the driver's name but he was very much in the James Hunt mould, perhaps the first flaw in the concept, as Hunt already seemed like a figure of the past. The manager's name was Bubbles. Bubbles was a sort of roly-poly, posh *bon vivant* who perhaps foreshadowed Arthur's later collaboration with Matt Berry, *Toast of London*. All I remember about 'Wheels of Speed' is that the first episode concerned the driver being on such a losing streak that he accepts sponsorship from a laxative company. It will not rock you to the core to discover that he accidentally takes some on the day of a big race and keeps having to stop to go to the toilet. Yes, I know. After my pontificating about dirty jokes! But come on, that would have been funny. At the pit stops? When you're talking about microseconds? Ah, maybe not. We'll never know, because you'll never see it. As a concept, 'Wheels of Speed' was not copper-bottomed.

I find it very, very difficult to come up with ideas. When you think about it, I've only had about five or six major ones. But in between, there have been countless failures, experiments and dead ends. An idea has to be copper-bottomed for me to move to series with it. It's so hard to gain an audience's trust that if there's a major flaw in your premise – one that can't be fixed, no matter how many stages your story moves through – that trust will leak from a thousand puncture holes. In every episode you have to get your heroes into a jam. And if along the way, your audience is asking, 'But why didn't they…? But why don't they just…? But couldn't they have…?', you are sunk. These questions are deadly to a comic set-piece and even if you have managed to secure a copper bottom for your premise as a whole, they will still arise in every scene and sequence, so you have to give yourself every advantage you can. A robust premise is essential attire for the well-dressed thirty-minute farce.

'Wheels of Speed' had a great (ie stupid) title, the funniest unseen climax to a sitcom I believe ever not filmed, and some good jokes. It did not have a robust premise. If it had, someone would have noticed and brought it to the screen. It was instead a kind of fantasy sitcom that could only exist in our heads; completely unfilmable. People would ask us how we would do the motor-racing scenes and we had our answer ready: 'Back projection!' – and the more fake it looked, the better, as far as we were concerned. We desperately wanted to create something uniquely our own. We envisioned a sitcom devoted only to being funny, and funny in the same magical way that Vic and Bob were funny. Comedy untethered by reality or sense. Pure comedy.

Arthur's word for it was 'stupid'. To us, 'stupid' was the highest praise. A sketch like 'Unfrozen Caveman Lawyer', with the late and much-missed Phil Hartman, was a direct hit, as far as we were concerned. Hartman plays a caveman, unfrozen from a block of ice, who becomes a lawyer and cynically uses his Palaeolithic identity as a tool to sway juries. It's hilarious. Not satire, not parody, not spoof... Funny because it's funny. Stupid, in other words. But so stupid it was smart.

UK comedy, on the other hand, was often very worthy. The cheerful, scatalogical chaos of *The Young One*s had come and gone, and the comedy had started to settle back into the old routines of Oxford and Cambridge poshos floating into the entertainment business to poke gentle fun at their MP classmates who had floated into Westminster. We weren't part of this, and we didn't like a lot of the comedy that came out of it. An early lesson for me was that if everyone was doing a certain kind of comedy, you should be doing the opposite. Fashion fades, and if something is wildly popular, it might already be too late to start writing about it.

We had an idea for a sketch that always began with an identical premise. Two management types are talking about a potential hire for their company who is about to come in for an interview. One of them says to the other: 'Listen, just bear in mind, he has a bit of an unusually shaped head. For God's sake don't mention it; he's very sensitive about it.' Then the guy comes in and his head looks like a miniature but still-operational WW2 battleship. During the interview, little planes keep landing on it. But the management guy is under strict instructions not to mention it.

Every week we thought we'd have someone come in with an unusually shaped head that you weren't allowed to talk about. First we'd have the battleship, then the following week it would be a man with a head shaped like a guitar and a flamenco musician would start playing it during the interview. Arthur said, 'How about one where it's shaped like a small fishing village, and in one of the windows you can see an elderly female crime author working on her latest novel?'

Griff and Mel had to think of their audience, who might stare at a sketch like this in complete bewilderment. They had a huge viewership – now that I think of it, probably the biggest audience Arthur and I ever had – and while they wanted to take risks, they also had to bear in mind the question producer John Plowman would often ask: 'Will my aunt in Weston-super-Mare laugh?' Ordinary people wanted to laugh too, not just comedy snobs like Arthur and me.

We wanted to write comedy and, with *Smith and Jones*, that's what we did. Visual gags, one-liners, working backwards from found footage… I remember once they gave us footage of tanks at some sort of military event and told us to put Mel and Griff at the controls. We came back with two or three pages of material, moving the footage around so it meant different things in different sketches. Working with Mel and Griff showed us that comic inspiration wasn't a sword being held up in the middle of a lake, something you just happened upon if you were lucky enough to be passing by. It wasn't something mysterious and external, it was more like a muscle that you had to keep in shape. We picked up enough of the craft of comedy writing that we began to feel more confident with our own material.

That wasn't the only benefit of knowing Mel and Griff. At the time, we were in our terrible, featureless flat in Bounds Green. I had a hunch – after a while when you're around rich people, you get little hunches like this – that if I said, 'Griff, do you have any properties in London we could rent?', he would say yes, and we could live there. I did; he did; and we did. It was the first flat owned by Griff and his wife Jo when they came to London. A humble two-bedroom in Kilburn. They rented it to us for something like three hundred and fifty quid a month – next to nothing. During this time, we were able to experiment and stretch ourselves creatively without worrying too much about paying the bills. Griff was almost like our patron in the classic Pope/Michelangelo sense, and I guess we paid him in sketches.

There was a variety club in London that I loved called Club Zarathustra. It was a cabaret with the emphasis on comedy. Stewart Lee, Richard Herring and Simon Munnery hosted the evening, the latter in character as a Nietzschean intellectual who despised his audience. Of course, the audience weren't insulted by Simon's intellectual hauteur because they knew they were actually being flattered, and Simon had the material to back up his self-regard. He was an audacious performer. When the band KLF burned a million pounds as an art prank, Simon burned a five-pound note on stage to horrified gasps from the audience. 'Look at that,' he said. 'All the shock of the KLF at a fraction of the cost.'

The Club Zarathustra team were all Oxbridge types, and I was eager to impress them because it was the Other Interesting Thing That Was Happening apart from *Vic and Bob* and *The Day Today*, Armando Iannucci and Chris Morris' current affairs parody. I was a little embarrassed to be writing for the more established and conventional *Smith and Jones*. Not embarrassed as such, just... Well, I'm sure both Griff and Mel knew they weren't the new gunslingers in town, and they had come to terms with that. But when you're young and arrogant you can't wait to show people what you can do, so I naturally drifted towards the iconoclasts and trailblazers at Club Z.

I performed at Club Z every now and again, but for the most part my only role was that of an audience member. As such, I did my bit, always happily entering into fights with people who were talking or otherwise being rude. If there's one thing I hate about live comedy, it's people in the audience who think they're a part of the show. Once, I went to see Noel Fielding and Julian Barratt perform *The Mighty Boosh* in a small theatre above a pub. They were great despite the drunk guy who was talking back to the stage as if it was required of him.

For some reason, I didn't do the usual build-up involved in such a situation – the half-turn and the peeved look – and instead went straight to 'SHUT THE FUCK UP!', which made him briefly go into another dimension before he returned to his senses and started making outraged noises. I probably scared Julian and Noel more than my intended target, who was so angry he followed me into the toilets and smashed the cubicle door open, Jackie Chan drunken-master-style. Thankfully he'd expended all his energy on kicking the door in so I was able to see him off with the force of my terrified stare.

Aptly enough, being an audience member at Club Zarathustra made me a bit smarter in my approach to hecklers. One evening, there was a guy who was so insulted by Simon's patter that he started answering back with a string of dispiriting, unfunny comments. Instead of flipping out again and frightening Simon (as if anyone could frighten Simon, a performer who might have been born onto a stage), I whispered to him, 'Hey, it's terrible, isn't it?'

'Yeah it is! It's crap!'

'You know you can ask for your money back?'

And he said, 'Yeah, that's what I'm gonna do!' He sprang from his chair and said to his girlfriend, 'We're going.' And they left to ask for their money back. Job done.

I don't want to be misunderstood here. I love audiences, and I think they bring out the best in me. When you're writing for a live audience, you have to make it smart enough for the smartest person in the room, but also clear enough so that even if he falls asleep, the laughter from everyone else might wake him up. It's like entering into diplomatic negotiations with a genius and an idiot and everyone in between. It's a direct line to humanity, and I love it. It's a pleasure to write for a live audience.

But if you're in the audience, you have entered into a contract with the performer that you will shut the hell up. That's why performers applaud the audience at the end of plays: they're thanking the audience for doing their bit. It takes effort and focus to be an audience member. When people rudely break this contract, you'd better hope I'm not the audience alongside you because there's every chance we might end up staring aghast at each other in a toilet cubicle.

Club Zarathustra was also where I first saw Kevin Eldon, with whom we were lucky enough to eventually work. He used to do a double act with a chap named Roger Mann that brought to mind Peter Cook and Dudley Moore's Derek and Clive. They were brothers, is the thing I remember, because I've never forgotten this improvised exchange:

ROGER: I saw Mum's bra last week.
KEVIN: Did you? Where?
ROGER: In the shed. A bird built its nest in it.
KEVIN: (pause) That doesn't count.

That doesn't count. Genius.

I made the stage only once or twice at Club Zarathustra. I had begun playing poker, and I had a small case for poker chips which looked a bit like a tiny briefcase. So I dressed in a suit and I just walked through the crowd growling and roaring, and called the routine 'Giant Businessman'. Comedy writer Andy Riley and myself wore big chunky fishermen's jumpers, strummed guitars and performed Kraftwerk covers in a British folk style. We called ourselves Craftwork. It was funny – once – so I think we only did it once.

I never liked repeating myself. In our Joshua Trio days in Dublin, when I first tried stand-up, I hadn't realised that comedians did the same stuff every night and just refined their jokes. Not knowing this, I used to go mad trying to think of a new act every week. I would go up on stage, perpetually terrified, thinking, 'Some of these jokes are OK I guess…' Comedians spend their time on stage getting to a place where they feel comfortable with the material, but I never gave myself that chance. I was doing a different act every week. I never took the time to really understand what it meant to be a stand-up, and it showed.

A warm-up guy for *Father Ted* once told a joke that explained the art of stand-up to me better than anything else I'd seen. He would ask the audience: 'What are those mirrors that kind of stick out? Concave or convex?'

And scattered people in the crowd replied 'Convex'.

'Convex, right. Those mirrors are weird. When you take off all your clothes and jump up and down, you look like the only person on the bus.'

I heard him do the same joke at the next show, and he asked the same question, 'What are those mirrors that kind of stick out? Concave or convex?' And the audience answered again, just as they had the previous week. I realised then that the question was a crucial part of the joke; misdirection, just as you might see with a magician. The question disarms each new audience and makes them think, every time, that what the comedian is saying is true. Because they engaged authentically in the first half of the joke, they leave themselves open for the punchline, like a boxer drawn too close by a feint. This is the craft, these are the things comedians unlock through time spent on stage. It wasn't a good fit for me. I didn't have the patience.

I was always fiercely protective of my performer friends. Breaking the contract between audience and performer was a form of bullying, to my mind. One loud-mouth and an evening is ruined for hundreds of people. My heart always belonged to people who could make me laugh. And you came through me if you came at them. I didn't mind. I knew if the tables were turned, they'd do the same thing for me.

5

WE'LL ALWAYS HAVE PARIS

OUR FIRST SITCOM was a painful early lesson, one we had no desire to be taught twice. Set in the 1920s, it was the story of a pretentious, talentless Parisian painter who loudly and persistently proclaimed his genius, drank too much and hung around with other no-hopers on the Left Bank. We were swinging for Ben Elton and Richard Curtis's *Blackadder*, which we loved: lots of jokes about the changes coming about in the early twentieth century, intellectuals discussing ludicrously outdated topics as if they were groundbreaking news, that sort of thing. I remember one gag went: 'They don't make films like they used to. Remember "Train Pulling Into Station" And "People Coming Out of Factory"? Now *those* were films.' This was years before Woody Allen had a rare late hit with *Midnight in Paris*, but we didn't catch the mood in quite the same way. *Au contraire!*

We'd been writing sketches for Alexei Sayle's TV show and he signed on for the main part, Alain Degout. The scripts made everyone laugh, but that turned out to be a mirage. *Paris* became a harsh lesson in how many elements are required to keep a successful sitcom on its legs, and how few are needed to topple it. For instance, if you're writing a sitcom that deals in wild anachronisms and absurd retellings of the lives of the Impressionists and Surrealists, it might not be a great idea to use painted backdrops that are renditions of Monet landscapes and Van Gogh's *Starry Night*, as we did. Most studio sets attempt a facsimile of reality. Ours was saying 'this is all fake'. If you're dropping heavy hints at the outset that nothing the audience will see is real, then they'll find it harder to engage with your world and invest in your characters. The set was beautiful but it gave the audience its first 'out'. Ben Elton and Richard Curtis never made that mistake.

An 'out' can be anything. A bad joke, a dislikable character, a failed pratfall... Audiences are always looking for a reason to stop watching a TV show. Your job as a writer is to prevent them finding one. So you can get away with letting one 'out' slip past you, sometimes two, but never three. I guess poverty was our 'trap', and there was nothing wrong with the gags, which were abundant – but *Paris* had a lot of outs. We wanted to go into hiding when the reviews came in.

It's a shame because we had everything going for us. Our cast was an incredible collection of comedy royalty, including Neil Morrissey, who had recently found TV stardom in *Men Behaving Badly*, Rebecca Front, and James Dreyfus, who played Degout's arch-enemy Beluniare. James would later break new ground in *Gimme Gimme Gimme*, playing an obnoxious gay character at a time when many would have been too nervous to even countenance such a thing. We were somewhat in shock to turn up every day and meet not just these exciting contemporaries, but the likes of Eleanor Bron, John Bird, John Barron and Windsor Davies, who guested in single episodes. We even had a young Patrick Marber as a Hemingway figure. Or was it Gauguin? Even if it was online I don't think I could bring myself to watch it to find out.

The magic of seeing actors whom you've grown up admiring sitting across from you at an audition never wears off. And we both loved Alexei. Once, in the pub, he explained to us why it was always posh people who owned production companies. 'After Oxford and Cambridge,' he said, 'they don't have any problems finding people to help them set it up. They're all "I know a good lawyer", "I got a great guy to do the numbers". Whereas working-class people are more like, "I know a bloke with a van".'

Alexei was our star power and probably helped us get the commission. Later on he said, generously, 'I was the problem in *Paris*.' To be fair, even a more experienced actor would have had a hard time with our main character, whose default oratory style was the rant. Degout was based on Kirk Douglas's turn as Van Gogh in *Lust for Life*, where he played the artist as a man suffering from a permanent migraine. It was one of those things that Arthur and I just latched onto, in a comic sense, and wanted to emulate or recreate or something.

There may have been a bit of Klaus Kinski in there too. Kinski was Werner Herzog's collaborator on some of the greatest German films of all time: *Fitzcarraldo* and *Aguirre, the Wrath of God*. He was an actor with terrifying blue eyes and a smile like a curtain rising on a graveyard. I had just finished reading (or thumbing through, as it's nigh-on impossible to read cover to cover) his autobiography, *Kinski Uncut*, and a little bit of his spirit was in our script. In *Neon* magazine – a short-lived but excellent film monthly that followed *Select* – I wrote a comic column imagining his daily life as an ordinary parent in the UK. Try reading the following in an outraged German accent and you'll get the idea: 'What idiots people who work in shops are! I asked for a Fruit Corner and was given an ordinary yoghurt! That's no good! I like to mix the fruit and the yoghurt! I threw the container in the man's stupid face! He shouted at me as if I was a child!'

What worked as a humorous piece in *Neon* ran out of puff over the course of a six-episode Channel 4 sitcom, but the book is worth tracking down. Written in the present tense, one chapter begins 'I must have a sunflower!', which still makes me laugh. He does appear to own up to at least one rape in it, with no apparent shame or regret (and little posthumous cancelling, as far as I'm aware), so it's not what you would call a comfortable read, but it's an extraordinary insight into a manic, psychotically uninhibited personality. You can see why we thought that would make the basis of a character for a sitcom. We had to make six episodes of it to learn that he wasn't a good *central* character for a sitcom.

At this early stage, we also didn't yet know how to rewrite. Every read-through ended with the same note – 'too long' – and it was. Each episode dragged itself over the finish line at eight minutes over, sometimes even ten. A page of script is supposed to roughly translate to one minute of screen time. We would write forty pages and refuse to cut anything. This situation was made worse by the fact that a Channel 4 half hour wasn't even half an hour when you allowed for advertisements.

At (around) thirty minutes, a sitcom really is the perfect length. As the 45 RPM single was to pop music, so is the half hour to comedy. Just as the manufacturing requirements and limitations of pressing hot vinyl into a seven-inch diameter disc gave the world 'Heart Of Glass' and 'Mr Blue Sky', so the sitcom's episode length lends itself to farces. Prone to collapse under its own weight when stretched to feature length, the thirty-minute farce, as perfected by *Fawlty Towers* and *Seinfeld*, is an achievable and noble aim.

On *Paris*, however, we kept handing in 'Bohemian Rhapsody' instead of 'Teenage Kicks'. If we had listened to the executives and written to the actual length of a sitcom, we might have found an audience. When the time came to pay the piper, all we had as leverage during the ensuing editing-room discussions was our earlier intransigence. And that's not actually leverage! I think I remember asking the producer to suggest to Channel 4 that they just not run ads. That's how desperate we were to claw back three and a half minutes. We had dug a grave for ourselves, moaned at them when they advised us to stop pulling the earth in after us, and then demanded they dig us back up at the expense of being able to fund the channel. The result was a miserable edit where all those jokes we were too proud to cut ended up in the bin anyway. All that was left was the exposition and the plots that the exposition served. Those plots were thin, to say the least, and we hadn't yet mastered the art of disguising exposition with a joke, so it was a sort of anatomy model of a show – all the bits that should have been hidden were instead on full display under brutal lighting.

The reviews were savage, but the pain was useful. Just as a rat learns to stop pressing the buzzer that makes smoke rise from his whiskers, so we would never again make the same mistake of putting any part before the whole. The writing, we knew now, was just the start. The final thing you see on screen within those twenty-four minutes – that's something else entirely: that's the thing people actually see at home. As comedy writers, we had a singular voice but we still needed to learn lessons of economy and craft. The target was smaller, harder to hit, and yet more beautiful than we first realised. Most of all, we learned this: you only get one chance to do it right, so you had better do it right.

Channel 4 had made a whatever-million-quid investment in us and we had delivered a stinker. I don't remember the show ever making it on to DVD, which is fair enough. There are fun things in it, but it was a swing and a miss. For this reason, and because I was about to meet a man named Geoffrey Perkins, I came to hate the 'executives are out to ruin everything' ethos. It annoyed me, even as certain executives annoyed me. Sure, executives can give unhelpful notes, but the fact that they feel the need to say anything at all often shows you your script isn't quite there yet. They're your first audience, and some of them have a great instinct for storytelling, so when they're unhappy, you should take notice; soothing their unease might make for a better final result.

I could see how the indie mentality had ruined many bands, who considered it a form of failure to get across to the most people possible. 'Selling out' was a big imaginary problem that hobbled a lot of otherwise brilliant people. The indie mentality prevented so many bands, and some comedians, from reaching their potential. Kurt Cobain had a bad case. Minneapolis band The Replacements were so messed up by it that they sabotaged every chance they had at reaching the audience they deserved. Legend has it that they once tried to take revenge on a record company by throwing tape masters *of their own work* into the Mississippi River.

The awful hipster idea that there's something corrupt about finding an audience is a pose echoed in the evergreen complaint about studio sitcoms: 'I don't need to be told where to laugh.' This was an early sort of memetic viral phrase that I would hear over and over again from countless people who each thought they were being lone wolves. It's not being told to do anything; it's about being a part of humanity. The orgasm scene in *When Harry Met Sally* was funny, but it was a thing of joy in a packed cinema, surrounded by men and women who suddenly saw their own sense of humour and playfulness reflected back at them, not just from Meg Ryan and Billy Crystal, but from each other.

I love audiences. They're smart. They keep you on your toes. The reason so much 'content' is so bad at the moment is because the audience is being edged out of the relationship. Writers no longer know who they're writing for. They may have in mind something like the average 'diverse' cast of a current American TV show. As Henry Ford might have said, 'Any colour you like, as long as they're middle class.' In representing everyone, they represent no one.

When you're writing for an audience, as opposed to a HR department, you're trying to grab the attention of the cross-section of humanity that these shows are ineptly trying to represent. You're addressing a collective intelligence and empathy and a shared understanding of the nature of stories that seems baked into our bones. Often during a studio recording, you might ask yourself something like, 'Will they need that extra line? The one that sort of explains the premise of an upcoming joke?' The answer is often no, and the way you can tell is because somewhere in the course of the evening, the audience responds to a key moment with a significant laugh and you know that they got there early.

If they're onto the premise that soon, you can't linger, or repeat information they already know and risk losing their good will. So you might cut that line on the fly. Audiences are fickle, and that too keeps you on your toes, or it should. There would have been few writers more acutely aware of the audience than Shakespeare. His plays were finessed in front of crowds that were raucous, unruly, prone to distraction, and often armed. He wrote for an audience that carried knives, which must have concentrated his mind wonderfully.

That's why we're still reading him: because he couldn't fake it. He had to tell the truth, he had to be funny, and meaningful, and engaging. And this collaboration with his audiences has given us his collected plays, the most influential body of dramatic literature in the English language. Back on earth with the much more humble sitcom, the studio audience draws funny, heightened performances from the actors, and for my part, I wouldn't dare write a joke that could be received in silence. That's why, for me, studio sitcoms are brighter, lighter, with that sprinkle of fairy dust from the crowd, lifting the performers up. So people can say 'I don't need to be told when to laugh' all they want. Maybe it's true. Maybe they don't. But my audiences reminded me that we had to be funny, and I wouldn't be half the writer I am without them.

6

GETTING THE GANG TOGETHER

FOR MANY YEARS, Father Ted was Arthur Mathews. In the Joshua Trio era, when Paul Wonderful was offstage, showering the glitter off his naked body or swapping his bloody robes for clean ones, Arthur would pop out from his place behind the drums, stick a priest's collar at the top of his black shirt and keep the audience busy with a stream of fake church announcements. The moment he spoke, you knew the character. Gentle, unworldly, easily flustered. You knew that this was a man who would never curse. 'Flip!' was as bad as it got. If someone stole his car, he'd say, 'Flip those flipping flippers!'

Arthur played Ted with an almost camp lilt, a gentle smile playing on his face as if there was immense wisdom behind the baffling, mundane things he insisted on saying. His presence at a rock gig was automatically funny, and Arthur was writing killer jokes for him right off the bat. Our favourite was when he would announce to the crowd, 'If there's anyone at the back who can't see, say hello to them. They're from St Kevin's School for the Blind.'

I loved the character so much and was, as ever, extremely protective and proud of Arthur when he was performing. Once, when a group of people started talking through his act at the Baggot Inn, I yelled at them to shut up so hard that I felt a vein pop in my eye. Arthur, like the Mighty Boosh when their turn came around, looked briefly undone at the weird, out-of-control screeching from some lunatic in the audience, many decibels louder than the drunken conversation that had prompted it.

After we arrived in the UK, we felt there was definitely something to be done with Ted, but we never thought a UK broadcaster or audience would accept an Irish sitcom. Also, in our innocence, we believed that it would be cheaper to shoot a mock documentary rather than a sustained narrative, and thus might attract more flighty executives to our bird table. We pitched 'Irish Lives' as a series of six fly-on-the-wall documentaries about different characters, the first one following Ted as he visited all the priests with whom he studied at the seminary. More like a collection of sketches than anything else, each scene in it ended with Ted disappointed and frustrated when his old colleagues turned out to be crazy or shy or constantly dancing, or whatever other quality we found we could give a priest to make a character.

Two people he met in the pilot ended up as regulars. The scabrous older priest, Father Jack, began life as a former mentor to Ted. In that pilot script, Ted engages him in conversation for some time before others enter the room and do their best to explain to a disbelieving Ted that the old priest died sometime during the night. 'What are you on about?' says Ted. 'I was only just talking to him.'

A version of the character who would become Mrs Doyle was in there. The housekeeper was a staple figure in most priests' houses in Ireland, recognisable at a pinch for viewers in the UK, which was the test that had to be applied to all of the characters. The character appeared and did her thing, pushing cups of tea on Ted and not taking no for an answer, and all in all 'Irish Lives' was a nice collection of funny, not hugely connected scenes. We didn't yet realise what we had.

We went in to meet Geoffrey Perkins of Hat Trick, who told us that a series of one-off documentaries, introducing a different character every week, would not allow an audience to get accustomed to the characters and form a relationship with them. He suggested we go away and reimagine the 'Father Ted Crilly' episode as a sitcom, the first of a series of decisions in which Geoffrey was hardly ever wrong.

From a solitary episode to a run of six, we had a lot of character work to do. We filled Mrs Doyle's head with repressed desire and an inability to imagine life not spent serving men. There was no dim younger priest at this point, but we did have the name 'Dougal McGuire'. In the Joshua Trio days, Arthur would read out letters sent to Ted from him, but he was very different back then, his comic utility being that of an unfortunate priest who keeps being placed in highly dangerous, far-flung parishes. We brought him home, made him younger, and quickly found that he and Ted got on famously, producing pages and pages of material. We were able to hit the ground running with the characters because the Catholic Church itself had provided *Father Ted* with the 'trap' that Griff had told us every sitcom needed: all three priests had been 'moved on' because of misdeeds in previous parishes. It was becoming clear that this was the Church's way of sweeping a problem under the rug, and it was perfect. We had an answer to why Ted would endure these people who were pushing him to his limits.

I think it was here I started thinking of the concept of 'joke baskets', which were categories suggested by the premise or the characters or any aspect of your show. For instance, one joke basket we discovered was Craggy Island's geographical features:

- British boats with nuclear symbols on the side patrol the

island;
- no west side because it 'floated away';
- not significant enough to be on any maps;
- only local landmark is 'The Field', which isn't really a field but has 'fewer rocks in it than most places'.

Once you discover a joke basket that ties in to the premise of your show, you're always on the look out for jokes to chuck into it. It keeps you scanning your life for material, even if you don't yet have a story to which it can be attached. In this way, we kept finding out new aspects to the world we were creating, even when we weren't writing dialogue.

On the other hand, writing the dialogue revealed our characters to us more than anything else. Their voices were so instantly familiar to us that it became like flipping on a tape recorder. Every word on the page told us a little bit more about them.

Dougal didn't necessarily believe in God; Ted didn't either but knew to keep it to himself.

Ted fancied himself something of an intellectual but the only books we know he's read are *The Shining* by Stephen King and a (fictitious) romance novel called 'Bejewelled With Kisses'.

Dougal regularly took Father Jack out for walks in his wheelchair and regularly lost him.

Mrs Doyle was boiling with repressed sexual desire.

Jack and Dougal were largely invisible to each other.

Ted felt pain, Mrs Doyle did too to a lesser extent, Dougal and Jack not at all.

Other characteristics became funny simply by virtue of being present in a priest. Dougal was deeply superstitious, an extremely unlikely and unfortunate attribute for the job, but it made us laugh. Everything either felt right, or it didn't, and laughter always pointed us in the right direction.

Being Irish, we knew we were sailing close to the wind with Dougal, an idiot, and Jack, an alcoholic. Ireland was the butt of many a Paddy joke as I was growing up. Put a step wrong with... with whatever this was turning out to be, and we would never be forgiven. But we also felt, well, why can't we have a stupid character? Like Manuel in *Fawlty Towers*, Baldrick in *Blackadder*, but especially like Trigger in John Sullivan's *Only Fools and Horses*, probably the best stupid character ever written. Were the Irish not allowed to be dumb, to be human, to take part in comedy? Because we were the butt of jokes, we're not allowed to be funny ourselves?

If American Jews had thought like that, there wouldn't be any comedy at all; the voices of Neil Simon, Mel Brooks, Woody Allen, Jerry Seinfeld, Larry David and countless others dominated American comedy in the latter half of the twentieth century, and as a result, American comedy is inextricably linked to the Jewish voice. In Ireland, we had Dave Allen and Hal Roach and precious little else. Irish people were naturally, instinctively irreverent and funny – our evenings at the International had shown us that – but there was little reflection of this on our screens.

We thought we'd show bravado. We didn't feel we had to edit ourselves to make allowances for anyone's feelings. I never for a moment felt any different to any other kid growing up at that time. If the Brits could have a show like *The Young Ones*, why couldn't the Irish? Besides, Dougal wasn't just a fool, he was a Holy Fool. Jack wasn't just a drinker, he was a heroic drinker. It all felt right, and it made us laugh. And anything that made us laugh was in.

Seinfeld writer Peter Mehlman – on one of the last cassette tapes I would ever own, a bootleg from a seminar he conducted called 'Writing Seinfeld-Style' – said, 'Laughter is a very strong spice.' In other words, if you make people laugh, they'll forgive you anything. We knew we could poke fun all we wanted as long as we were funny.

Waiting patiently for our efforts to materialise was Geoffrey Perkins, already our producer, although I'm not sure we even knew it. Soft-voiced, cheerful and magnanimous, Geoffrey was also properly posh, with all the good qualities associated with his class and none of the bad. Most of all, he loved comedy and trusted the intelligence of the audience. Geoffrey looked and sounded like the stuffy BBC square who just didn't get it, maaan, but he got it better than a lot of the people who thought they knew better than him. He was a uniquely gifted comedy producer.

Arthur, with his ethos of 'funny and stupid and to hell with everything else', gave *Father Ted* an energy that was punk in flavour. (Someone once said to me that *Ted* was 'Ireland's punk rock', which I still think is the highest praise.) But Geoffrey gave it something we didn't even know it needed: a heart. After reviewing his first album in the pages of *Select*, I had remained friends with Neil Hannon. We asked him to give us a theme tune, and he auditioned two pieces. The first was a silly, plinky-plonk number that later became the intro for his song 'A Woman Of The World'. The other was lusher, more conservative, more 'Irish'. We were suspicious of the golden melody in the latter and felt concern that we were already slipping into paddywhackery with it.

'We're making fun of sitcoms,' we told Geoffrey. 'The first track sounds like a parody of sitcoms. That's what we want.'

Geoffrey looked wounded.

'People will *love* these characters,' he said. 'Why would you want to make fun of them?'

We didn't have a good answer, and the golden melody became our theme.

On another occasion, looking through the photographs of suggestions for the Parochial House, Arthur and I okayed each one, not really knowing what criteria to apply.

'This seems fine.'

'This one?'

'No, no, no!' said Geoffrey, again looking wounded. He couldn't believe we failed to see how *wrong* they all were. Then he came upon one – boxy and isolated, like a child's drawing of a house –

and shouted in triumph, 'This! This is the one!' And sure enough, as we stared at it, we realised that none of the others came close. The Parochial House in the photo immediately replaced the fuzzy outline we carried in our heads, and Geoffrey again saved the show from being only a fuzzy outline of what it would come to be.

On the set of *Paris*, we weren't exactly unwelcome, but neither were we encouraged to participate. And why would we be? At that stage, we had no idea what the work involved. Luckily Hat Trick Productions, being at that time a writer-led production company, encouraged us to take part in every aspect of the show. We resolved to interfere in *Father Ted*'s making to a molecular degree. This was partly self-preservation. Much as I love the form, studio sitcoms are often creaky, old-fashioned affairs. A good studio sitcom – that is, one filmed in front of an audience – has to be far better than a good single-camera sitcom (like *The Office*) if anyone is even going to look in its direction, and if it didn't work, the paddywhackery charge would kill us. We didn't want to go back to Ireland and be chased everywhere, like a kind of evil Beatles.

We became unofficial co-producers, attending each casting session and location scout. Consulted on everything from set-dressing to costume choices, I drove the art department a little bit crazy by constantly picking up on details I thought too 'Oirish'. They were responding to their own research photos; I was responding to years of seeing Ireland misrepresented and romanticised. The truth was somewhere in the middle. I hope we both got what we wanted, but the fact that they never at any point tried to kill me is a great testament to their professionalism.

Casting was a pain. I've never gotten used to the process. Most people who come in for a part won't get it. You know it, they know it, and they can usually sense it. It's an awful thing to 'test' people in this way and it's why I love the modern trend of sending phone videos as auditions. We saw a young Aidan Gillen, long before Littlefinger in *Game of Thrones*, for the Dancing Priest. For his audition, I played dancing Ted, because Arthur was shy and I

had no dignity. Aidan stared unhappily at his script for the length
of Ted's dialogue and then, when the time came for him to speak
his lines, he literally ran out of the room. Derrick Branche came
in to read for the overdubbed Cuban priest in the episode 'The
Passion of St Tibulus'. I recognised him from *Only When I Laugh*,
the ITV hospital sitcom, in which he played Gupte, the extremely
stereotyped Indian nurse. It wasn't a show I particularly admired
but it was a part of my childhood nonetheless.

'Oh, you were Gupte!' I said without thinking, honestly
delighted.

He stared at me for a moment or two as the temperature in the
room abruptly dropped. 'Do you want my autograph?' he hissed.
I quickly decided against asking him for any funny memories from
the show.

The actor Alan Devlin came in for Jack. Devlin's major claim
to fame was when he walked off the stage during *The Pirates of
Penzance* ('Fuck this!'), went into the pub next door to the theatre,
still wearing his radio microphone, and started ordering booze
and slagging off the production. When he auditioned for us, he
was already grandly drunk. The script described Jack 'barking'
a line so he barked, went down on his hands and knees, and bit
Geoffrey in the leg. He retook his seat and looked at Ros Hubbard,
our casting agent.

'I've not got it, have I?'

He had not. We didn't actually need Father Jack on the set, just
someone who could play him.

Frank Kelly floated in, bringing the Abbey Theatre with him.
Frank was as far from Jack as you could imagine. Almost dainty
in movement and speech, he was closer in character to the flower-
scattering, puppy-loving version of Jack that popped up in a later
episode. But we had him in mind from the start – he might even
have been the first we mentally cast – because of his work on an old
Irish satirical show called *Hall's Pictorial Weekly*. Arthur's memory
of it was clearer than mine, but I did have a shimmering childhood

vision of Frank playing what you might call 'gombeens' – dodgy wheeler-dealers – in that show.

Understandably, Frank, a fine wine-loving, old-school thespian – straight, but with a hint of Oscar Wilde in the way he carried himself – was initially a little suspicious of the part. Jack's scenes were somewhat one-note, to say the least, and we could see Frank trying to use his training to figure the character out. But there was nothing to figure out. Thankfully for us, in that first audition he put his doubts to one side and his face curled into the cunning grimace Arthur and I had had in mind from the outset. He shouted 'DRINK' and finally we heard the word ring the bell the way it needed to be rung. We had our Jack.

Ardal O'Hanlon, who played Dougal, is such a strange one; not the man himself, just the roundabout route we took to getting our hands on him. Back in the *Hot Press* days, while Arthur and I were sitting in the cellar of the International, Ardal was honing his stand-up act upstairs in the International's comedy club – called The Comedy Cellar (yes, it's confusing) – and in my memory we didn't cross paths at all until we started thinking of him for the part. In fact, I remember trying to slip the deadpan Irish comedian Kevin McAleer a copy of the script at a gig in London. McAleer politely turned me down, showing none of the horror that leaps onto my face when someone asks me to read a script.

One day Arthur came into the office with a video tape (one of the last times in history someone would perform that action) and showed me a clip of some sort of youth Shakespeare RTÉ thing. Ardal was in a scene, but I didn't think he was doing anything special.

'Wait until he's alone at the end of the scene,' said Arthur.

Sure enough, as soon as the other actor left the shot, Ardal stared after her in a sort of cartoonish fog of bafflement. And there, suddenly, was Dougal. Ardal would often use that baffled look to great effect in his stand-up act. I remember one of his jokes went:

'My dad was mad crack. One day I took a sticker off a Mars bar and put it on the fridge. Then I said, "Dad, look, the fridge cost sixty-nine pence."

'"No, it didn't, son. That fridge cost three hundred pounds."

'Mad crack!'

It's barely a joke. In fact, I wonder if it's just a true story. But delivered by Ardal, with his wide-eyed wonder at everything that happened to wander out of his mouth, it was exquisitely funny. When *Father Ted* took off, Ardal's sense of artistry led him to gradually drop that Dougal-ness from his act, so in a sense, he sort of gave Dougal to us, and I'll always be grateful. Casting Ardal provided us with an immediate win that made the process less nerve-wracking than it could have been. Later, he said he thought he was doing a bad job because we were talking to everyone else more than him. But that was just because his line readings were so good, we never had to give him notes. We had nothing for him. He couldn't say a line wrong.

We knew Ardal would be funny, but I was less sure about Dermot Morgan, the satirist and impressionist that everyone fancied for the role of Ted. I knew about Dermot only from a character he used to do on the RTÉ Variety Show The Live Mike: another priest, as it happens, Father Trendy. I was less familiar with his political radio satire, *Scrap Saturday*, which had made him a star in Ireland, but a star who was running out of road. RTÉ's growing timidity in the face of his lacerating satire and Ireland's increasingly draconian libel laws were helping to strangle his ability to make topical comedy.

As well as not having followed *Scrap Saturday*, I was also, in my puppydog, lovestruck way, outraged that Arthur wouldn't be taking the role of Ted himself. For me, Arthur *was* Father Ted, and the idea of anyone else doing the character was sacrilegious. 'Dermot's the one,' Arthur assured me. I wondered if it was only because he had him in his head as Father Trendy. 'No, it won't be like Trendy. He'll be more like he is in the pub.'

More powerful than the memory of Father Trendy were Dermot's late-night phone calls campaigning for the role. I would never meet anyone again who wanted a part so badly. It was burning a hole through him. His energy alone could have powered the show, although he must have found me a frustrating audience. Dermot was a skilled impressionist, but his targets were generally Irish politicians and sportsmen. Having little interest in either, most of the time I had no idea what he was talking about.

I had little understanding of the technical aspects of acting, and I couldn't imagine anyone but Arthur taking the part. His voice, his mannerisms – these were what we had used to write Ted's dialogue, and while Ardal was exactly what we envisaged for Dougal, Dermot wasn't as natural a fit – at least to me, at least not initially.

David Mamet says that 'there are no characters – there's only actors and dialogue'. In other words, in a visual medium, it is the combination of dialogue and actor that gives you what the audience perceives as the 'character'. Change the words, or the actor, and you have a completely different person. So when Dermot sat with Ardal in a pub in Dublin and we watched them read through the scenes for the first time, I finally started seeing the version of Father Ted that he would bring with him. Arthur's Ted was quiet and camp, someone who didn't draw unnecessary attention to himself. Dermot brought much of his own ambition and drive, which in Ted became a carnivorous and conniving approach to the priesthood.

Arthur couldn't have played a schemer, and the Ted we had created was a schemer. Dermot also grounded Ted in the real world, giving us another anchor that prevented the show floating away entirely on a cloud of whimsy. He also gave us his imposing physicality. Whenever I think of what Dermot brought to the role, I see him as Ted, snapping his Zippo lighter shut upon making a decision, something Arthur's Ted would never have done. Arthur's Ted wasn't a smoker, wasn't ambitious, wasn't bursting to escape the priesthood in the same way Dermot was bursting to escape his

Pauline was much younger than Mrs Doyle but our brilliant makeup department soon put that right

stalled Irish career... These new elements, far from diminishing the character, enriched both Ted and the rewrites and the show.

Mrs Doyle, we could not find. We thought it would be a breeze for some reason, but no one quite got what we were after. It didn't help, probably, that we were getting each actress to read a speech that involved saying the words 'go on' over and over again. It was around this time that we started learning to write scenes as part of the casting process. Just little sketches to give another flavour of the character. There's a famous scene we later wrote for Mrs Doyle in which she complains about the bad language in a book she's read – 'It was a bit much for me Father: feck this and feck that' – and then proceeds to repeat all of it virtually verbatim to an increasingly mortified Ted. That speech probably grew from just needing something else to do in casting sessions, sessions that would otherwise have been unbearably awkward as yet another actor tried to find variation in repeating the words 'go on' over and over.

Being a comedy writer in the nineties meant being in white rooms with one or two small boxy televisions that had a slot beneath them for VCR tapes. One day we popped one in, glancing at the note from Hubbards casting which told us that the video held one more possible candidate for Mrs Doyle. 'She might be too young, but have a look.' By now, we had a ton of new material for the character after we got tired of torturing actresses by making them do the 'go on' scene in different ways. Mrs Doyle was coming into focus just as our hopes for finding someone to play her were dimming.

But Pauline McLynn hadn't received that material yet. When she appeared on screen, she did the 'go on' scene and killed it. She was much younger than the character but, as with Jack, we didn't need Mrs Doyle, we needed someone who could play her, someone for whom the wracking cost of being alive, and of being a woman who existed only to serve men, was making such demands on her body that she sometimes staggered beneath them. In this case, Pauline found the character in a scene that had barely changed from its first appearance in our mock documentary, a scene that had begun to feel to us like toothache. The difficulty of finding comic variation in a speech that simply repeats the words 'go on' turned out to be part of an automatic winnowing process. We thought the problem was the scene. We might have lost faith in it entirely had Pauline not come in and made us realise there was only ever one woman who could do it.

The Hubbards were right – she was too young for the role; but the problem was solved with plenty of makeup and a travelling mole that sprouted on different parts of her face every week.

7

'PUT ON THE STROKES TAPE'

I HOPE IT WON'T BREAK anyone's heart to learn that Craggy Island doesn't actually exist, as such. Most of it was filmed well inland, in Clare. The magic of the title sequence, eh? We worried about yet another Irish show starting off with a helicopter shot of rolling hills but the fourth-wall-breaking crash at the end allowed us to have our cake and eat it. The music, the titles, the rolling hills, the crash into the house. Scene, characters, tone, all introduced in under thirty seconds. I sense Geoffrey's invisible hand guiding us through many of these early decisions.

A month or so before we started filming in front of the audience, we went to Ireland and grabbed all the exterior shots – anything with Ted running out the front door or being chased around the garden by a nun or hanging from a crane or whatever it might be. After location filming, there followed a week or two in the editing room getting this footage into a good enough shape to show to the studio audience on monitors. The short-term aim of this location footage was to get the biggest laughs possible from each fresh audience, who waited at the end of every studio rehearsal week like a jury. On location, Declan Lowney, our director, kindly let us stand beside him, firing dumb questions as we watched the monitor.

'Oh, you haven't got that shot of him reaching for the thing? Are we going to get that?' I would say.

'Yeah, we're just moving cameras now to get that shot.'

'Oh. OK.'

That conversation must have replayed in different ways a thousand times. I couldn't seem to get it through my head that not every shot was the last. I just knew what I wanted to see, and I would panic when time was moving on and I hadn't yet seen it. I didn't think in terms of scenes either; it was the jokes, each one a toothsome treat waiting just ahead. I knew the flavour of laugh we were looking for on each joke because Arthur and I had already laughed at it ourselves in the 'correct' way. So when it didn't taste right, I immediately knew it. That's what I love about comedy:

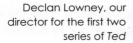

Declan Lowney, our director for the first two series of *Ted*

you can't fake it. I just did everything I could to ensure that at least once, we got a take where a certain line was said just so, and if a member of the crew had to look away and bite his fist to stop from laughing, well, then we definitely had it.

Once, we were shooting part of the montage of Ted's memories of Jack. In one, Ted's playing golf and Jack runs him over in a car. I looked at the frame, and I saw Ted playing golf, but the car was a tiny dot in the background, moving closer to the screen, visible throughout. I nearly had a heart attack. 'No, no! It's got to be a surprise! It enters from the right and leaves on the left!' It took time to realise that the images that had frozen into their perfect form in my mind were not necessarily shared by those who had read the scripts. A dozen readers will interpret a moment in a dozen ways.

There are techniques one can use to guide the reader's eye. For instance, if you write:

> Ted takes the key out of his pocket...
> ...and slides it into the lock

it suggests two shots. A shot of Ted wide enough to show him reaching into his pocket, and then a close-up of the key sliding into the lock. In this way a writer can 'direct' a scene, or at least leave a trail of breadcrumbs that the director can follow if he wishes. But we hadn't yet mastered that craft so we spent a lot of time crowding around Declan at the monitor. Our purpose on set was not entirely clear to the crew. The only place writers should be, ideally, is in a room, writing, but they were patient with us as we hung out with makeup and costume, and anyone else whose jobs paused while the cameras were running.

One freezing morning, just after dawn, my friend Ken was driving us to the set, which was located in the hills of County Cavan. None of us had the slightest idea that there was black ice covering the winding roads. As we approached a tight corner, Ken turned the wheel but the car continued stubbornly and sickeningly in the direction it had been going before he did so. Suddenly we were sliding sideways towards a looming brick wall.

I was putting a lot of thought into screaming in terror by this stage, but then, just before we hit the wall, the car, more or less entirely of its own volition, came to a sudden stop. Ken turned the engine off and we all took a few moments to remember how to breathe. For a few moments, it was almost as if nothing had happened, as if we had merely decided to park there. When we worked up enough courage to set off again, Ken had to gently nudge the accelerator to get the car the rest of the way to the shoot. If we went up a hill and the tyres went even slightly too fast, they would start to spin and we'd slide back down to the bottom of the hill again. We crept towards the top of each hill, and then he'd put on the brakes and we would just slide down the other side. We got there in the end but that wall nearly finished us.

And the reason it took us by surprise was because we didn't get the early-morning memo that there was black ice on the roads. This memo was given to every single member of the crew, except us, because we were the writers. So I used to joke that I had to learn how to direct so as to avoid being killed on the way to the set.

Why was *Ted* a success where *Paris* was not? First, and I know it sounds strange to say, *Ted* was a much more grounded show. Everything about *Paris* – from the writing, to the painted backdrops to the performances – was over the top. By crying out so loudly for attention, we were easily ignored.

Most importantly, *Ted* had a secret weapon, which was Arthur Mathews. Sure, Arthur had also done *Paris*, but *Ted* was a perfect meeting of writer and subject. Two of Arthur's uncles were priests – Tom and Paddy – and he had a deep affection for them that couldn't help informing the show's tone. We knew there was a developing scandal within the church. One headline-making story in Ireland at the time was that of Father Michael Cleary; he had an affair with his housekeeper that began when she was seventeen and he was thirty-four, producing at least one child, while she acted as his housekeeper and he carried on being a priest. Awareness was growing of these kinds of tales, so it was a sort of dark iceberg beneath the surface of the show, but it needed to stay below the surface. One of the many problems with Catholic sex scandals is that they tended not to be very funny.

The scandals were never going to be a major part of the show. We weren't going to hurry along the Catholic Church's truth and reconciliation process with our dumb jokes. That process of horror and recrimination and contrition was taking care of itself, and it wasn't our area. Unlike our compatriot, the late comedian Dave Allen, who viewed religion as oppressive and menacing, we took a similar line to the Pythons, who just thought it was a chance for men to dress up in giant hats. (One of the funniest and greatest aspects of the human race is surely the belief that high hats bestow authority.)

Besides, in our experience, priests were largely benign. We knew many who did not end up being drawn by a court sketch artist. For instance, Arthur's uncles were the very picture of innocence. One of them, Father Tom, once surprised Arthur by telling another priest, while he was preparing some tea: 'Put on The Strokes Tape.' For a dizzying second, Arthur thought his uncle had become a fan of the early noughties New York indie band. The other priest pressed play and after a moment, Arthur heard: 'First, rest the patient's head on a pillow or coat...' The Strokes Tape was a recording on how to help someone who'd had a stroke.

I grew up hating how priests dominated not just the actual but the cultural landscape in Ireland. As a teenager, my dream was to write Raymond Carver stories about embittered, divorced men (hang on a second! My wish came true!) but there was a priest and a parish in every other contemporary short story out of Ireland and early on I swore I would never write anything with a priest in it.

But the more Arthur told me about the hidden world of priests and parishes, the more I realised we had something truly unique. I would quiz him endlessly on what I suddenly realised was a whole universe of comic possibilities, as deep and strange as anything in *Vic and Bob*, and one that had been under my nose my whole life. My mother, for instance, was Mrs Doyle, fiercely refusing any offer of payment from her friends after two cups of tea and a bit of cake. 'PUT your money away!' she'd yell, flapping at their hands. 'You're mad! You're mad! Put your money away!' a scene that replayed throughout my childhood with various aunts and neighbours cycling through a series of taekwondo manoeuvres to shove the opposing side's purse back into a handbag. Moments like these had begun to glitter in my memory. Arthur gave Ireland back to me, after years of my thinking I had no use for it. And every time he told me another priest fact, I fell deeper in love with the group I had promised to never, ever write about.

'Every priest knows every other priest.'

'Priests often hate talking about religion and will try to change the subject.'

Some of the facts weren't facts at all.

'Priests' socks are made from a special extra-black kind of wool; only priests know where to buy it.'

Twin Peaks was fresh in our memory too, and we admired how David Lynch took a hermetic, mysterious world – that of the FBI – and just decided out of nowhere that they investigated things like David Bowie magically appearing in hallways. Once you have any kind of mystery surrounding an organisation, you can make up whatever nonsense you like about it and no one will contradict you. Our ear for the idiosyncrasies of Irish speech gave us the rough crackle of authenticity to sell the jokes and enhance the credibility of the world we created on Craggy Island. We did zero research. Soon, almost every fact about the Catholic Church was made up off the top of our heads, but we hoped people would be laughing too much to care.

We decided that we would never show our priests at work.

That was one of the rules: never show them doing Mass or Holy Communion or confession. Show them talking about it afterwards, sure, but never doing it. At first I didn't quite understand the rule, but I adhered to it because after *Paris* I was keen to create strictures to guide the writing and keep us on track. Never again would we hand in a forty-minute episode for a twenty-four minute slot.

Arthur pointed out that we weren't the first ecclesiastical sitcom. There was *All Gas and Gaiters* in the UK and there was even an Irish one called *Leave It to Mrs O'Brien*. These shows would all have scenes in common – a christening that goes wrong, a drunken sermon… 'This has to be about them in their downtime,' Arthur said, although he probably didn't use the word 'downtime'. 'If we have them doing Mass, it'll just look like one of those shows.'

Once we had a scene where Ted needed to do a really short Mass, but according to our rule, we couldn't see him do it.

'Couldn't we just break it this one time?' I asked Arthur, eager as always to find an easy fix to a problem.

'Absolutely not.'

And so we had him going through a church door, which swings wide and then slowly starts to close. We can hear within a Mass delivered at breakneck speed and just before the door finally slams shut, Ted bursts through it again, having already finished the entire Mass. It was exciting to discover rules and boundaries can sometimes take you to ideas you wouldn't normally have considered. Our rule had given us a joke we otherwise wouldn't have had, and once again, no one would mistake *Father Ted* for *Leave It to Mrs O'Brien*.

As with any success story, a few myths have grown up around *Ted* but by far the most persistent was that we had offered the show to RTÉ and they turned us down. No matter how often we told people it wasn't true, it kept coming back to us in different forms: interviews with journalists, in the back of taxi cabs and then finally on social media… It just wouldn't die, even when Arthur gave an extraordinarily memorable quote: 'Why would we give Ted to

RTÉ? That'd be like giving it to Waterford Glass.'

We weren't trying to be mean. The truth was just that RTÉ didn't have the infrastructure to make good studio sitcoms. We needed the experience of Hat Trick and Channel 4. Creatively, *Ted* is an Irish sitcom, but it was made within the British tradition, and it wouldn't have been half the show it was without the Harrow-educated Geoffrey Perkins making us better writers on the job. Geoffrey's notes gave us tantalising visions of the scripts as they could be, of the heights our show could reach. He never had to tell us to write anything; he just said, 'I think you're missing a trick here,' and suddenly we would make the scene take another turn and reach a level of comedy and sophistication we may not have found without him.

There should be an almost poetic density to a finished comedy script. Shakespeare's dance with his audience gave us language packed with allusion and beauty and plays overflowing with seventeenth-century content: advice to teenagers; reflections on mortality; physical comedy; violence; satire; sarcasm, horror; awe. Nothing less than the entire span of human experience, sometimes within a single speech. But this was only possible because of the simplicity of his stories. Arthur and I didn't know we were learning this lesson, but we learned it nonetheless: lose as much plot as you can, boil everything down so that you can put it in a newspaper TV listing. When the story is so simple that people can say 'it's the one where Ted is accused of racism', then you can start to enrich it further with layers of gags, set-pieces and subplots that keep people coming back to watch it again and again.

Geoffrey Perkins was inspiring and rarely put a foot wrong. The only decision to which we objected was the *Deliverance* moment in episode one, where the camera team sent to interview Ted recreate the classic 'Duelling Banjos' scene from that movie with a unique-looking local. Once filmed, we took against it. The guy dancing in the background tipped it dangerously close to paddywhackery for us, and we were still anxious about the show's reception back home. It certainly felt wrong for episode one, and we fought till the end either to remove it or make that episode the second in the run rather than the first. We lost that battle and in the end it didn't matter, because now no one even remembers which episode *is* the first.

Thanks to Geoffrey, we felt we were in good shape to finally present our show to the studio audience. We had our cast and six scripts that were pretty good, and getting better all the time.

At this point, while we were waiting to go into the studio, the show was still called 'Father Ted Crilly'. It had been called that since we began working on it because, well, that's what it was called. It's something no one – not even Geoffrey – ever thought about. One day we were hanging out with our mate Glenn Rickwood, a graphic designer we knew through music journalism. Glenn was a big genial galoot with a heart as expansive as a Yes live album. I only realised this thirty years later, during my removal from polite society, when he was one of the few people decent enough to ring me and ask if I was OK.

Back in the nineties, over drinks in that Kilburn flat, Glenn was peering at one of the scripts. He was too nice a bloke ever to look visibly annoyed but a range of emotions seemed to play over his face as he stared at the show's title. He seemed agitated about something.

'"Father Ted Crilly"…' he said, finally. 'You should change it to *Father Ted*. It'll look better on the DVDs.'

So that's what we did.

8

THE CAT AND THE PIANO

FOR MANY DEVOTEES OF THE show, each of *Father Ted*'s twenty-five episodes has the familiarity of a hymn. But so many disparate things had to come together to make it happen that I don't think you'd ever get the full story of why the notes fell in the particular order that they did. We were always looking for material. I was so in love with our creation that I thought about little else. It was a treasure to me, Craggy Island. So small it was invisible on a map, yet big enough that it felt we had staked out an entire continent of comic potential. I felt lit up by its promise and the real world was useful to me only in what it could provide for the show.

For instance, one evening, queuing for a recording for a terrible TV show in the old, iconic BBC building at White City, we realised that we could put any adjective in front of the word 'priest' and it would create a character. The Sarcastic Priest, the Laughing Priest, the Boring-Voiced Priest, the Exciting-Voiced

Priest. We ruminated happily on this and might have populated the entire show on that short walk through the BBC's corridors were it not for the fact that we saw some sort of promotion for a David Attenborough wildlife programme and one of us said 'The Monkey Priest'. This was how Father Fintan Fay popped into existence. We could think about nothing else beyond him. 'Just a priest who's a monkey. That's it.'

'He can't talk.'

'He walks like an orangutan.' I demonstrated, bending my legs while extending my arms above my head and letting my hands randomly flap about as I changed direction.

After an hour of happily discussing it we were rosy pink from laughter and all was well. But if I had thought about the journey that joke would take to reach the screen, I would have been sick with anxiety. First, you have to put him in a story that makes sense, where his existence doesn't slow things down. He can't be in it too long either, because after a while he might become annoying. Once the script is right, you have to cast someone who understands the idea and can embody it. Worse yet, maybe it's all for nothing. Maybe the Monkey Priest, after performing so graciously for us in our imaginations, would become awkward and shy when released in front of an audience.

Thankfully, Geoffrey's Zen-Englishness saved us from descending into this kind of unhelpful reverie. He had that quality of the best producers – a manner that said 'everything's going to be OK, trust to the process, listen to what the audience is trying to tell you'. And 'audience' here means the various audiences along the way. From the giant men shifting the lighting equipment around in the rafters, all the way down to the executives in the viewing gallery grazing from bowls of sweets. As fine a sample of humanity as you could wish for. Every laugh told a story, every silence another.

As I mentioned earlier, it may be hard for today's young 'uns to fully appreciate this, but *The Simpsons* was once appointment television. To those of us who experienced these early seasons as they first aired, the episodes etched themselves into our shared consciousness like few other cultural artefacts. There are moments in *The Simpsons* that constitute a shared inner language among my generation. Many of us can't hear the phrase 'I'm seeing double here' without mentally combining it with 'four Krusties!' This was from 'Homie The Clown', which, along with *The Phil Silvers Show*'s 'The Eating Competition' and 'Communication Problems' from *Fawlty Towers*, are rare examples of a perfect sitcom episode. They don't happen very often, but when they do, they are something to study closely.

The Simpsons at its best had a rhythm that you didn't see in live-action sitcoms. Because it was animated, they could have someone say a line, and then cut to a location halfway across the world where a completely random character would say something to provide some sort of humorous counterpoint. We wanted some of the same energy. We weren't *Yes, Minister*, we were Homer shooting Marge in the face with a 'makeup gun', the gun for women who only had 'four-fifths of a second to get ready'.

The script had to look a certain way on the page. Too much dialogue without a visual gag and I would get antsy. The opposite could also be true, with too much activity revealing a plot that was working too hard. If the characters didn't know what to say about a matter, there was a chance it didn't belong in the show. The pieces either neatly fell into place like Tetris blocks, or they were out.

We were aiming for perfect. Every single second of it had to be funny. If it wasn't funny for even a moment, there had to be something EXTREMELY funny coming up. We were laughing all the time when we wrote it, and it was important to us that the same joy we had writing it carried through the process. Again, a long journey for a joke to take and not everything made it to the screen in quite the way we imagined. But for every joke that wasn't

The lads, Ardal
and Dermot

quite how we visualised it, a startling decision from one of the actors would make up for it. Ardal delivered a line reading of the simple question 'Who are you?' with such unexpected rudeness that we made it a permanent part of his character. We only realised midway through filming that Pauline was the most gifted physical actor of the bunch, the one who should have all the gags that involved falling out of shot.

As soon as Dermot stepped in front of the first studio audience and heard how explosively Ardal was going down, he lost a bit of confidence in his character. Dermot was more of a satirist, and I guess we were doing what you might call whimsy. But whatever you called it, we thought Ted was a hilarious character. We were giving him some great lines but they weren't funny in the same way that Dougal was funny. In *Only Fools and Horses*, Trigger is always going to get bigger laughs than Del Boy, but Del Boy is still the star. Dermot was the star of a show with his character's name as its title, but his drive was such that he still thought he was only halfway up the ladder. And it couldn't have been comfortable for him, listening to the great delighted explosions of laughter that dependably followed Dougal's non-sequiturs. On top of that, he was eager to introduce himself as a satirist and writer to UK audiences, so, during series one and two, he was often engaged in lining up other work. He would take phone calls for future jobs during rehearsals, which is something you really don't do.

One day, I said to Declan Lowney, our director, 'This is driving me mad – the phone calls. Can we do something about them?' And Declan did the director's trick of making it a general announcement, so as not to embarrass Dermot by singling him out. At the start of the read-through, Declan said, 'Just to say, everyone, this week we're not going to have any mobile phones on during rehearsals.' Dermot's whole body shot up from his script like a meerkat. As soon as the read was over, he sprang up, darted around the table to Declan and said, 'The phone-call thing – that doesn't apply to me, does it? Because I've got some *crucial* calls coming up.'

My mum told me a story that we tried to give to Ted. She was in a house belonging to someone she didn't know very well, and this woman left her for a moment to make some tea or pick some tea or do something to do with tea. Among the objects in the room where my mother waited was a piano with the lid up and the keys exposed. Across from the piano, an open window was admitting a pleasant breeze and then, presently, a grey cat, which poured itself over the sill, dropped silently into the room and padded towards her.

'Hello,' said Mum and held her hand out to the cat.

The cat sniffed my mum's hand, considered it for a moment and then, in my mum's telling, proceeded to go absolutely mental. It started to run laps around the room, jumping up behind Mum and running along the back of the sofa, and every time it reached the piano, it ran across the keys.

BANG, CLANG, DRANG, GLANG.

Then, again, another circuit of the room and again across the keys.

BANG, CLANG, DRANG, GLANG.

Then it leapt up and disappeared out of the window again.

There was a brief pause and then the woman who owned the house appeared around the door and stared at my mother in shock.

After a moment, Mum said, 'No, no, I wasn't playing the... It was your cat.'

The woman said, 'I don't have a cat.'

So not only did this woman think my mum was whacking the piano keys like a toddler, she thought she had gone on to blatantly lie about it. We tried to have the same thing happen to Ted, but Geoffrey nixed it. Too far-fetched, he told us.

'But it happened,' I protested. I had questioned my mother like a police detective and she swore on our lives – my brothers' and sister's and mine – that it was true.

'Doesn't matter,' he said. Another one of Geoffrey's lessons. Being true isn't enough. It has to *feel* true.

Sometimes inspiration was mysterious, other times much less so, to an almost embarrassing degree.

The scene in episode six where Ted walks in on a deceased Father Jack ('I was only just talking to him!' says Ted, again, oblivious that he's been doing all the talking) is actually almost beat for beat the same as a similar scene in the *Fawlty Towers* episode 'The Kipper and the Corpse'. Arthur didn't spot it, Geoffrey didn't spot it, none of the actors spotted it, or if they did they thought it was deliberate and kept it to themselves. Worst of all, I didn't spot it. *Fawlty Towers* is for me almost a religious text. If there was a fire, and I had to choose between saving a human being, and saving the last digital copy of *Fawlty Towers*? Well, it really would depend on which human being we were talking about.

But even I didn't notice it. When *Paris* came out, we were accused of copying the storyline of Tony Hancock's film *The Rebel* for the plotline of the first episode. But neither of us were particular fans of the film and the accusation took us by surprise. On the other hand, when someone finally did notice the similarities between the scene in *Father Ted* and 'The Kipper and the Corpse', we realised with horror that they were right. It would have been much more reasonable for people to accuse us of plagiarising John Cleese than Tony Hancock. And yet, no one ever made that charge. Charm is a powerful thing, and in the same way that people don't notice audience laughter if they enjoy a show, we somehow seemed to get away with our unconscious daylight robbery.

Wearing their Sunday best, my terrified mum and dad came over for that very episode, the last studio recording on series one. 'Is it good? Is it good?' they asked everyone in the green room. They just couldn't tell. The episode they watched was the first we ever wrote, Jack coming back from the dead because drinking Toilet Duck wasn't fatal to priests. The experience had frazzled their

Dermot meets my mum, the real Mrs Doyle

brains. They didn't know how to take the apparent attack on the priesthood, even if our ferocious assault was conducted with jokes about spider babies and toy cows.

'Mum, Dad, this is Geoffrey. Geoffrey produced the show.'

'Hello, Geoffrey. Lovely to meet you. Is it good?'

'Yes, hello Geoffrey. Is it good?'

'It's very good,' Geoffrey assured them. 'Don't worry. '

We were buoyant. The crew had been laughing throughout, which Geoffrey told us was a great sign. TV crews are hard to please, and they're trying to do their job. If they're laughing, it's significant. Sure enough, the show was an almost instant success. A few early reviewers had that reflexive distrust of comedy that marks the breed (I should know; it's my breed), but for the most part the notices glowed. Even so, we didn't realise we had a hit until we saw, in the audience of the first episode of the second series, a pair of nuns who were obviously not real nuns. We pointed them out to each other excitedly. People were dressing as characters from the show! That had to be a good sign. It made sense on another level too, as one of our central satirical themes regarding the Catholic Church was 'literally anyone can do this job'.

And then we won a Bafta. This began a lifetime addiction to winning awards which is a REALLY BAD THING because it means that you're ceding control of how you feel about your work to others. I couldn't help it. Ever since I was a kid, I'd always loved awards shows. When we finally won, given the award by no less than Vic and Bob themselves, I arrived on stage so suddenly that Bob let out a small cry. I carried on loving awards shows until the first time I went to one and didn't win anything.

Early success has proved something of a double-edged sword, but overall I would recommend it. A part of me that had been anxious and restive suddenly found some peace. There was no need to prove I could create another show like *Father Ted*. I was already relaxed about my legacy, if such a word can be applied to the cardboard and plywood world of studio sitcoms. That meant

The whole cast and crew in the front room of the Parochial House. Frank didn't even have to move from his chair. I'm off to the right, next to the bookcase

I could enter into later collaborations with a light heart, even as expectations remained high. Even now, if people meet me and their faces light up, ninety-nine percent of the time it's because of *Father Ted*.

The second series was substantially easier to write because we were now writing for our cast. Frank Kelly *bounded* into the rehearsal room on the first day. As soon as he had seen the show in its entirety, he loved it. Jack, being the most extreme regular character, had to be activated only every so often, like Godzilla, so Frank began working very carefully to protect the scattered comic moments that he had. At the read-through for 'Are You Right There, Father Ted?', he was worried that the joke about Jack being addicted to small spaces wouldn't play because no one would believe he could fit in a grandfather clock.

In addition, the lessons of *Seinfeld* inspired us to refine the scriptwriting process even further. A *Seinfeld* story for a single character might only consist of three scenes, placed at intervals along the show's running length. But when you have one plot line for every character, the show rapidly acquires the necessary poetic density. Three characters means nine scenes. With four characters you have twelve! That's a whole show already, more than one, actually. You might even have to lose something; keep it in the fridge for another episode.

We learned how to write by writing. One of the problems we kept facing was exposition. Arthur wasn't troubled by it, but it maddened me to hear characters telling each other the plot rather than simply talking to each other and accidentally revealing it. We hit upon something I think was ours alone – perhaps *Blackadder* did it to some extent, but I think we properly went for it – which was leaning into the exposition and turning its obviousness into a joke. For instance, the short speech where Ted goes on and on about the perfectly square bit of black dirt on a window – indeed discusses the very unlikelihood of a piece of dirt having such perfect dimensions – was intended only to hammer it into your head that it was there, and explain why people looking in through the window thought that Ted was doing a Hitler impression.

Often we would throw out pages of script that didn't add anything to the very simple premise, and I learned that you know you're in a good place when you're cutting jokes you love. It means the story has taken over and is almost telling itself. Anything that doesn't fit falls from it naturally like something vestigial. In the episode 'A Song For Europe', midway through series two, we originally had an entire sequence of Ted and Dougal in a sound studio recording their Eurovision entry with a frazzled hippy named Beep, based on Dublin music personality B.P. Fallon.

At one point during the recording of the song, the permanently stoned Beep runs in and congratulates Ted and Dougal.

'That was amazing, guys! Best take yet! Shall we call it a day?'

Cut to Ted and Dougal, bent over their equipment, looking at him in confusion.

'We're still setting up, Beep. We haven't recorded anything yet.'

We loved the scene, but it would have brought the show to thirty minutes – six minutes over a Channel 4 half hour. Also, it brought up too many questions about Ted and Dougal's musical aptitude;

Dermot Morgan with Geoffrey Perkins, and me deep in conversation in the background

suddenly they're 'setting up equipment'? We took it out and felt great about it. We knew by then that the episode was special, and that if something that good had to go, then it must mean the rest of it was in great shape.

On series two, Geoffrey left his post as producer to become head of comedy at the BBC. Although we acquired a brilliant new producer in Lissa Evans, my role grew in Geoffrey's absence, and by series three I would take over from Declan as director. Suddenly I had a place on the set, which meant I'd get the memo about black ice on the roads. The likelihood of my living through the shoot shot up, although Arthur would still have to take his chances.

The idyllic days of hanging out with my notebook, flirting with the wardrobe and costume departments and trying to think of more jokes were over. I learned that directing, as Stephen Fry so memorably put it, is the job of being pecked to death by a million questions. From the moment you wake up to the moment you go to sleep, you're being asked, 'This jumper or this jumper? Do you want this to go here or here?' Elements to which I had never given a moment's thought, such as, 'What should the extras be doing?' nibbled at me. These questions hurt my brain because they didn't have anything to do with the comedy.

The only time I knew what the extras should be doing was when they were part of the joke. Like when Ted has his grand Hercule Poirot moment at the end of 'Chirpy Burpy Cheap Sheep', and the crowd's shocked murmurings are punctured by a single voice going 'Fucking hell' (mine). If it was in the script, I knew how to shoot it. Anything that wasn't written down came as an unpleasant shock.

But I came to like directing well enough. The only thing you need to know is what you want. Robert Rodriguez, who made the *El Mariachi* films, had a memorable piece of advice. He said you should sit in front of a white wall after you've written your script and 'watch' your film. Then, on a blank piece of paper, you write down all the shots that you see in the order that you see them. And that's your shot list.

It really is that simple. But then you get the questions.

9

SHAME ABOUT YER MAN

DERMOT WASN'T YET famous on the first series so, while wearing his character's costume, he would be met with funny looks by passers-by when greeting his wife and new baby with kisses and hugs. Similarly, Ardal and Pauline were just, as far as everyone knew, a young, fresh-faced priest and a strangely sprightly old woman who swore like a docker. By the final series, all of them were so well known that they would be followed down the main street in Ennistymon by groups of children as they made their way to each new camera set-up.

Kids especially loved Jack, because they were terrified of him. As Dougal might have said, he was the anti-Santa. Frank told me that at the height of his *Father Ted* fame, crowds of local Dublin scamps would come to his home so he could sign his autograph on their clammy, crumpled pieces of paper. He would maintain his somewhat posh, somewhat camp, charming manner throughout

Frank, a natural storyteller and bon vivant, would often find himself eating alone because no one could bear to sit with him while he was in makeup

the exchange until, with the ceremony completed, the kids would just stand there, looking blank, unsure how to close the transaction. Frank would then snap into character and shout 'FECK OFF!' at them, causing a sudden multi-directional scramble for safety.

Despite the attention that came with success, we were all getting exhausted. This would be our third season of Frank sitting on his own in the cafeteria because no one from the crew could bear to look at his makeup job while they were eating. At a distance, Father Jack's ghastliness was comic, and when he first wandered out of the makeup van there was widespread delight at the job done by our makeup team. But as soon as the details came into focus over a lunchtime plate of curry and chips, it lost a lot of its appeal.

So Frank, a born raconteur, someone with incredible stories to tell, including working briefly with Michael Caine on *The Italian*

Job, was usually found sitting off in the distance doing a crossword to the soundtrack of conversation from nearby cast and crew. After I could bear this no longer, I defocused my vision enough to join him and hear a few of his stories. Frank had several strings to his bow. He once had a novelty hit record with his comic version of 'Twelve Days of Christmas', in which each additional gift inflicts further chaos and bother on an increasingly frustrated and angry narrator. 'Seven swans-a-swimming is a most romantic idea but not in the bath of a private house! We cannot use the bathroom now because they've gone completely savage and rush the door every time we try to enter!'

I'm not sure in what capacity he did it, but Frank was touring Ireland at a time when the 'showbands' were at their peak. In the postwar period, these were professional, live bands made up of a tour bus full of musicians, travelling from rural town to rural town playing a mix of pop, rock and country hits. They were wildly successful, because there was nowhere else to hear the music; at the time, the Catholic Church kept a firm grip on how much culture we were permitted to absorb from the heathens to our east and west. The songs weren't even played on the radio, so the bands had record players on the tour bus in order to learn any new numbers on their way to gigs. There are stories of these bands playing shows alongside The Beatles. In fact, Brendan Bowyer of The Royal Showband had his Mercedes tour bus admired by the Fab Four when they were still in quiffs and leather.

The day I finally braved sitting with Frank over lunch, he told me one of his own stories. One time, he said, at a gig out in the middle of nowhere, the manager came onto the stage, put his hands up to shush the audience and made an announcement. 'Could everyone PLEASE use the toilets instead of doing it up against the wall outside,' he said. 'There's a stream of urine flowing all the way down the front walk. It's disgusting. People shouldn't have to put up with it. If you need to take a slash, do it in the toilets provided, not up against the fucking walls, for God's sake. You're not animals.

'And now, ladies and gentlemen…DUSTY SPRINGFIELD!'

By series three, Dermot was famous. He would sometimes repair away from filming to have a quiet pint on his own and look at the newspapers. On one such occasion, the barman approached and nodded towards a lone drinker, a man at the other end of the bar.

The barman leaned over and quietly said to Dermot. 'Do you see yer man? He murdered his wife, put her in the trunk of his car and pushed it off the edge of a cliff.'

Dermot took this in.

'So you're not the only celebrity in town.'

I remember Dermot telling me this, and I laughed but he didn't. He seemed tired. But we all were. Arthur and I now felt we had strip-mined Craggy Island pretty conclusively of all its comedy. For instance, we had a running joke about Ted always phoning his friend Larry Duff on his mobile phone (cellphones being still something of a novelty at the time) and distracting him to such an extent that he would have a disastrous accident. The first one was the best, with Larry driving off a cliff in a bit of impressive stock footage we tracked down. But there were one or two later ones that made me wince.

The flip side of being able to write for our cast was leaning too heavily on the things we knew they could do. It comes to a point where you're not exploring the characters with them but running in place. It's the sad fate of many sitcoms, with audiences turning up not to be surprised and elated, but reassured and placated that their old friends haven't changed – and never will. And when you can't run in place, you run the risk of breaking the character. Rather than fill another episode with Jack shouting abuse at everyone, at one point, we had Ted say of him, 'Oh, today is the only day of the year when Father Jack becomes full of the joys of spring, and becomes a lovely man,' or something along those lines. Then we cut to Jack playing with puppies and dancing in a field. We were breaking the character, just to give us something new to do with him. I thought, well, you can do that once. What are we going to do in series four? We couldn't keep on breaking his character, or before long we wouldn't be able to find Jack in the wreckage.

We suspected also that if we went into a fourth series, Dougal's childishness might start looking a bit melancholy. Unlike John Sullivan, who brought the severely confused Trigger onto the *Fools and Horses* stage only every so often, we had our Trigger up there all the time. Dougal, again, was someone who would run across the room if someone threw a sweet. You could get away with that for a while, but maybe only for a while, before he started growing visibly older and his eccentricities began to look like a predicament.

We knew also, from being comedy fans ourselves, that there's often a series too far. Say you're enjoying a show so much that you consider yourself a fan, and then one day someone says 'Did you see it last week?' and you realise you forgot all about it. That's what I mean. You don't quite know when it happened or how it happened, but somewhere along the line it stopped being an essential date in your calendar. My beloved *Seinfeld* never recovered from the loss of Larry David. When he left, the characters suddenly felt to me like ghosts, and my attention drifted away.

Perhaps the saddest example is *The Simpsons*, which began by satirising disposable culture, and then became, with each subsequent season, a progressively worse example of it. If they'd quit in time, they'd never have had to deal with the Apu scandal – where the formerly beloved Indian 7/11 employee, whose character satirised Indian culture in the same way that Homer was the lunkhead American everyman, was suddenly deemed problematic by a generation who found everything problematic. But it was true that the character had withered with age. We didn't want that to happen to our guys. Who's to say? If fate hadn't got in the way, maybe we could have been lured back into writing a fourth series. But I kind of hope we would have stood our ground. Out of the twenty-five episodes, I think you could say about eighteen were pretty damned good. And that's a hell of a strike rate for a two-man team.

Here's a scene for you. Me, Arthur and Frank Kelly, maybe even Neil Hannon, because his music was the soul of the show and it would fit if he was there at this precise moment, all of us in a silent black Ford Galaxy gliding over the Thames with the London skyline glowing gold and red around us. Frank would frequently tell the story, which is the only reason I can still visualise it. Apparently I said something like, 'Look at this, going over the Thames, on our way to making the last few episodes of our multi-award-winning sitcom. It won't get better than this.'

And indeed it didn't.

The final day of shooting a series like *Father Ted* is a bit like the final day of school. There's a giddy, loose atmosphere. We'd been through a lot – the cast and crew, Lissa and Arthur and I – and we were finally going to be free of each other. Dermot had really given us his all during the third series. He was still easily distracted by the studio audience, to whom he would wander over between takes so he could regale them with material, but he was also generous and open and doing the job brilliantly. Having found his groove as an actor after three years of on-the-job training, Dermot was focused, his energy was keeping us all going, and his anxiety at not getting the same kinds of laughs as Ardal was a thing of the past. That series contained some of my favourite *Ted* moments, and Dermot powered through it, giving us every ounce of his energy. Once we wrapped, we expected him to join us to celebrate, but a fleeting appearance at the wrap party was only to make his excuses and leave. He looked beat. I stayed up and danced with my girlfriend of the time, or more likely watched her dance, and we used Saturday to recover and celebrate again.

By Sunday, Dermot was dead. He had a heart attack over dinner with friends at his home in West London and died shortly afterwards in hospital. He was forty-five.

I heard the news from John Fisher, Dermot's trusted friend and assistant, trying to make sense of his words through the fog of a 7am hangover. 'What are you on about? I was only just talking to him' – one of the first lines we'd written for Ted – played through my mind on a loop. I had to call Arthur to tell him the news. He thought I was joking. The phone calls, the confusion, lasted only for an hour or two, to be replaced over the next few days by that grim march through the process of saying goodbye to someone who has left the room forever.

I was only just talking to him.

Just a few days after the funeral, we had to go back into the editing room and make the show. There was Dermot, facing us from several screens, messing about between takes, waves of audible mirth from the audience greeting his every word, and yet, he was gone. Editing was usually a process of laughter and lively debate but we cut series three with the insane fact of Dermot's death ensuring we never enjoyed it too much. The third series also brought our first billboard poster campaign. Dermot, Ardal, Pauline and Frank, towering over traffic and pulling silly faces. But one of them gone. There, bigger than ever, but gone.

In our football episode, 'Escape From Victory', there was a scene where Ted cannot accept his star striker is dead, so he ends up sitting on the guy's chest in the coffin and giving him CPR to bring him back to life. I got a call from John Fisher again. 'Listen Graham, we have to lose that scene. It's going to be upsetting.' Similarly, we had to change our ending to the series, which originally had Ted ready to commit suicide at the idea of spending the rest of his life on Craggy Island. We replaced it with a montage – memories of the show, running under the suddenly devastating title music – and almost accidentally created something so moving that it allowed people to grieve Dermot's death. The montage was a strange ending to *Ted*'s story. As powerful as it was, it closed the show on a melancholy note, instead of the joyful chaos we had planned. Even now, a quarter of a century later, when people discover I wrote *Father Ted*, their first words are often, 'Shame about yer man.'

After nearly a decade of working together, and four years of being flatmates, Arthur and I had developed a form of telepathy. I remember once sitting beside him watching telly and I started to say something. He laughed before I said it. He knew what the joke was and pre-approved it. Even when he moved out of Griff's flat, we spoke every other day on the phone. I dreaded the thought that he might return to Ireland, or indeed go anywhere, or do anything that meant we wouldn't be able to continue writing together. Together, I felt, we made one great comedy writer; I was the strategist who sat down and thought about structure and character consistency and tried to ensure things made sense, whereas Arthur followed his nose down endless labyrinths of nonsense. Sometimes we'd switch roles, but that's how it usually worked, and it worked well. I was twenty-nine, still too immature to realise that a healthy bit of distance was probably going to be better for our future as collaborators.

In the pub or just chatting about an idea, Arthur said little and hit the target every time, whereas my route to a laugh was more circuitous. I rambled and tripped across jokes. On the page, we swapped roles, Arthur producing pages and pages of hilarious dialogue, while I only committed things to paper if I was certain they would work. Sometimes Arthur's material wouldn't fit logically, so I would fish through his pages, find stuff I liked and try and make it knit together by writing a bit myself. Then he would do the same to mine. It was a lovely to-and-fro.

I was always trying to figure out how stories worked, what made a story a story. For me, at that time, it was a mysterious thing. It still is. How do you know when a story is a story? In America, they have page counts and act breaks. We just had a list of ten things we wanted to happen. As we wrote, we would discover the answers to story problems just by stumbling upon them. Later on, I adopted *Rick and Morty* creator Dan Harmon's story circles, which simplify the mythic structure of stories as laid out by Joseph Campbell in *The Hero's Journey*.

Harmon draws a circle to represent each character's journey:

1. The character…
2. …has a problem.
3. He enters into a 'new world' to solve the problem.
4. He tries various ways of dealing with the problem.
5. He gets what he wants…
6. But suffers as a result.
7. He returns to the normal world….
8. Having changed.

A young writer once told me he didn't like using these kinds of guides. He said he preferred the idea of something like we had done in our episode 'Entertaining Father Stone'. Out of interest I went back to that episode and discovered it fitted the story circle in the years before we knew such things existed.

1. Father Ted is relaxing in bed with no responsibilities.
2. He discovers Father Stone is coming.
3. Father Stone arrives.
4. Ted and Dougal try to continue their normal lives with Stone, but it's impossible.
5. Ted prays to God to get rid of Stone, God hits Stone with lightning.
6. Ted suffers much embarrassment and guilt, meeting Father Stone's family while he's in a coma.
7. Ted prays to God, promising he'll change his ways and Father Stone miraculously awakens.
8. Ted sits miserably with Stone, realising he's stuck with him.

While writing the episode, we were for a while hopelessly lost around point five. We had Stone, who was being awkward and silent, and Ted and Dougal were having a rough time. It was funny enough, but any more awkward, protracted silences and the show would have dropped dead. Suddenly, it hit me that Ted was a priest, and could actually use the power of prayer to get rid of Stone. The crack of lightning spun the show in a new direction, and gave us Stone's family and lines like: 'Sure, wouldn't it have been better if he'd been killed?' Had we had Harmon's guide, we might have reached that moment of inspiration much sooner. All these systems, these handholds and guide ropes, are just there to support you while you're trying to get to your destination. They're not a replacement for creativity, they're a framework to allow for it.

Stone was based on a real priest who used to visit a married couple, some friends of Arthur's, every year. This priest would stay with them, not talk at all and refuse to do anything that might alleviate the awkwardness and boredom. Not only this, but he could not be dissuaded from coming, no matter what. Finally, one year the wife had had enough, grabbed the phone from her husband and said desperately, 'Please don't come! We have nothing in common!'

'We'll *find* something in common,' said the priest.

The best writers disappear, leaving only their characters behind. It was a sign we'd done our job right that when Arthur and I went on RTÉ's *The Late Late Show*, an uncomfortable Ryan Tubridy could barely think of anything to ask us. We were an impediment to people enjoying *Father Ted*, a reminder that the show is actually a collection of decisions, casting, writing, shooting, and the suspension of disbelief is just a little bit harder for an audience to achieve. No one cared that Arthur created the character on stages in pubs, that we wrote 'Flight Into Terror' in one weekend, or that

Arthur had a cameo in the episode 'The Old Grey Whistle Theft', playing an irate picnicker

we called one character 'Fargo' because *Fargo* was the only film you could rent on the location hotel's video channel, so we saw it every night as, every night, a different crew member put it on for the first time.

Among the writer's duties is an ability to step off the stage, and nowhere was this more obvious than when Arthur and I attended one of the *Father Ted* weekends that cropped up once the show had achieved mainstream and cult success in Ireland. *Ted*'s victory in Ireland was always particularly sweet to us. I'd heard stories of pubs going silent and closing the blinds while it was on; bringing an Irish pub to a stop – that's an achievement I can take to the grave. But the *Father Ted* weekends were on another level of fandom entirely, an event where fans could step into the show and lose themselves. It was quite a thing for us to see people dressed up as various characters from the show, and just as our costume department had astonished us by providing a spectrum of colours and choices (watch Dougal's jumpers change from episode to episode) so here the fans reflected our show back to us in a way that left us moved and marvelling at the world within a world that we'd accidentally created. We were the only people not dressed as priests or bishops or cardinals, nuns or cleaning ladies.

Every so often, someone would nod over at us quizzically, and be informed that we were the writers. The effect was instantaneous. You could see them shrinking in their cassocks, suddenly self-conscious. Just as visitors to the Parochial House in Clare express disappointment that the interior looks nothing like the *Father Ted* living room, which existed only as a set at the London Studios, so we were, merely by our presence, puncturing a fantasy and rudely intruding on it. We didn't go back.

It's heartbreaking, in a way, like seeing a kid off to college. A wave goodbye and suddenly, that's it, a whole part of your life is over. For the best part of a decade, we were our show's biggest fans, because we had to be. All our rules and ambitions, our attempts to play with the form, to subvert expectations of the sitcom and of Ireland and ourselves, all that was leading to this moment, when we would have nothing more to do with it.

We only broke our rule about never seeing the priests at work once, in our episode based on the Keanu Reeves film *Speed*. Ted and his mates decided that the best way to help Dougal survive driving a milk float with a bomb on it was to perform Mass while driving alongside it. The visual was so funny that even Arthur abandoned his objections. Not only that, he performed the service himself, and audiences finally got to see the two Teds together, rattling alongside a milk float on a trailer pulled by a tractor. Dermot, our friend who had made the character his own, and Ted's first incarnation, embodied by the gentle, punk comic genius, Arthur Mathews.

10
SHORT FORM

HAVING REPEATEDLY pooh-poohed the idea that our attention spans were getting shorter, dismissing it again and again to my own satisfaction as Luddite scaremongering, I now find myself watching film trailers for film trailers. Each trailer has, just before it begins, another trailer, which shows highlights from the main trailer. Human curiosity, satisfied moment to moment by the endless scroll of social media posts, is no longer a sufficient engine for the job of watching a two-minute advert for a film. I myself have found that every time I think of something I need to google for this book, at least half an hour disappears I know not where, but I do return to my writing with the knowledge that Jordan Peele has a new film out.

I didn't recognise the attention-shattering aspect of the internet because it was just my speed. I loved writing sketches for much the same reason. A sketch burns brightly and disappears, like the head of a match, whereas a sitcom is more like a furnace that you have to keep feeding with the fuel of character development, story arcs, set-ups/payoffs and so on. Feeling the pressure from the raised expectations after *Ted*, we decided to make a sketch show to 'relax'. It was called *Big Train*, after an easy-listening song that we both liked because it was funny and didn't seem to mean anything.

For the first part of my writing life, my treasured book of Fry and Laurie sketches was something of a Comedy Bible. I hope I'm quoting it right – I lost my only copy somewhere along the line – but when we were writing we always aimed for something as funny as this exchange between an eccentric therapist and his patient:

THERAPIST: Do I scare you, Kenneth?
KENNETH: No.
THERAPIST: suddenly screams.
KENNETH: AHHH!
THERAPIST: Did that scare you, Kenneth?
KENNETH: Well, yes.

Other obsessions were the snippets of *Saturday Night Live* sketches we saw on DVD compilations. We wore out the laser watching a *Best of Phil Hartman* DVD, which I think is where we discovered our beloved Caveman Lawyer. When the internet came along, and I finally got to see entire episodes of *SNL*, I realised that these snippets were highlights of what were often cavernously long sketches, under-rehearsed to such an extent that the actors spent much of the time staring, not at their colleagues in the show, but off-screen at cue cards. It's strange to me that *SNL* places such store in being 'live'. Creative spontaneity comes at the beginning and the end of the rehearsal process. At the beginning, because the lack of familiarity with the material leads to creative interpretations and enhancements of it. At the end, because easy familiarity with the material allows actors to improvise at a micro level. *SNL*, by contrast, seems to bring its audience into the no man's land at the middle of the process, where the players' footing is uncertain and there's still ambivalence about where they find the cues and cameras. Still, *SNL* often manages to overcome the obstacles they put in their own way. We loved that selection of Hartman moments; his impression of Admiral Stockdale, running mate to the billionaire presidential candidate Ross Perot, in which he shouted random political slogans like 'GRIDLOCK' at no one in particular, formed a major part of Father Jack's DNA.

Another obsession was *The Day Today*. Working in the Talkback offices while we were writing *Father Ted* were Armando Iannucci, Chris Morris and Steve Coogan, who were co-captains of the groundbreaking news satire, along with the soon-to-be famed playwright Patrick Marber. A news parody that sold nonsense situations to the viewer by playing them dead straight, *The Day Today* had that perfect mix of derision and affection towards its target – the BBC's pompous news division – that makes for the best satire. In one episode, they had a couple of actors in a story about wild horses running loose in London Underground's tunnels. Well, to be precise, they had one actor playing the tube driver, and another man who was an actual tube driver. The actor couldn't quite get what they were after. He didn't have that thing that people have when they're interviewed by the news, where they zone out and give flat answers like cops giving evidence at a trial. But the real driver had that quality, so he's the one who made it into the show. He instinctively understood that if you're going to have a joke about horses loose in tube tunnels, the thing you must not do is act.

It seemed to us that *The Day Today*'s approach to comedy was entirely new. Thrilled by what they were doing, we even contributed a few ideas, but we also wondered about transposing their approach onto a narrative sketch show. Hyper-realism didn't suit every concept, so our fondness for the silly and the stupid gave us a choice of styles that allowed us to experiment occasionally while still keeping an eye on Jon Plowman's aunt in Weston-super-Mare.

Gary Larson's *Far Side* cartoons were also in the mix – I think he was the first person to hit on the idea that animals can spell, just not very well, which went on to become the internet's predominant comic meme – as was Luís Buñuel's *Phantom of Paradise*, which is really just a collection of sketches played straight. In one, a man with a rifle kills several innocent people and is found guilty of murder, whereupon he thanks his jubilant defence team and walks from the court a free man. In another, desperate attempts to locate a missing child play out despite the fact the child is in every scene, begging for attention from the adults, who either ignore him or distractedly shoo him away. There's a thing in comedy I call a CBA, which means Could Be Anything. If a guy's walking down the street and an elephant falls on him, that's a CBA. It could've been an elephant, could've been a bus, could've been a whale... It Could Be Anything so it's not funny as a result. Buñuel's sketches, on the other hand, possess a gripping and coherent internal logic. We thought we'd reach for Buñuel because experience had taught us that when you aim high, you tend to fail better.

Confident that we now had a multiplicity of comic dynamics and influences going for us, we found actors who did 'silly' and 'dead straight' with equal gusto: Simon Pegg, Kevin Eldon (from my Club Z days), Amelia Bullmore, Julia Davis and Mark Heap. All of them enormously talented and game for anything. One sketch had pop duo Hall and Oates – creators of 'Maneater' and many more unbelievably catchy, smooth pop singles in the eighties – being asked to clean up a rough area of inner London. Kevin Eldon and Simon Pegg didn't even do an impression. We just put a curly wig on Kevin and got him to kneel down so he looked really short. Simon and Kevin wandered around, trying to get prostitutes off the streets, cleaning up dog mess, the residents playing it for real, saying, 'Why are they doing this? They have no skills.' It was a matter of just playing it as straight as we could, and showing the frustration of the locals, as these two pop stars wander around the estate, completely out of their depth.

It was like a comedy laboratory in which we were running various experiments: if you make something as realistic as possible, but it's a ridiculous situation, will it become funnier the longer it goes on? We wanted to have people wheezing with laughter. Unfortunately, while working on *Big Train*, I was still struggling with the urge to become a Director with a capital D. Our use of improvisation helped us to build a sense of reality, but I was so besotted with our actors and my role behind the camera that I sometimes left too much of it in the final cut. My advice: include just enough improv to convince people it's real and then make with the jokes, folks. Cut everything that doesn't make you laugh and you'll look like a genius.

But on the whole, it worked just fine. I remember how much we laughed when we came up with the 'Spoon Phobia' sketch, how we laughed all through the filming of that sketch, all through the editing, and even now it's something I would place at the very top of my career. In it, a fresh-faced and charismatic new manager strolls into the office and quickly wins over the staff. He then announces that he has a fear of spoons and asks for some sensitivity around the matter. Someone enters the meeting late, stirring a cup of tea with a spoon, and the new manager immediately jumps out the window and kills himself. We wrote that one and took the rest of the week off.

Bloopers from the nineties sitcom *Friends* fill me with a mixture of envy and horror. Between takes, the actors, RELAXED TO THE POINT OF GIGGLING, play practical jokes on each other because American budgets allow them to run each episode in front of two separate audiences on consecutive nights. Part of the reason why making a studio sitcom in the UK is so stressful is that we only get one shot. An entire week of rehearsals – not to mention the months of writing, rewriting and pre-production leading up to it

– converges on a single three-hour recording. If we failed to shoot something within those three hours, we'd have to find some time the following week, which left even less time for the episode we had to shoot that night.

Still, there's something to be said for a tight budget. Some of the best sketches in *Big Train* came about purely through necessity. We wrote a sketch set in an office, and our producer Sioned Wiliam said, 'We've got this office for the whole day. Will you write more stuff set in an office?' So we would write fifteen more sketches set in an office. And there were often better sketches among those fifteen than the ones we'd actually pitched in the first place. This is another reason I can't bear lazy writers. The idea that the first thing out of your pen, everyone has to kiss its arse, is ludicrous. Writing is rewriting, and writers who don't rewrite are a liability.

Where we fell down with *Big Train* was not understanding the essential role of live audience laughter. We thought we could replicate it by presenting the show as a finished programme in a cinema. When you're doing a studio sitcom, the audience is a key part of the show, and you can draw from them a very live, responsive laughter. I would sometimes ask to show a location clip for a second time and tell the audience, 'Don't laugh at the first joke; hold it in so that you can hear the second joke, because the second joke is really good.' The crowd would then listen attentively, give you the right kind of laugh you needed for the first quiet joke, and then boom! An explosion when they heard the punchline. It is a kind of music soundtrack, I suppose, the audience transforming into an orchestra, reacting to the material in an engaged, dynamic way as if led by a conductor. But *Big Train* was shot entirely on location. We just plonked the audience down in a cinema and pressed 'play'. So the laughter was kind of a flat, weird thing. As if that wasn't bad enough, at one recording, some schoolboys in the audience started laughing sarcastically. 'We've got sarcastic laughter over the show,' I said to Sioned finally. 'That is surely not a good thing.' So I had to keep going out into the audience and saying, 'The people who are doing sarcastic laughing, please stop it.' For years, I've groaned at the memory of that moment, but now, writing it down, I see it's the stuff of exquisite comedy.

I didn't make it to the second series of *Big Train*. Perhaps because of our cheap rent, I saw comedy less as a business and more as an art project or an experiment; we had successfully produced a show in the style of *Big Train* and I felt it was time to move on to something else. Our limited budget had meant a gruelling shoot and the thought of doing another one was too tiring to even contemplate. In retrospect, all I needed was a break. If I'd known it would be one of the last times I worked with Arthur, I'd have made the whole thing last a bit longer.

Shortly after that, we were already scouting for another sitcom idea, and Arthur had a hunch that Richard Neville's book *Hippy Hippy Shake* could contain it. Neville was part of the editorial staff on the infamous *Oz*, a counterculture magazine in the sixties whose editors wound up in court for various outrages against good taste. I couldn't get through the book. It consisted of Neville saying, as Arthur put it, 'We met this hippy, and then we met this hippy, and then we went over here and interviewed this hippy, and then this hippy came in...' This amused Arthur no end. Being a punk, he found the hippy movement intrinsically comical, and he related to the era because it was the generation he was rebelling against.

The subject may have rung Arthur's bell but for me, the hippy era was a bit of pre-history. By the time we pitched *Hippies*, which at that point I still could only describe as a sitcom about a bunch of hippies, I was feeling uneasy. I just couldn't figure out what we were saying with the show, even though Arthur seemed to have it down. His key comic principle was that young people tend to believe they're the centre of the universe, even when they're not. This was appealing in a theoretical way, but for some reason I couldn't engage with the world we had to build around them. I always had a firm handle on Craggy Island. With *Ted*, I knew what the rules were, what to avoid, and what to pursue. But with *Hippies* I felt unmoored.

As a result, I just mentally shut down. I couldn't sleep. I was finally giving in to exhaustion at five or six in the morning and then coming in late. Arthur was rattling along, saying, 'I'll just keep writing; you can look at it later.' Finally, he wrote two episodes without me, and I took them away to rewrite. I tried to make them work for me. I thought I would imprint on the episodes my usual principles and style. But sadly, Arthur wasn't present when I was doing all that; we didn't have our usual dynamic; our back-and-forth had just broken down completely, so my changes just looked like vandalism.

'If you're not into it, Graham, you shouldn't do it,' he said. I was too immature to realise that I should have sat down with him and pitched the approach I had taken. I should have said, 'Look, this is how I think it can work, and this is what I changed and why I changed it.' But I didn't. I was so nervous about the whole concept that I just took the opportunity he gave me and escaped.

Geoffrey Perkins was really annoyed by my departure and refused to accept it. When I went to a recording to give Arthur some support, the studio teemed with people I knew from past shows – technicians and actors alike – all congratulating me. Someone handed me their copy of the script and I saw with bewilderment that the episode was credited to both Arthur and myself. One of the main actors told me how much he had loved the scripts. I responded that I was looking forward to reading them myself.

Still, somehow, Arthur and I remained friends.

But then I did a stupid thing, and I include this sorry tale as a warning to any young kid starting out, who has found, by some miracle, a friend, a raw genius, with whom they share a telepathic link, with whom they will work and find success. I wish I was the author of a guide to tending the garden of such a collaboration, rather than how to trample through the tulips towards no collaboration at all. One day, you see, I had this simple thought:

'I'm always calling Arthur! Arthur never calls me!'

And then, disastrously: 'I'm going to see how long Arthur goes before calling me.'

Guess how that turned out? Oh, my God. I was outraged. Week after week passed, and after a while I gave up staring moonily at the phone and instead let that precious friendship wither through pointless neglect. Arthur just doesn't call people. He's delighted when you call him, but he's one of these people that seems to think it's somewhat presumptuous to think anyone would be interested in him calling them. When I did eventually give in and resentfully dialled his number, it was months later, and I was surprised at how happy he was to hear from me.

But there was no way back for us as collaborators. The confidence I would gain from working on other shows disrupted our dynamic, and when we tried to sit down together again, I'd lost the knack of a certain kind of etiquette and diplomacy we had always used to work, an invisible binding agent that I hadn't realised had been keeping us together for years.

11
WHO DO YOU THINK WE SHOULD GET?

BEFORE THE INTERNET wrought havoc on our reading habits, we had in bookshops a refuge. You felt the people lucky enough to dwell behind the counter of these magical places were on your side, and that's why Bernard Black, Dylan Moran's character in *Black Books*, was so instantly recognisable as a comic character. Bernard was on no side but his own, the customers in his shop merely impediments to his vague plans for the day. I saw him first at the Channel 4 Sitcom Festival, a showcase of pilots presented to a live audience in a theatre. The only other one I remember was about three men who pass kidney stones at the same time, a sitcom 'trap' from which I'm afraid I was easily able to escape.

As the lights came up, the audience was presented with Dylan, in a bookshop, being rude to a customer. And that's all they needed. In less than a minute, the audience knew the character and the premise. A rude bookshop owner. Instantly, you knew where you were and why it was a funny character. The hard labour of reducing a premise to its essentials had been completed. My heart started racing, because everything about it was *almost* great. The only thing that was keeping it from being viable was the surrealism. The show was sometimes that bit too mad, which is something you see with a lot of writers who are just starting out.

But even the mistakes were thrilling. The whole thing ended with a group of students committing suicide in the shop. I vividly remember seeing their legs hanging from the ceiling, fake legs strung along the top of the stage. The story turn made no sense, but it was thrilling to see Dylan and his team attempt this ambitious visual joke – making theirs the only show that kicked against the limitations of the festival. I knew the gag wouldn't make the journey from stage to screen but Bernard would – as would the supporting characters, Manny and Fran. Bill Bailey was already cast as Manny, more like a fairytale character at times, a sort of magical hippy gnome. Tamsin Greig would arrive later, via auditions, to play Fran, giving us our third element, a nostalgic scent of a certain type of English comedy royalty: Joyce Grenfell, Eleanor Bron… High-born elegance and poise undermined by a disobedient, comic physicality.

When I met Dylan after the staging, I could barely keep still. 'This is fucking great; you just need to cut out all the mad stuff.' At that stage I was already obsessed by *Seinfeld*, and Dylan's set-up of two guys and a girl reminded me of George, Jerry and Elaine. It seemed to me a bookshop was the ideal setting for those endlessly engaging conversations about ephemera that *Seinfeld* did so well.

I'm a bad person to be around charismatic people because I just do whatever they do, and as I began working with him, I kind of fell in love with Dylan. When he felt like clocking off, well, who was I to argue? With Dylan, we'd write for an hour, then he'd go, 'Should we go to lunch?' and that was the end of the day. At one point I actually had blood in my urine from drinking so much with him. Despite or even because of this, I had a good time writing that first series with the guy. Dylan smoked cigarettes and railed against the modern world, and I focused on the scaffolding of the show.

I spent too long feeling a vague annoyance that my comedy compass always led me back to surrealism. It felt like 'easy' mode to me, but then again, that anxiety would make me interrogate an idea until it started to glow, and become hot enough again to command my full attention. A concept couldn't just be surreal; it had to feel exactly right, tuned to a precise frequency. Manny goes to hospital because he swallows *The Little Book of Calm*. The actual book is really thick and you could never swallow it, but because it was called *The **Little** Book of Calm*, you could convince the audience in a dreamlike way that the impossible has occurred. And because that book's title had achieved a certain brand awareness among the wider public, we wouldn't leave John Plowman's aunt in Weston-super-Mare behind. That's a special kind of surrealism, about as far as you can get from a CBA, because it knits together a few things in your head that somehow make sense. Once you've got a foolproof set-up like that, the rest of your job is easy. The *Little Book of Calm* premise led to four or five brilliant scenes in the *Black Books* pilot, each setting off the other like a cascade of dominos.

Having chosen Larry David, the genius behind *Seinfeld*, as my North Star, I decided that the most perfect form of surreal comedy is where you accumulate realistic events so that you're finally able to deliver a surreal set-piece that the audience feels is legitimate. The 'Puffy Shirt' episode of *Seinfeld* is a perfect example of this build-up and pay-off. Early on, we learn that Kramer, Seinfeld's louche neighbour, has a new girlfriend who is an unknown fashion designer but also a 'low talker' (first gag, giving a name for that quality), then we meet her, and we see her 'low talking' in action. She's completely inaudible (second gag). An awkward Jerry just agrees with everything she says (third gag). Later, just before he's due to do a major TV appearance, he finds out that he's actually agreed to wear a ridiculous puffy shirt that the woman designed (fourth). He tries to get out of it, but learns she's been inundated with sales on the basis that Jerry will be wearing the shirt on TV. Again the stakes are so high, he has to go on TV wearing the shirt (fifth). And gag five is such a deserved and massive payoff that every moment within it – every pause and gesture – resonates and rings and produces cascading laughter. A system of incremental steps led to this surreal, beautiful visual gag, and the audience didn't question any of it because each step was disguised as jokes and authentic minutiae. That's the art of it. It's beautiful when you get it right.

I co-directed that first series of *Black Books* and was happy with the result, if not the process, which was fraught from the first day of rehearsals. Writing together was a joy, but it was the last stage Dylan wanted to share with me, and seeing the cast and crew ask me questions used to drive him mad. He'd bound across the room and suddenly find himself deep into a debate about what book a background extra might be reading, exactly what I was trying to protect him from so that he could concentrate on the comedy. Also, in one episode we had a particular actor who I will never forget. Just a monstrously rude and arrogant person who clearly hated the fact that she had lowered herself to being in our show. At one point she said, 'You don't want it to be, like, a sitcom, right?' And I thought, 'Well, yes, because it's a sitcom.' I guess I should thank her, as I would never cast someone now without speaking to a few of their previous colleagues first, an integral part of any director's workflow.

We'd been spoiled with *Father Ted*. Geoffrey's Buddha-like patience had set the tone on the first series, and our crew was committed and proud because they knew they were working on something special. That made for a happy set and a good show. But *Black Books* lacked a Geoffrey and I felt the difference keenly. When making a TV show, the process itself has to be its own reward. The amount of time spent scrutinising and fine-tuning a television programme makes it nearly unwatchable when you've wrapped. You never get to enjoy your own show. So the thing itself is the thing. The day-to-day doing of it has to be enjoyable, or at the very least bearable, because, as the song sort of goes, that's all there is.

Almost as soon as we began filming, the joy of writing the thing became a distant memory as Dylan and I failed to find a way of working together that suited us both. I loved Bill Bailey, as a person and an actor. You couldn't imagine a more gentle and convivial man, even though we used to get turned away from restaurants because the staff took him for a Hell's Angel. And Bill and Dylan's loose, overlapping acting style was something I had never seen in any other studio sitcom. We were onto something special with it, no doubt about it. But the process was needlessly slow and painful. Afterwards, I felt I had to have assurances we wouldn't be having another nightmare during rehearsal.

Sometime after series one I sat across from Dylan and the show's executive producer in a Soho restaurant and was told, 'Well, you know it didn't really work out – you as director.'

'Er, we won a Bafta!'

'We're going to get a new director.'

'OK,' I said.

'Who do you think we should get?'

I said, 'Cool, let me have a think about that,' left the restaurant and that was that.

The one person I always wanted to be was Geoffrey Perkins, in respect of how he handled such moments. He never let his ego decide on matters. For him, it was all about the show going on. But I'm too easily hurt, something I imagine I have in common with most who would 'identify' as victims of childhood bullying. So I walked. The second and third series were done without me, and I've never seen them.

12
DO NOT CAST MILO O'SHEA

THE MOVIES WERE MY first love. For years I wanted to be one of the gunslingers. Scorsese, Truffaut, Tarantino, Mamet – all the standard film school male crushes. My busted tailspin trajectory swung me into the *Hot Press* office instead, into Arthur, and a career in writing television sitcoms, which were neither film nor theatre but the bastard, cardboard, conjoined offspring of both. It was an internal demotion that sometimes troubled me: not a gunslinger but a piano player in a saloon. Remembering my dad and me creased up in front of *Fawlty Towers* put my mind at rest. It can be a grand calling to give people something else to look at when they can't see eye to eye.

All this wisdom came to me much later on. First, I had to try and fail to make movies. Well, that's not entirely true. I did manage to land some rewrite work. Rewriting movies is a great gig when you can get it. You're paid a handsome sum for not taking a credit and doing everything you're told. It's why you see sitcom warhorses like *The Likely Lads'* Dick Clement and Ian La Frenais using it as a retirement plan. The heavy work of dragging a first draft from a laptop has been completed, a series of producers and executives having already cleared the dead wood, battened the hatches and removed the mixed metaphors. With a script that's sixty-five or seventy-five percent of the way there, rewriting is like completing a crossword puzzle with answers to many of the hardest clues already filled in. But Hollywood sees writers as mechanics, so most offers came to me because I was in the same geographical location as the shoot. You wouldn't fly a mechanic over to fix your car if it broke down abroad, would you? No, you'd get a local one. They'd hire the village idiot from *Father Ted* with his ageing (even then) I SHOT JR T-shirt, if he could pull off nodding at a director for a couple of hours every day for a fortnight.

While rewriting a story that works is pure pleasure, a lot of the time the film has a structural flaw that no one has noticed. Or there's no comic engine behind the story so the comedy takes the form of a series of gags, and lives or dies moment to moment by the quality of each one. Often you're told it just needs a dialogue polish, but the micro of bad dialogue is often shackled to the macro of a flaw in the premise. I only ever mention a flaw in the premise if I think I can fix it, and I won't take a job if I don't. If you can't fix a flawed premise, all that's left is panic as the cast and crew do everything in their power to stop the flaw spreading to other parts of the script like a cancer. It can't be said often enough: when you're running an unhappy set, it's because you didn't spend enough time on the script.

I had collaborated with Arthur on the first film I rewrote, *The Matchmaker*, starring Janeane Garofalo. She was one of the reasons *The Larry Sanders Show* was so good. In the nineties, she was midway through a short period of being, as she herself said with her usual, self-lacerating wit, 'America's sweetheart'. We tried to write the character of the titular matchmaker in such a way that he would break some of the Hollywood Irish tropes of which everyone except Irish people can't get enough. Our efforts were well enough received so I phoned the charming director, Mark Joffe, and said, 'Listen, you've got to promise me one thing: do not cast Milo O'Shea as the matchmaker.' No offence to the late Milo, who specialised in Irish characters with a bit of an ol' glint in the eye, but I knew it would undo all the work we'd done. The character had to be cast against type. The comedy would ONLY land if it didn't have his cheeky Irish grandpa energy. Milo O'Shea, I assured Mark, would be an absolute disaster in the part.

'We've already offered and he's accepted.'

'Oh, I'm sure he'll be brilliant.'

There was a run of this kind of movie afterwards in which an uptight American woman would finally give in and start smooching the incorrigible, unkempt Irish man who she hated until she went to a pub with him and someone played a fiddle. I would stop reading the instant I realised what they were. My gaze also screeched to a halt in a script as soon as it tripped over the word 'priest'. Russell Brand once got in touch and asked if we could have a chat about an idea.

I said, 'Absolutely, as long as it has nothing to do with priests.'

Never heard from him again.

The film company Working Title came to me and said, 'We want to do a drag comedy.' I told them I'd only be interested in it if we were doing something new, so I had the idea of two guys who sneak onto an ocean liner and are mistaken for the famously masculine lesbian couple Gertrude Stein and Alice B. Toklas. Alice and Gertrude ruled artistic Paris in the 1920s, were very much women, but when a young girl, the daughter of an artist who had recently been graced with a visit, was asked her opinion of the duo, she said, 'I liked the man, but why did the lady have a moustache?' A premise struck me: a drag comedy where the two men looked nothing like women, where the passengers on the ship were too worried about being unfashionable to acknowledge the truth. My nose for comedy had hit upon the very theme that would smash my life to smithereens!

There's a key bit where the captain of the ship says to the steward, 'I must tell you something. It has been said that Misses Stein and Toklas have a very masculine quality. On no account draw attention to it or talk about it or reference it in any way.' The steward goes and knocks at their cabin door, and when these two obvious men open it, the steward swallows his shock and speaks to them like they're women, and they have no idea why. Soon the whole boat is pretending that they're women. A straight woman falls in love with Gertrude, and believes this now makes her a lesbian, and the captain of the ship, tortured by his own homosexuality and his love for one of his past lieutenants, falls in love with Alice, believing it makes him straight.

I still think it's a great concept, but I was too young and inexperienced to pull it off. My problem was a basic one: I didn't know how to write movies. Also, I originally pitched it set in a country house, and when I changed it to a cruise ship the only note was, 'Where's our cheap comedy gone?!' They were so annoyed they lost interest in the idea. But can you imagine if that film had been made? A drag comedy about two fraudsters glorified as divine beings? The very thing practised en masse by a generation of fraudsters glomming on to transsexual rights?

I don't know if my life would be better now, or much, much worse.

Some Americans talked about making *Father Ted* in Boston with Ted Danson. It's a shame it didn't happen because it would have aired around the same time as the Boston sex-abuse scandal started breaking – a huge network of paedophiles and paedophile-enablers within the Catholic Church exposed by dogged American journalists.

'Father Crilly, someone's on the phone from the *Boston Globe*.'

'The *Boston Globe*! My favourite newspaper!' [into phone] 'Hello? Ooh! The Spotlight team, you say!'

'Who's that, Ted?'

'They're a special investigative group that covers big stories. You know – like really grave scandals involving hugely powerful institutions and things like that.' [into phone] 'So what are you guys working on at the moment?'

Write your way out of that cliffhanger.

There have been a few moments in life where I have found something so funny that I sort of bypassed laughing and developed an entirely unreciprocated romantic bond with the person responsible. Arthur falling down the stairs at the *Hot Press* office formed the basis of my first love; but Steve Coogan saying 'GOOOOOAAAL!' as his badly cut-out digital head zoomed around a football pitch in *The Day Today* came a close second. Kramer drinking an entire glass of beer while smoking a cigarette is in there too. Then, nothing – until I saw Richard Ayoade rapping, 'She's smooth, like ice, cold to the touch, and it isn't very nice,' wearing a fedora tipped down over one eye while pretending to mix cocktails. Once again, I fell in love.

It was a scene from *Garth Marenghi's Darkplace*. Billed as horror parody, the Channel 4 show is a tricky one to explain: it has a structural premise similar to Nabokov's *Pale Fire*, which is a novel that pretends it's a serious work of non-fiction about a supposedly famous poem, when in reality the poem only exists within the pages of the novel. Similarly, *Darkplace* is a fictional comedy series that pretends it's a serious documentary about a fictional famous television show.

If you're confused, don't worry about it. Richard was in it; that's the important part. I had no premise, no title, but I knew I wanted Richard to be at the heart of whatever I did next. I only had the image of him sitting in an office. At first I thought the office would be a travel agent. Richard in the middle; two people – opposites: a man and a woman – on either side of his desk, arguing. A big fiery 'will-they-won't-they' *Cheers*-type relationship, maybe. Whatever it was though, Richard dead centre, near a phone, for some reason. Maybe because in *Darkplace*, Richard had once said goodbye to a phone after he had put it back in its cradle.

Every time I create a new TV programme, I only have one aim: I want it to be a beloved classic that people can watch again and again and is enjoyed by multiple generations forever. I want it to be perfect, unassailable. It won't be, in the end; it'll be a little short of that. But if you aim for perfect, you're on the right track. Sitcoms are despised, outdated, in perpetual need of reinvention. The form itself conspires against quality. So you have to give yourself every advantage when starting out on a new one. As we've established, you can recover from the odd bad decision, but there's never a way back from a flawed premise.

My expectations of myself were set by *Father Ted*. But *Ted* had a solid-gold premise, and they don't grow on trees. They don't grow anywhere, in fact, annoyingly. So you can be forced to set out with a premise that's maybe eighty percent of the way there, something that takes just a little bit too long to pitch. In that case, you have to make sure that every component is shining as brightly as it possibly can to make up for that missing twenty percent, which might be characterised as the inability to sum the premise up in fewer than ten words. 'It's about the worst priests in the world in the worst parish in the world' is pretty damn good, as premises go, but even that's five words over.

I had Richard in an office, a man and a woman arguing. And nothing else. But Robert Popper, a brilliant sitcom writer himself, and a commissioner at Channel 4, had told me that if I wrote something, it could be on television in under a year. Under a year! I finally stopped tinkering with 'Gertrude and Alice'. My pistols hanging up nearby, I sat back down at the piano and got to work.

13

UPSTAIRS, DOWNSTAIRS

WHEN THE *FATHER TED* DVD money was still rolling in, my main indulgence was owning both a PC and a Mac. The Mac I liked for writing and the PC was for games. PC games have a lot of depth, and they're often quirkier than games you see on consoles like the Xbox and PlayStation. Unfortunately I bought a piece of junk that was advertised as a gaming PC. It had a little alien face on the front that would light up when you turned it on and that was about the end of its utility. As a high-end gaming rig, it was just a little worse at running *World of Warcraft* than the Speak & Spell I had stabbed answers into as a child, but as a machine that made a little alien face light up, it had no equal.

And that's how I came to meet so many IT people in such a short space of time. If I'd known I was going to write a show based on the experience, I would have taken notes, but instead I slowly absorbed their essence through proximity. Picture me sitting there with a series of these guys trying to make conversation. They're often a certain type: dry; sardonic; not much sign of a riotous inner life.

There was one guy who I had spoken to on the phone and when he came round, my wife answered the door. Instead of saying hello like a normal person, and introducing himself, he said to her, 'You're not Graham.' And my wife said, 'No, no I'm not. He's, uh, this way,' and brought him in. Later, I asked him, 'You don't see many people doing call-out services for PC stuff, fixing PCs... Why is that, do you know?' And he says, 'Ah, most of them don't have the people skills.' After straining to find something to talk about with this guy for the past half hour, and hearing that story from my wife later, something about the whole situation struck me as funny. I started thinking about guys who fix computers, and this bloke ('You're not Graham') who thinks that others don't have people skills.

That's fine as far as it goes. But one point of view does not a sitcom cast make.

Years earlier, I had taken a two-day comedy writing course by Danny Simon, Neil Simon's brother. The man worked for Phil Silvers on Bilko, the gold standard, so I was eager to hear what he had to say. I didn't retain much from the course except one crucial piece of advice, which was worth whatever exorbitant price he was charging for the afternoon. He said that sitcoms should be attentive to societal change. *The Mary Tyler Moore Show*, for instance, was a reaction to the emerging phenomenon of women entering the workplace in greater numbers. Adorably, Danny used the term 'women's libbers' to describe the shift, but the advice itself was timeless and valuable and directly led to *The IT Crowd*.

There was an obvious societal transformation happening at the time, and it was the internet. Everything changed overnight. I was always frustrated that people couldn't see it, couldn't see what computers could do for us. I used to use all these apps for coordinating teams, and try to encourage all the others on a crew to use these tools so I wouldn't have to use emails all the time. They'd always send emails anyway and I'd be insisting they use the tools and it actually just added an extra step that was annoying for everyone. But it was also funny. The situation was ridiculous. I was ridiculous.

So for me at this time, the world was divided into two types of people. There's one type of person who would respond with a cold glare if you asked them if they knew what a browser was, because of course they did. And there's another type of person who has no idea what you're talking about when you say browser. Like, 'What do you mean, browser?' And you go, 'You know, like Safari.' They go, 'Oh, yeah, yeah, Safari.' Which they just think of as the thing you press to go to the internet. That seemed to represent a compelling set of opposites that might make for entertainment when communicated loudly over Richard Ayoade's head.

I started writing *The IT Crowd* around the time I got married. Just before I met my wife, my love life was very chaotic. It was the kind of chaos in which I think a lot of men possibly find themselves before they settle down. It's like a feeling of freefall. A feeling of, if this goes on, something terrible is going to happen – the evidence being all the terrible things that had already happened.

But Helen came into my life and I suddenly realised there was a lot to be said for the kind of order and calm a relationship brings. I realised, as we all do, eventually, that routine and familiarity could be good things, almost necessary at some point, if you don't want to die of a cocaine-induced heart attack in your forties. And of course, fatherhood provided the kind of joy I didn't even realise was possible. Until I met Helen, I was largely alone, and falling in love gave me another societal change I could track, this one in the microclimate of my fictional office. I wanted to write about the effect of a woman coming into a male environment, which my flat at that point very much was, and transforming it.

So all these things together, the woman coming into the male environment, and the two kinds of people in terms of computers,

Fatherhood apparently induced in me a desire to wear terrible shirts

the change that computers would bring, they seemed to me to clip together nicely. But I still didn't have a premise.

Then Ash Atalla, our brilliant producer who also made *The Office*, looked at all the disparate materials and said two magic words: 'Upstairs, downstairs.' A two-word premise that guided most decisions we made in that first series.

Richard is fond of telling the story that, introducing him to his character, Moss, I said, 'You're playing the biggest nerd who ever existed. A big nerdy nerd who doesn't know how to behave with regular humans.'

'What kind of voice would he have?' he said.

'Oh, you know,' I said. 'Just your regular voice.'

Roy was more of a music nerd than a computer nerd, with some of the same attitude of the men who had once outraged me by offering me fifteen pounds for an electric typewriter in Notting Hill. He was meant to be a version of myself, an avatar in the same way that Larry David used the character of George in *Seinfeld*, but I wanted to disguise the relationship as much as I could and so felt he shouldn't be played by a fellow Irishman. Chris O'Dowd, born and raised in County Roscommon, somehow charmed his way into the audition and he nailed it. I used to joke that I had to hire Chris; he was so good that not hiring him might have resulted in my being questioned for discriminating against the Irish. Katherine Parkinson was also a joy in auditions for the role of Jen, the head of department who is clueless about IT, and never stopped being a joy. She gave it an energy I recognised from the very best musical comedies; you might call it 'zip'. I'd been watching a lot of *Singin' in the Rain* – one of the very few Golden Age musicals I truly love, as it has zip up the wazoo and every song is a corker – and sometimes the relationship between Katherine, Chris and Richard had that feel. I could see the three of them thinking it was great to stay up late and talk the whole night through. I also thought they were a

Katherine
Parkinson never
stopped being a
joy as Jen

good match for the will-they-won't-they storyline I had planned. The upstairs, downstairs premise simply demanded there be some hanky-panky between the upstairs people, represented by Jen, and the basement dwellers who had Roy as their champion.

Thinking of the last episode of *Garth Marenghi*, in which Matt Berry sang a ludicrous soft-rock ballad 'One Track Lover' while showing off a perfectly commonplace pair of black underpants, I knew I wanted him for the boss. But Matt wasn't available so Chris Morris kindly stepped in to give Denholm Reynholm, owner/patriarch of Reynholm Industries, some of the British steel we required for the role. As Kevin Eldon later said to me, 'Chris is officer class,' so I was slightly stunned when he accepted it.

While our team was scouting locations and gathering research photos – which confirmed my suspicion that IT offices looked more or less like my own office: computer parts, books, comics, CDs and DVDs, 'stored' away as if someone carrying them had received a fright in the centre of the room – I went over the scripts again

I was slightly stunned – in the best possible way – when Chris Morris stepped in to play Denholm Reynholm

140

and again, trying to find and seal any cracks in the story through which the audience's engagement might escape, and responding to whatever compromises our budget demanded.

Again, rewriting was the best part of the job. It's like a series of puzzles, at the end of which is a moment that neither you nor the audience could have ever seen coming. You were solving a problem, a flaw in the script, that you did not place there deliberately. So the solution has come about partly through chance, through things that had nothing to do with your first draft, when your ego held the pen and the story went where you commanded. As long as you keep some sort of true north in your mind (true north might be 'no cheap jokes', or 'this episode is about cats' or 'everyone thinks Ted is a racist'), you'll end up getting to where you need to go, and often by a better route.

There's usually a point in the process for me when the old story falls away like a collapsing industrial chimney and behind it, shimmering in the sun, is a golden palace, a vision of what the show could become. Then *that* becomes your true north and writing becomes even easier. You subject each scene on which your attention alights to the same question – does it belong in The Golden Palace? No? Then lose it quickly to give you time to think of something that does.

Any hope that my years on *Father Ted* would have acclimatised me to the pressure of recording in front of a studio audience was quickly dispelled. Show nights were always brutal. Stomach-churning anxiety all day, until the moment I heard the first laugh, which is the one that tells you whether the audience has decided to put their guard up. It's always a strong joke, because it's the on-ramp for the show, so if they don't laugh at that, it's going to be a long night. I could never eat on recording day, not until I heard that laugh. I would stand by a monitor, watching the warm-up greeting the audience, a chicken sandwich in my hand. As soon as we got that first laugh I would suddenly become famished and tear into the sandwich.

In poker, you don't push your bad hands; in comedy, if an audience doesn't go for something, you don't moan about it, you simply adjust and move on. There's a million ways in the edit to minimise the damage done by a joke that doesn't land. For instance, you can cut it tightly so it no longer looks like it was meant to be a joke at all. I do that in real life too. If I'm telling a joke and I realise it's not going to get a laugh, I sometimes start pretending that it's a true story. You'd be surprised how often that works.

There will be many audiences on the way to a final cut, and each one will tell you something important about your story. I should say that by 'audience' I mean everyone from the first reader of the first draft to the final studio audience, should you be so antiquated as to require one. The ancestors of the audience were audience members themselves. Why wouldn't you tap into that great sea of storytelling knowledge we all carry within us? The director Edgar Wright did a wonderful interview with Steven Spielberg in which the great man suggested that one of the reasons *Jaws* was so good was that the crew weren't afraid to approach him and suggest ideas. Then he became the man who made *Jaws*, and they stopped approaching. Luckily, sitcom writers sit at the children's table, to paraphrase Woody Allen, so my crews never had any qualms about approaching me.

You can survive losing the odd joke if you write enough of them. Most of the time, the compromises that I have to endure when I'm making things is balanced out by the magic that the actors bring to it. This is the thing I say that makes me sound most like my dad: actors are the greatest special effects. Ardal O'Hanlon and Matt Berry were good examples. Ardal was just so good from the off that writing for him was a joy. Matt has a similar kind of magic. I believe Christopher Walken will get someone to send him a script with all the punctuation removed, so he can do his Christopher Walken THING of emphasising...whatever THE HELL he

Chris O'Dowd in his 'bad boy' outfit

chocolate moment

WANTS. Whether that's true or not, you never forget Christopher Walken in a film, and you never forget Matt. In one episode, we tried to recreate John Travolta and Jamie Lee Curtis' sexy workout from the film *Perfect*, but because it was in the studio it just looked... well, like a sitcom. But it didn't really matter because Matt Berry and Katherine Parkinson were there.

Chris O'Dowd had the hardest job because he was ostensibly playing me. He's an actor who likes to build his characters, so when he asked for information on Roy, my answer – 'Me, it's just me' – wasn't helpful. After all, who the fuck was I? Even I don't know. Writing this book gives me a fright every day. My own confusion over Roy was reflected in the fact that I didn't give him a surname until, I think, series three, and I still have to google to remember what it was. (It was Trenneman, since you ask, which sounds a bit like my often-mispronounced name.) Chris thought the guy might be into early eighties rock or something, and wanted his T-shirts to reflect that, but when he saw the T-shirts I had been saving in

143

a little file he brightened up immediately. One of them just said 'NO', which did more character work in a single word than I had managed in pages of dialogue.

Noel Fielding's character, the reclusive member of the IT department, banished to the server room, began life as a death metal fan, then became a Goth, and I never really resolved it. But again, an actor saved my arse, and after a while he was just 'Richmond', someone who clung to ceilings and spoke like a member of Pink Floyd. What is it they say? Start with a character, you get a type; start with a type, you get nothing. My inability to define Richmond as a character might have made him a bit more interesting – given Noel more space to play. Similarly, even though Chris O'Dowd built in the slouch that turns me into a walking question mark, it's still not 'me' in the show. It's a weird mix of me and Chris. Roy is the horrible baby we had together.

Elvis Costello said the history of rock music is people trying to copy other people and getting it slightly wrong. With *The IT Crowd* I was trying to write *Seinfeld* again. I set out with a more realistic show in mind, and I just couldn't do it. *IT Crowd* is ostensibly set in reality, but being in this office block and having Chris Morris and then Matt Berry as bosses meant I could create another hermetically sealed world where logic didn't have to apply. On top of that, I was writing it on my own, and surrealism was my comfort zone during what was always a stressful process.

Still, I was always trying to find the rough crackle of authenticity in each plot and subplot. I knew these moments when I saw them, but they were hard to deliver consistently without a dedicated writing team. *Seinfeld* was constructed out of these specific details that convince you something is true. The team on the show quickly learned from Larry David that all they had to do was to become a 'spy in the house of me'. In other words, the material that was valuable to the show was the ludicrous but precise nonsense that flashes through your head, often in moments of stress, which you shake off as soon as soon as your logical mind takes over again.

Noel Fielding's character Richmond spoke like a member of Pink Floyd

It's comedy that makes sense at a gut level, and so provides consequences that are impossible to anticipate.

In America, showrunners have little golf carts in which they can pootle around the lot. In the UK, you literally have to run. A year's exercise in six weeks. I was running to the editing room to work on the location stuff, then running back to the studio to watch rehearsals, running up stairs to look at costumes; everything happening simultaneously, running, running; always late for something, every decision vital. I had to be across everything; it's just such a subtle shift sometimes, from when something is funny to when it suddenly is not. And every joke has to receive all your love and attention because the tiniest detail can throw an audience.

I had some great producers on *The IT Crowd* – among them Ash Atalla, who set the template for the show, and Richard Boden, who became a friend and regular collaborator – but I still took on too much. I thought I had to fix all the problems in the script, rather than rehearse them out. We would do a read-through, and I would be in despair. Richard Boden always wanted to get it on its feet and start rehearsing but I was too embarrassed. 'I'll take it home. I'll fix it!' Then the rest of that day rewriting, maybe even the day after that, while Richard was back at the studio rehearsing what he could. It was so unnecessary. Had I listened to Richard and got it on its feet, we would have done just as well with half the stress. What I'd forgotten was that the actors were like this giant creative brain that I had access to, four or five people who are seeing the story through their eyes. And I was sitting at home, writing into the night and grinding a few more years off the end of my life. My mind was usually racing to such an extent that I couldn't sleep, and I became dependent on Zopiclone to knock myself unconscious. After a few weeks of steady use, I bawled out Chris in the middle of a show because I thought he was giving me attitude. And all this because the read-throughs were throwing me into a panic. It took me forever to realise, but read-throughs are always terrible. If I could go back and tell my younger self a single thing, it would be that: read-throughs are always terrible.

During *Father Ted*, when the internet was becoming what we now understand as the internet, we began a competition to come up with an extra word for Father Jack. We thought, we have FECK, DRINK, ARSE, GIRLS – the fans can vote for the next word! What fun! We announced this competition online somehow – it was the dawn of the age where you could do such things, and because we didn't go through Channel 4, we began getting cheerful messages from them like, 'What have you done? We're getting all these emails! What competition?!' I don't think we picked anything in the end, let alone make Frank actually say it.

Similar miseries awaited my poor design team on *The IT Crowd*. 'The office has to be a living set,' I'd say. 'There has to be more stuff every week: different posters; everything moving around and growing.' Which was fine for me to say, but a pain in the arse to implement. I would ask fans of the show to send us their fanzines and comics – anything they wanted on the show – which meant tons of eye candy arrived weekly, and it kept the set feeling alive, like a place where people actually worked. I loved fanzine culture, comic culture, music culture, nerd culture, so finally the set began to look like my office. I also littered the set with posters for the Open Rights Group in the UK and the Electronic Frontier Foundation because I believed they stood up for internet freedom.

Around 2006, I had a website called 'Why That's Delightful', with which I could stay in touch with fans, talk about projects and share silly videos. On the episode where Moss becomes involved in 'Street Countdown', I used the site to put out a call for nerdy extras. It worked out great. On the day, they were listening to our conversations to find out what each scene needed, so they barely needed any direction. Once again, the fans were able to cos-play as characters from a world I'd helped create. But unlike the *Father Ted* weekends, this time they were actually in the show, so they stood up prouder in their costumes whenever we made eye contact.

But the flip side to an audience is a mob. When I had the bright idea of creating a post for every show so I could answer questions about them as they went out, the mob arrived in the form of a Chris Morris fansite populated by young men for whom, it seemed, life was not working out. My guess is that they confused Chris Morris with the character he played in *The Day Today* and *Brass Eye*, and adopted this tone in all their dealings because they thought he might phone them and ask to hang out. Whatever their origin story, they arrived with the confidence only ever found in people who have never created anything, flooding the page with accusations of plagiarism, complaints about every other joke, expressing themselves in such a tone of sneering superiority that they quickly turned the site into a toxic ghetto. I always assume the best of people. It's a real shock when they turn out to be frothing lunatics.

I get this outlook from my dad. I fought with him as soon as I was able to think but in the end I'm just a second draft of him. He

147

loved music and movies and literature and theatre and anything in those forms that was charming and added to life. When I went through a horror movie phase, Dad would respond to my *Cryptkeeper* enthusiasm with the same line every time: 'Why do they make stuff like that, when there are so many *beautiful* things in the world?' Put us both in front of *Singin' in the Rain* or *Fawlty Towers* and we were happy. We argued over almost everything else.

But when it came down to it, he always chose people over ideology. After some time in London, I arrived back home one year and got into one of our traditional rows, this time about abortion. In Ireland, abortion was illegal, and even though the country was drifting towards secularism, abortion was one of those issues that seemed, to me at least, buried so deep in Irish people that you would never even reach its roots, let alone work to remove them. Religion was at the root of most of our disagreements – and abortion was a major battleground – so when we got into this particular fight over it, I argued that there was no such thing as banning abortions, only banning safe abortions. That in the United States, before abortion rights were granted in the Roe v. Wade ruling, desperate women would throw themselves downstairs or take poison to induce a miscarriage. That it was particularly dangerous to the poor. Nothing worked. He found it all theoretical and unconvincing.

My girlfriend at the time had told me of her own abortion. A few years earlier she'd been seeing a man who had revealed, some way into the relationship, that he had a wife and child. She was so disturbed and appalled by this that she broke off all contact. When she discovered she was pregnant, the idea of having the baby was so intolerable to her that she had the procedure as quickly as she could.

As quickly as *I* could, I deployed this fact against my father.

'Dad, you know Susan had an abortion?'

He looked shocked for a moment.

'Oh. Well, I'm sure she had her reasons.'

Then, when Ireland was voting in a referendum on same-sex marriage, I travelled back to vote and, after some persuading, my dad voted for it too. Once he had mortified me by using the phrase, 'the gay agenda', but like everyone else, he saw the images of gay newlyweds and it troubled him to stand in the way of anyone's happiness. He began questioning some of his lifelong beliefs enough to allow some of my arguments to penetrate. We both went to vote, doing our bit to usher in what we thought would be a new era of acceptance in Ireland, and went to the pub.

As for *The IT Crowd*, somehow we all made it out the other side as friends, and the show became another cult hit. Danny Simon's analysis of sitcom successes like *The Mary Tyler Moore Show* had proved to be superb guidance for us. The internet was revealing itself, changing everything at an exponential rate, and my characters were there to talk about it. How early is *The IT Crowd*? Friendface was our parody of Facebook, as if Facebook was this crazy novelty, which to us, it was. 'Just sign up with Friendface by giving us all of your personal information... We won't use it to do anything bad, we promise!'

'The Speech', an episode in the show's third series – one of the best, in fact – featured a transsexual character and was based on a really rather admirable story about Des Lynam. While on a date, the transsexual model and actor Caroline Cossey supposedly told Lynam what he was bound to find out sooner or later, namely that Cossey was trans and, despite what outward appearances might suggest, male. Apparently, Lynam just shrugged and continued eating, completely unbothered.

Arthur and I were always impressed by his insouciance. The story stayed with me until I gave it to Matt Berry's character, couldn't figure a way out of it, and rested a very important story point on the balsa-wood foundation that Berry had actually misheard his new sweetheart, April, saying that she/he was a man; he thought she was saying she was from Iran. (Years later, sitting in a restaurant, I clapped my hand to my head and thought:

'Oman! He should have thought she was from Oman!' But by then it was far too late.)

The rest of the story involved an extended fight sequence for no other reason than that I wanted to film a *'Matrix*-style' fight sequence. When the pushback came, from some of Twitter's early adopters of trans ideology, a lot was made of the fact that Berry's character Douglas won the fight by throwing April through a window. Maybe if April had won the fight, I wouldn't have got into trouble, but I doubt it. The reaction to the show was oddly ferocious and very male, throwing up the same debating tactics and personality types that I had first encountered in the bitter Chris Morris fans.

Brushing it all off as just another routine internet drama, I waited for it to pass, and finally it did, or so I thought.

14

IT ALL COMES TOGETHER.
NO ONE CARES

I WORKED ON A SHOW where some of my collaborators on the production were stiff and slow and argumentative, and the scripts always had a tangled mess of dead wood in them, because they refused to do that part of the process that is absolutely vital when you're rewriting, which is clearing that stuff out; anything that muddies the plot, disrupts its flow or puzzles the audience, you have to get rid of all of it. Twice, I was hired on a sketch show by friends, ostensibly as a script editor, and twice, I was fired when those friends realised they would have to do some work. Punching-up jokes on a flawed premise is like mopping ice off the deck of the *Titanic*.

For a show to be a living thing – for it to have that special something that holds your attention throughout a lengthy process – you must be open to feedback. Your actors are your first audience. If something is bugging them, listen carefully. Each actor sees the story as a timeline they're passing through, and if something is obstructing them, it might get in the way of the audience's engagement too. Just as audiences will ask 'But why didn't he...?' or 'Why doesn't he just...?', actors will raise the same kind of questions. They are your scouts, warning you of treacherous ground ahead.

To extend the metaphor for a moment, the crew are your soldiers. They're your next audience and, like your eventual audience, they are discerning people who know what they like. You're surrounded by dozens of people who could give you a single idea that might raise the show from a conventional experience to one that is truly unique. Keep your antennae twitching. A member of the cast or crew might tell a joke that gives you a solution to a problem you didn't even know you had.

But to allow that process to happen, you have to get out of your own way. 'Rewriting' is too prissy a word for the early part of the process. Think of your story as a bonsai tree hidden somewhere in the chaos of an overgrown yard. With the micro-scale of a bonsai tree, the imperfections are clear, and you can set about them with those clippers that make a tidy *snip*. But those clippers arrive at the end of the process. The tools you need for the overgrown yard are a machete and a skip.

Now don't get me wrong. It is possible to sort of accidentally write a perfect script. The *Father Ted* episode 'Flight Into Terror', for example, barely changed from its first draft to the last. But for the most part, a first draft will not have: foreshadowing (because you don't quite know where you're going); set-ups and payoffs; consistent characters; and a comfortable, confident tone that carries through the whole thing. That's your target, and ninety-nine percent of the time you're not going to hit it with your first draft. As someone said, 'You have to write the ending to know what the beginning should be, but you have to write the wrong beginning to get there.'

'The Beast of Craggy Island' began life as an episode in which

Ted and Dougal can't get down the stairs of a double-decker bus because of a small yapping dog. After fifteen pages of this, we realised we didn't know how to get them down either. A few days banging our heads against this half-idea, and Arthur and I were getting fractious with each other. The looming deadline made us realise all of a sudden that we had a great title and a great fictional duo to transpose on our fictional duo: Ted and Dougal could become Holmes and Watson, and our script could become a whodunnit.

Out of that came a sheep called Chris, corrupt farmers wearing crowns and riding bikes in fur coats, and this speech from Dougal about the legendary 'Beast of Craggy Island':

> They say it's as big as four cats and it's got a retractable leg so's it can leap up at you better. And you know what, Ted, it lights up at night and it's got four ears, two of them are for listening and the other two are kind of back-up ears. Its claws are as big as cups and for some reason, it's got a tremendous fear of stamps. Mrs Doyle was telling me that it's got magnets on its tail, so if you're made out of metal it can attach itself to you, and instead of a mouth, it's got four arses!

Jokes just tumbled out of the thing. It quickly developed a beginning, middle and end. The small yapping dog blinked out of existence along with the bus, and in their place was a bonsai tree.

Another thing that helps create a solid first draft is some fresh experience that informs the writing. 'Flight Into Terror' happened because I once had to travel to Dublin to write an episode with Arthur. I was suffering from a sudden terror of flying because I had convinced myself, in the manner of George Costanza from *Seinfeld*, that all the foreign interviews I did when I was a music journalist were about to catch up with me, odds-wise. When I was a music journalist, I used to love these little jollies, because the rest of my life was pretty hardscrabble in comparison. Now that I was

153

successful, respected, wealthy and the owner of a Bafta, I felt it was about time that God did a Father Stone lightning strike on the engines of every aircraft I boarded.

On the flight over to Dublin, I was in the first row of seats, facing the air hostess, and the plane actually landed and then TOOK OFF AGAIN.

'Don't worry,' she said, reading my mind or perhaps noticing that I had almost removed both arms of my metal chair in terror. 'It's just a crosswind making it unsafe to land.'

'Oh, I'm fine,' I said, perfectly calmly. 'But if it happens again I should warn you, I'm going to be a control problem.'

I have no idea where the words 'control problem' came from, but she visibly blanched. When I realised she was more frightened of my potential reaction than any possibility of a crash, I immediately relaxed and passed the whole thing off as a joke. The plane landed safely, so joke it remained. But I really would have been a control problem.

It was this story I brought to Arthur, and gave us 'Flight Into Terror', which barely changed from the moment we wrote it to the night it aired. And yet, I don't think the words 'control problem' are in there at all.

Once a story is cleaned of everything that doesn't: a) add to character; b) add to the story; or c) add to the comic premise provided by the setting/situation, then you usually end up with a show that has two or three clear plots (one plot and two subplots), and it's ready to shoot. But I've worked with people who fall in love with their first go of it, and as a result they stumble forever through the overgrown yard. They don't know what's a good joke, what's a bad joke. The only answer is to plant a camera down and shoot all of it while the crew tries not to nod off.

'Gertrude and Alice' had good jokes in it, but it didn't have any forward momentum, it didn't make you want to turn the page, it never really made clear what it was about. It was an overgrown yard, and I couldn't find the garden in it, let alone a bonsai tree. I also made the classic rookie mistake of not letting it go. I thought that I just had to get it right and then it would be filmed and everything would be great. I spent four years working on that script. And then *The IT Crowd* came along and saved me. I thought, my God, I could have something on screen in a matter of months! That's what happened: I wrote it and it was made.

After that, I came to a decision, which was tied to my fear of climate change. We were all wearing T-shirts later and later in the year – you really shouldn't be wearing a T-shirt while watching fireworks unless you're at Burning Man – and every year was going down as 'the hottest on record'. But if we were all going to drown in, say, 2016, I didn't know if there was anything that I could personally do about it, so I came to a decision. 'I'm good at my job, which happens to be making silly sitcoms. So maybe I should just keep doing what I do best – making these shows that bring a lot of joy to people – and perhaps give them a break from all the darkness life throws their way.'

I decided that was what I was going to do. I felt it was a good way of living the second half of my life. Forget my ego; make people laugh, bring people together in front of the telly. There was always a bit of me that still wanted to be a great director, but that ship had sailed and sunk and been filmed by James Cameron. Cardboard sets that wobbled when you hit them, that was my natural arena, my true home.

Some time after *The IT Crowd*, I was in an HMV store and there was a whole rack with the words 'Graham Linehan Section' written in felt tip over a display of DVDs of all my shows. Here's how stupid I am: I didn't take a photograph. It was one of the nicest things. And I realised: I've got a style; it's playing out in the form of these sitcoms, and not one of them has fucked it up. I'm going to keep going, and keep trying to make people happy.

Then I made *Count Arthur* and no one watched it.

Before I move on to the Count, let me tell you about yet another project that contained a sympathetic portrayal of a cross-dressing man.

The transatlantic route between the British Isles and Hollywood tends to go only in one direction, but William Rose bucked the trend. Born in Missouri, he was stationed in Scotland in the Second World War and ended up marrying an Englishwoman and settling in Britain. He was the man who, one night, literally dreamed up *The Ladykillers*, in which sweet old Mrs Wilberforce (played by Katie Johnson) inadvertently rents a room in her house to a bunch of crooks including Alec Guinness, Herbert Lom, and Peter Sellers.

It is a perfectly engineered story, the pacing and structure calibrated like the workings of a watch. When Mrs Wilberforce uncovers the truth, her house guests decide to do away with the old lady, as she is now the only witness to an audacious armed robbery. But none of them can summon the required steel to do her in and so, one by one, they do each other in. The comedy has a sort of medicinal cynicism and sourness to it, and yet it's one of Ealing's most optimistic and dreamlike films, which is appropriate as the whole plot came to Rose in his sleep. Waking in the middle of the night, he told every detail to his wife Tania, a writer herself. The next morning, Rose couldn't even remember the conversation. Fortunately, Tania had crept downstairs in the night, written down every detail and it was waiting in the typewriter to be turned into a script.

One day I got a message from theatre producer Ed Snape. 'You like *The Ladykillers*, right?'

'Sure.' I'd always liked the film. Who didn't?

'Could be funnier, though, right?'

That's a great pitch for a writer. While it is a very funny film, and has a structure that works like a Rube Goldberg machine, the comedy is somewhat muted. Once I got my hands on it, with the blessing of William Rose's son, I was able to zoom in on the big, big laughs I knew were contained within the situation. Restricted to the stage, it blossomed as a farce. When Mrs Wilberforce has her friends round for tea, and this gaggle of little old ladies listen to a concert by the crooks, who are masquerading as musicians but cannot play a note, I was able to have them pass their efforts off as the work of a dangerously innovative avant-garde composer. The joke that kicked off my first sitcom – the one we didn't steal from *The Rebel* but one I didn't mind stealing again – finally had a worthy home.

In addition, I made the character of Major Courtney a closeted, cross-dressing gay man, which gave his death some pathos and provided further foreshadowing of the insanity that lay in store for me. In my version, just before he falls to his death from the roof of the house, the Major takes a moment to look around him at the surrounding city and says:

> Always liked King's Cross. It has a…reputation but I've found people here to be lovely. Very compassionate. Very understanding, if you get my meaning. In general, people can be cruel if they detect even a whiff of…originality. But not in some of the places round here. No, I've always loved King's Cross.

I was thinking of Graham Chapman from *Monty Python*, dressed as a sergeant major, standing up from his desk to reveal stockings and suspenders. The liberation that Chapman, a closeted gay man, must have felt at these public transgressions might have been tempered had he known cross-dressing would come to mean anything but subversion, that it would begin to represent the strict enforcement of gender stereotypes, forcing many young gay people – those masculine girls and feminine boys – back into a closet made of their own bodies.

When I was in my twenties in Kilburn and still had a digestive system worth boasting about, I would eat fry-ups every other day. A huge pond of beans and sausages and fried bread that had formed in a plate. It was an early commitment to the work that gave me the voluptuous body I have today. The cafés that contained these feasts were decorated in bright yellow and red colours, with huge laminated menus covered in photos of the food, and regulars. The regulars didn't sit together; they just kind of shouted to each other over the rows of chairs and tables, which were all bolted to the floor as if people running off with them had been a perennial issue.

It seemed the right milieu for Count Arthur Strong. His creator, Steve Delaney, had initially developed the character of an eccentric former music-hall performer with comedy-club audiences in mind. Played by Steve with what looked like several advanced zones of sciatica fighting for his attention, the Count was a tortured tangle of frustrated showbiz dreams and half-remembered routines. He would limp around the stage, often apparently forgetting the audience was there, and tuning in and out of a structure which only he could identify. When Steve was commissioned to write *Count Arthur Strong's Radio Show* for BBC Radio 4, the character changed to adapt to the new medium, becoming more human, less physically wracked. Both worked equally well but for different reasons.

When Steve and I brought the show to TV, it made sense to us to change him again. The radio show was heavy on monologues, with interruptions from various regulars. On TV, we couldn't have that. On TV, you have to see the other people, and if the show was monologue-driven, the actors, aside from Steve, would have nothing to do except stand there, listening.

Another goal was to anchor the Count in the real world, which meant developing the character's background and inner life more than Steve had ever had to do before. Certain things made him restless – the Count had his limits, the things that Steve felt the character just wouldn't do – and I enjoyed working within these boundaries. But Steve also proved willing to dig into the Count and discover aspects that didn't find expression in his chaotic live shows or the endless digressions of his radio incarnation. For the café regulars, we tried to create a sort of 'wheel' of characters with the Count as the central hub connecting them all, the idea being that all the other characters would bring out different aspects of his personality. We were also thinking of the regulars in the *Cheers* bar. So we watched a lot of that show, and we watched a lot of Bilko because, like Phil Silvers' beloved army sergeant, the Count was a schemer.

Finally, most importantly, we needed a central relationship – someone off whom the Count could bounce his opinions, someone whose oddness could befuddle the Count in the same way the Count's oddness befuddled everyone else. Rory Kinnear turned out to be a comedy natural who just didn't usually play comic roles, as he wanted to escape expectations brought about by being the son of the great Roy Kinnear. We wanted someone who could embody the cringing self-consciousness of the liberal Englishman, and we couldn't have done better.

The Count had a heart of gold, but we tried to keep that a secret until the end of every episode, if we mentioned it at all. As with Bilko, you have to hide and delay the heart-of-gold reveal because people with hearts of gold are not funny. This means that Bilko spent the entire episode (like, say, a notorious one about an eating contest) behaving like a complete louse, until at the end he revealed himself to be, deep down, a friend, a good boss, a fellow soldier – lots of good qualities that, if you saw them and they were what you thought of when you thought of Bilko, you'd never watch the thing. Similarly, we wanted Arthur to have a heart, but hidden, mostly.

In the rehearsal room, I had a nice combination of two approaches to acting that I'd seen throughout my career: Steve, a comedian who's been refining a specific character his whole life, and Rory, a trained actor with complete command of his craft. Rory struck me as someone who could start acting upon waking up from a deep sleep. 'Ah! Is it the morrow?!!'

This time, I listened to my long-suffering producer, Richard Boden. He said, 'Sort the problems out in the rehearsal room. Don't go home. Do it all here.' I discovered the rehearsal trick that instantly made my life better, and it was simply this: I would write down every problem, every laugh that didn't happen, every plot turn that left the audience behind, every logic bomb that waited until it had a read-through audience before going off – whatever it happened to be – on a big whiteboard. We'd start the week with, say, fifteen problems on the board. And the next day we'd come in and in the morning someone would say, 'I was thinking about that thing that happens in the third scene – maybe we could do this.' And that would work, so you'd cross out that problem, and then you start rehearsing it. Then you hit the next bit that doesn't work, talk about it, swap ideas, sort something out, then cross that off the board. So by the end of the second day we have about six things crossed off the board, nine problems remaining. And so on and so on. It meant I could leave work at the end of the day like a regular person, and have something like a normal life.

There was always one issue left by the end of the week, one thing we couldn't quite figure out. But we tended to sort that one out in front of the audience. I think there's a part of your brain that's been working on the chewy little nub of a problem from the start of the week, and at the very last moment, just when you need it most, the answer bubbles up from your subconscious.

So on *Count Arthur* I found a way of working that would keep me going for the rest of my life. Easy-going, pleasant, satisfying. It was one of the best working experiences I've ever had. This new-found method, which Richard Boden had finally hammered into me, provided me with working habits that stood me in good stead for a few productions. I went to Chicago to work on a smart little comedy called *Shrink* with Tim Baltz. Tim and the team around him and his co-writers certainly didn't mind putting the scripts through a series of stress tests and I hope they think I helped, but working with them allowed me to let go a little too. In the end, it was their show.

Then, a sweet Irish programme for RTÉ called *The Walshes* in which I like to think I did something which hadn't been done before, which was to put the Irish mammy on television. They're not as much of a clear archetype as, for instance, Jewish mothers, so I felt it was a worthy aim. I also wanted to show a Dublin eejit. Eejits are actually found everywhere, but the Dublin variety was instantly recognisable to me. Blokes who know they're not brilliantly smart, and are a little bit embarrassed about it and make up for it in other ways, like playing pranks on each other constantly. I remember seeing a documentary in which Paul Gascoigne and his friends crept up on a sleeping mate and dumped a big bucket of ice water over him. Just horrible. Imagine having people like that as your friends. It'd be like living in hell! Eejits!

The cross-pollination that has always existed between America and the UK in cultural matters extends to comedy. One of the earliest mock-documentaries, and an all-time classic of the form, *Spinal Tap*, was still fresh in our minds when we wrote 'Irish Lives: Father Ted Crilly'. But Geoffrey told us to turn it into a studio sitcom and suddenly monkey priests started leaping out of it. When the fashion turned to single-camera sitcoms in the UK, they became more realistic, and in the US, the same fashion made the shows sillier, and in my view more 'British'. Tina Fey's *30 Rock* is a good example, with certain kinds of jokes in it that you don't usually see in American sitcoms. For example, someone walking in front of a camera and it's adding fifteen pounds, but on the monitor you see it really exaggeratedly – the actor in a fat suit – and it's funny partly because it's so clearly fake.

On the rare occasions that America wanted anything from me, I suspect it was this kind of explosive, surreal, boundary-breaking comedy. But I was more interested in achieving the kind of sustained quality of American sitcoms like *Frasier*, *Taxi*, *Cheers* and my beloved *Seinfeld*. I was thinking Cole Porter rather than Rik Mayall, though I still loved both. Perhaps writing *Ladykillers* had given me a renewed taste for the autumnal tones, theatricality and class of a *Frasier*, but I was becoming a little embarrassed about surrealism because I felt it was my default setting, and I don't think anyone who cares about what they do should have a default anything. It was coming too easily to me, and I longed to achieve what the best episodes of *Seinfeld* achieved. Once again: the surreal outcome arrived at through the accumulation of realistic and authentic detail.

I tried to make the proposed American version of *The IT Crowd* more like what I valued in those American sitcoms, but I happened along at a time when American executives wanted to lose many of those elements that I always treasured, chief among them the studio audience, which had become passé following the success of *The Office*. Purely on the level of craftsmanship, American studio sitcoms have always held a special place in my heart. Nothing inspired me more than the way Larry David and Jerry Seinfeld waltzed around the restrictions of the format.

What I wasn't prepared for was the pressures of pilot season. I can honestly say that making an entire series of the UK *IT Crowd* was less stressful that writing a single pilot episode for an American network. I had a vision for how the new version would work, but I was in the UK, so I was getting notes sessions at the end of the day, when I was exhausted, and told to hand in fresh drafts within impossible time frames. This culminated in a terrible holiday on the end of Norway's coldest nipple, which my wife and I had arranged when we thought the date safe. This added to the stress exponentially as I continued to take notes and hand in fresh scripts.

Of course, after all that, they passed on the project.

The Walshes is still online, if you know how to track it down. I made it with a troupe called Diet of Worms, who I thought were an extremely talented bunch. Sadly, no one saw it. People just didn't take to it, which is a shame because it had some great moments, and I think we succeeded in capturing both the mammy and the eejit with hilarious performances from Philippa Dunne and Niall Gaffney. Not all of them feel the same way about me though. Recently, I was allowed back on Twitter after being banned for a few years and when I got in touch to say hello, one member of the troupe deleted his Twitter account rather than reply.

Not many saw *Count Arthur* either. In terms of what is deemed acceptable for audience numbers, it might as well not have been on. I thought a family show would be in safe hands with the BBC, but they never knew what to do with it. It was on too early, then too late, then not at all. The trailers failed to mention that it was partly the work of the man who created *Father Ted*, *Black Books* and *The IT Crowd*, which might have generated some heat. But the BBC and Channel 4 comedy departments inhabited a sort of Marvel/DC Universe where neither can admit the other exists, just as Batman and Spiderman are unaware of each other's existence. We might have survived the drubbing we got from the critics (the usual 'canned laughter' accusation, which they delighted in repeating even when they must have known it was untrue), but the reception from the fans meant we had no support on the ground either. Our changes to the character established in the radio show caught them by surprise, and I think they justifiably felt slighted after supporting the one-man show that Steve had been running perfectly well on his own for years. There was nothing you could do about it, though. *Father Ted* could easily have been put at the wrong time in the wrong spot, been seen by the wrong critics, and disappeared without trace.

The success of *Ted* made for a great couple of decades. When the royalties dried up, as they do after the third or fourth repeat (first repeat you get a hundred percent of your writing fee, second repeat gives seventy-five percent, third fifty, until you're finally getting next to nothing), we still had the video and DVD sales to keep us sitting pretty in the fabled catbird seat. Once we released a DVD package called something like *Father Ted: The Ultimate Collection* and a few years later there was another release planned. 'We can't put out another one!' I protested. 'We called the last one *The Ultimate Collection*. It's dishonest!' I didn't realise that this was the business. Finding new ways to sell *Father Ted* DVDs over and over again was paying my mortgage while I worked on shows that never quite did the same numbers. If DVDs and video hadn't gone the way of rotary phones and asbestos, we'd still be trying to sell *Father Ted* DVDs. I finally found my peace with that situation just as it disappeared forever.

Then the internet came along, the internet I'd been waiting for, which I didn't realise would prove disastrous to my income, first by destroying physical sales and then moving on to my reputation, which received the death of a thousand cuts when I began standing up for women's rights.

A little over a year ago, I saw *Count Arthur Strong* pop up on Netflix, which was welcome news at a time of increasing financial insecurity. I rang my agent in full tizz.

'*Count Arthur* is on Netflix! How much will I be getting for that?'

'Oh! Good point, I'll check!'

While I waited for her to call back, I thought about what I might be able to spend my Netflix money on, which was basically just tax. When your career drops through a hole in the floor, you're still paying tax on the money you made when it was at eye level. A few moments before, I'd had a mortgage, a career and a family. Now I just wanted to get out of the white shoebox I lived in and put some distance between me and the rest-home-to-graveyard pipeline.

The phone rang.

'Hi, any luck?'

'I'm afraid not. You don't get any money.'

'I don't get any money? I get no money? For a Netflix show?

How does that work?'

'The thing is, you still haven't paid off the advance you got from the BBC for writing it. So it has to keep on making money and then you'll get money.'

'I owe *them* money??'

I'm used to my shows not doing the same kind of numbers as *Father Ted* but this was ridiculous.

Even before my fall in fortunes, the sobering truth hit me that the skill set I had honed for years, namely the creation and production of television sitcoms, was no longer a reliable source of income. On top of that, the stress of filming it nearly finished me off. If I wanted to survive, I'd have to make other plans. Sitcom writing suddenly looked like another trap from which I might have to escape.

But if you can find it, *Count Arthur* is up there with anything I've done. Do please give it a go. And if you watch it enough times, I may one day get paid for it.

15

THE INTERNET IS COMING

SOMEWHERE WHILE ALL this comedy was going on, and I was building a life, the internet arrived. That life split into two, as it probably did for you, dear reader. Two personalities, one swimming through 'meatspace' and the other through the internet's wires and dots and numbers. My presence on Twitter made me blink into existence for the kinds of people who were booking panel shows and I was invited onto programmes like *Have I Got News For You*. It was nice being in front of a live audience again, but I had the feeling that I shouldn't be accepting these invites just because I'd been asked. Blowing my kazoo and bashing my knee-cymbals together suited the format, which is mercifully edited from three hours down to thirty minutes, but it was perhaps not good for my soul to have that sort of thing encouraged.

The flip, conversational tone of Twitter suited my temperament. As a critic, I had learned to present my dipshit opinions as if they were written on tablets of stone, so I had, built in, the certainty

166

you needed to thrive on the platform. Like everyone else, I didn't understand it at first, but then Stephen Fry got trapped in a lift and it partially clicked. 'Oh, OK, so this is happening...now, somewhere. Stephen Fry is *currently* trapped in a lift. Right.' I still wasn't sure of its utility to people who were *not* trapped in a lift. Then, Jonathan Ross asked me if @Glinner on Twitter was really me. When I told him yes, he tweeted about it and I watched my follower count soar from a few dozen to four thousand human souls. Something within me turned and fell into place as I realised I had access to another audience.

Both publisher and stage, Twitter suited the dormant singles reviewer *and* stand-up comedian in me. My therapist friend Stella O'Malley suspects I may have undiagnosed ADHD, and this instantaneous, multi-perspective human drama was just my speed. I even gave a talk to Twitter's London HQ on how excited I was by the site's possibilities. Oh, it was quite the love affair, with Twitter at least. Facebook, I immediately hated. I don't think people should be in touch with everyone they ever knew, like a tribe of cavemen. Twitter reminded me of the bar full of outsize personalities from our first sitcom, *Paris*, or from the cellar at the International in Dublin, literally the first place outside of my family where I felt entirely welcome. The heady, salon-like atmosphere of the internet suited me and where it did not suit me, I adjusted.

The future was bright! We had developed an instantaneous method of communicating with practically anyone in the world, granting humanity what felt like a form of telepathy. We were making great strides as a species, in our own chaotic way, flapping and gasping into a new, exciting part of our existence like prehistoric lungfish, exhilarated on the first few gulps of air. In this new world of transparency and connection I simply couldn't imagine how an epoch-defining darkness like the Holocaust could ever occur again. If we were all keeping an eye on each other, then everything should be fine, shouldn't it?

My benevolent view of Twitter reached full cry in my Beatles Theory, where I drew from our sudden interconnectedness a joyous vision of the future based on a reading of Ian MacDonald's *The People's Music*. A brain-expanding piece of social history disguised as music journalism, the book charts the transformative course of the Beatles and Dylan through the sixties. I always thought the sixties – in the cultural sense – just sort of happened, but MacDonald shows how Dylan and the Beatles *made* it happen, and how it wouldn't have happened without them. The Beatles in particular flooded the anglophone world with colour and nonsense, qualities badly needed by a generation shaking off the trauma its war-scarred parents had tried not to inflict on it.

The Beatles turned the lights on and the world was never the same. My theory was that if two crucial figures of world-changing musical genius – Lennon and McCartney – could randomly meet because they happened to be born near each other in Liverpool, what would a connected world bring, now that we didn't even need to be in the same geographical location as another person to come to know and collaborate with them? Might we see a new era of Lennons meeting McCartneys all over the world? And what would happen when scientists of equivalent gifts ran into each other online? Or doctors? Were we entering a new Renaissance?

I had a dismissive attitude to people who weren't using these new tools. I thought, 'Oh no, you're hanging on to the past. This will ring in the future much quicker, and the future's wonderful and it's people working together!' I remember, in the early days of Twitter, apologising to some journalist friends for talking about it so much. 'Why wouldn't we talk about it?' replied my fellow hack, Andrew Harrison. 'If it was the seventies we'd be talking about Bowie.' Two music journalists rhapsodising about social media was an early surrender in a war we didn't even know was taking place.

But Twitter was nice back then, and fun. I was still enjoying myself immensely. When you're a comedy writer, you're hanging out with other comedy writers, so you're already primed to be a proper Dick Quippington. Everyone can be Oscar Wilde when you have a moment to think. I once had an idea that Oscar Wilde was actually a mediocre wit but a scientific genius who built a time machine that sent him only two minutes into the past so he had enough time to think of a good comeback. Twitter was the next best thing.

Steve Martin said a very true thing about Twitter – that it was like radio in that both were very literal mediums. For example, I once pretended to live-tweet the running of the bulls in Pamplona. 'Live tweeting', for those lucky enough never to have had a Twitter account, is simply a running commentary on an event, as it happens, tweet by tweet.

'We're all getting ready, I've got my white shorts on and hat.'

I gave it a few moments to settle and then, chortling fondly at my own material, followed it up with a series of tweets that outlined my experiences at the event.

'A bell is ringing. I'd better—'

'The bulls are—'

'Oh my God, I—'

'Someone just got—'

'Help, they're—'

Many animal lovers just instantly believed it was true, and were furious at me for attending an event that was actually taking place hundreds of miles away.

Another time I jokingly tweeted that Osama Bin Laden had been killed while watching *The IT Crowd*. There was an old gag Hollywood screenwriters would tell each other, one that took the form of a moral conundrum: 'You're walking through an Argentinian jungle. You knock on a door and it opens to reveal an elderly but still sprightly Adolf Hitler. He recognises you and says he loves your show. Do you turn him in?' I was just ripping off that joke. The gag was, if Bin Laden liked one of my shows, could he really have been that bad a person?

To my astonishment, people missed the joke and took me at my word. So, naturally I tried to keep the rumour alive. I asked all sorts of people to share it. I wrote to followers in different countries and asked them to tweet about it in their native languages. I asked people to say, 'Is this true?' or, 'I've asked Glinner but there's no response as yet.' I knew that kind of uncertainty would actually help amplify it as a rumour. I retweeted all of these fake replies to help them circulate and then deleted my own retweets to erase the trail that led back to me. My motive was to fabricate a buzz around the affair, and it was so easy I realised later I could have done it without any of that effort. Next time you're wondering why so many people think J.K. Rowling is a bigot, remember how easy it was for me to persuade everyone that the last thing Bin Laden ever heard was Matt Berry shouting 'FAAAATHHERR!!!'

The next day, I tweeted that the FBI had been in touch and had given me a DVD containing a video of the assassination. Once again, I live-tweeted the experience and during it revealed that Bin Laden was actually watching a rival show, *The Big Bang Theory*. I pretended to be furious and immediately began tweeting again about what a monster he was. I thought people would love it. But there was disquiet below decks. One follower said, 'It's fine. I just won't trust him on anything ever again.' At the time, I didn't see it as a problem, thinking, 'I'm a comedy writer, so it doesn't matter if people don't trust me.' Boy, did that bite me in the arse.

One freezing winter, my wife and I set off to see a band play on the other side of London. I had a big coat on, like the one George wears in an episode of *Seinfeld*, a padded Gore-Tex number that made me look like a giant toddler. My arms were hanging like George's, and I asked Helen to take a photo. I tweeted it, and in the next tweet I said, 'I've fallen and I can't get up.' That was the joke – that the coat was so ungainly that it turned me into a big turtle. We were about to get on the Underground to go to Wembley, which was miles away, and I thought, 'Hmm, people might actually take that last tweet seriously. They might have thought I was somewhere, lying on my back in the snow.' So I wrote, 'By the way, that's a joke. I haven't really fallen in the snow,' and pressed send.

We were in the tunnels beneath London with no phone signal for more than an hour, and of course, the tweet hadn't gone through. When we got back to ground level there were dozens of worried texts and voicemails from friends. It was nice of them to worry, although I did feel there was a performative aspect to some of the concern, perhaps because I was friends with so many performers. Of course, when I did actually fall, this time by tumbling outside the bounds of polite dinner-table conversation, those same performers were suddenly nowhere to be seen.

When the music press was still around, the review pages would often centre on the derisive or the divisive. In 1986, two albums were reviewed in the *NME*: *Parade* by Prince, and *Liberty Belle and the Black Diamond Express* by The Go-Betweens. There was a ludicrous dance-music-v.-rock-music beef going on at the time and both albums were given to the critics who would hate them the most. So there was a terrible review for Prince's masterpiece in the same issue as a terrible review for The Go-Betweens' masterpiece, all because someone thought that the readers were getting bored of seeing enthusiasm and joy. This was a pre-internet version of the worst thing that ever happened to human communication, the Hot Take.

The Hot Take is basically just, 'You believe this widely accepted thing? Well, I believe the opposite, and here's why.' It is a rhetorical manoeuvre that could only have sprung up in an attention economy, where the spiciest opinions drive the greatest numbers to your account. The Hot Take is distinct from mere disagreement in that it is largely performative. The people who indulge in it receive the same kind of endorphin hit I would imagine is granted to flat-earthers and 9/11 truthers. It ran amok on Twitter where the language and values of American academia began to taint public conversations. Wealth never trickled down but, thanks to Tumblr and Twitter, academic posturing and obfuscation began dripping into the public sphere with devastating results.

American academia had begun to take leave of its senses, to the point where peer-reviewed journals were publishing meaningless papers so long as they adhered to a suddenly fashionable ideological framework. To expose the situation, three people – Peter Boghossian, James Lindsay and Helen Pluckrose – carried out what has become known as the Grievance Studies Hoax. Between 2017 and 2018, they submitted twenty ideologically freighted and absurd papers to peer-reviewed journals. Seven of them were accepted. The titles sound like parodies but will give you an idea of the kind of intellectual the trio were satirising: 'Going in Through the Back Door: Challenging Straight Male Homohysteria and Transphobia through Receptive Penetrative Sex Toy Use' and 'Who Are They to Judge?: Overcoming Anthropometry and a Framework for Fat Bodybuilding'.

Perhaps their finest contribution was 'Our Struggle is My Struggle: Solidarity Feminism as an Intersectional Reply to Neoliberal and Choice Feminism'. This paper was accepted by the feminist social work journal *Affilia*, even though it was actually a translated chapter from Adolf Hitler's *Mein Kampf* with some added quasi-feminist jargon sprinkled over it like sesame seeds. With the Grievance Studies experiment, Pluckrose, Lindsay and Boghossian had exposed the practice of 'idea laundering', wherein fraudulent or insane or merely stupid academics cited each other's papers – all of them filled with identical levels of obscure jargon – to construct what can only be described as a fake body of knowledge. A Library of Alexandria containing the work of dummies, charlatans and porn addicts.

The Hot Take ran out of control on Twitter to such an extent that a hashtag opposing it trended saying *#twoplustwoisfour*. I didn't follow along with the drama, but from what I could tell it was something of a last stand for the dwindling numbers of reality-based Twitter users. To the English-speaking world, thanks to Winston Smith's desperate attempts to hang onto it in Orwell's *Nineteen Eighty-Four*, the simple sum is an effective shorthand for truth and sanity and resistance to tyranny, so naturally, Twitter's army of hot-take merchants eagerly rose to the challenge of disproving it. 'As a biologist, I know that sometimes 2+2=5 because chromonoids often divest their menubrae in three layers.' That sort of thing. Twitter was fast evolving from a platform that connected people into a colossal stage for intellectual self-stimulation. A whole generation of attention-seeking mediocrities swept onto it and got to work. Many of them started putting pronouns in their Twitter bios, which I was beginning to recognise as a cat bell for idiots.

This hyper-contrarian climate showed its ugly side in 2015, when two gunmen claiming allegiance to Al-Qaeda opened fire in the offices of the satirical French magazine *Charlie Hebdo*. They killed twelve people, including cartoonists, journalists and police officers. Since the magazine had recently published a series of satirical cartoons of the prophet Muhammad, regarded as a blasphemous act in Islam, it took only a few hours for Twitter users to start openly declaring that the cartoonists deserved to be shot in cold blood. The American laptop class displayed its deep knowledge of French culture by casting the cartoonists as racists, using a caricature of then-Minister of Justice, Christiane Taubira, who was born in French Guiana, as evidence. Robert Wilson, a *Charlie Hebdo* writer, described it to me as one of history's great stitch-ups. He said: 'They cut off the text beneath that showed it was a response to an absolutely gobsmacking, racist article in *Valeurs Actuelles*, the Front National's weekly paper. The cartoon was perfectly, impeccably anti-racist and skewered the psychotically allergic reaction to her amongst the Right.'

The bad faith was dizzying. Taubira attended several of the funerals and delivered an especially moving speech at one of them, for Bernard Verlhac, who was a good friend. Moreover, she attended the memorial service for Mustapha Ourrad, a Muslim copy-editor who received scant media recognition because he didn't conform to the developing narrative, which portrayed a group of predominantly elderly left-wing satirists and cartoonists as bigots.

At a time when the world should have been united in grief over the image of coffins covered in cartoons drawn by their grieving colleagues, the empty chatter of these predominantly American commentators filled the air. I was horrified to see the 'bigot' narrative spread outside the US, too. Michael Ondaatje and Peter Carey, who both wrote novels very dear to me as a teenager, took part in some of the collective madness by withdrawing from a PEN Gala to protest an honour for, again, a group of elderly, left-wing cartoonists murdered in cold blood.

That was a bit of foreshadowing. I would soon see the full extent to which supposedly smart people can be bamboozled by the high priests and enforcers of online activism, and the ease with which the rest of the world tends to fall into line with The American View On Things.

I was fairly active on Twitter, politically. I turned down a major deal to make a version of *The IT Crowd* with Fox, partly because the network was owned by Rupert Murdoch, whom I hated, and I didn't want to be a hypocrite. But now I believe the only undeniable positive outcome of my online activism during that time was the role Helen and I played in repealing Ireland's draconian abortion laws under the eighth amendment of the republic's constitution. When Helen first got pregnant, we learned that the foetus had an abnormality which would have resulted in death moments after birth. Presented with the choice of continuing the pregnancy or terminating it, we of course chose the latter. Working with Amnesty International, we later appeared in a video interview in which Helen spoke of the trauma she suffered, and her subsequent horror at discovering that our decision would have been illegal in Ireland. I wrote a piece in the *Irish Times* saying it was time for the country to grow up on the issue, and authored a terrible, doomy advert that had the distinction of being voiced by Liam Neeson. But it was Helen's testimony that really broke through.

Helen and I tried to attend every protest we could, and at one of these events, I remember some strange person with a bullhorn trying out this nonsense:

'WE WANT THE STATE TO PAY FOR ABORTIONS!'
[general cheering]
'...AND SURGERIES FOR TRANS PEOPLE!'
[puzzled mumbling]

Looking around, I saw the same question in the eyes of everyone there. 'This is an abortion rally. What do 'trans people' have to do with anything?' It was one of the earliest times I began to feel uneasy. Sure, let's talk about trans rights, but first things first, eh? We hadn't yet won the fight we'd taken on. In retrospect, this was the first sign I had of the sleight of hand that would allow a sinister movement to attach itself to a number of progressive causes and wrap itself in their stolen banners. The abortion battle was a fight that women were winning on their own, and men couldn't stand not being at the centre of it. And so they did what men tend to do: they shouldered their way in. One of these men was an Irish trans activist who left his very young family to embrace his new identity 'as a woman'. This took the form of taking selfies of himself in women's toilets while giving the camera the finger. For achievements such as this, his image was projected onto the side of Dublin Barracks as part of Irish celebrations for International

Women's Day.

These were only the first ripples of a gathering tsunami of madness. Online, people had started to go dangerously insane. It was such a slow process that I didn't notice it at first, and was in fact seduced by the language and attitudes I was unconsciously absorbing from left-wing activists in the States. These activists were full of fire and fury and hated no one more than the heretics on their own side, for whom they reserved the worst punishments. In this new political climate, words began to lose their meaning. When we first heard 'transwomen are women' we didn't realise it was meant literally, and when we first heard about 'literal trans genocide' we didn't realise it wasn't.

Making *The IT Crowd* was the result of a story I'd spent my whole life telling myself. My dad threw his head back in laughter when I told him at the age of nine that *Star Wars* changed my life. But it really did, and among the dozens of ways it did so was that it gave me my first tribe. Because of my strangely shaped face, which made me a target in school, I always felt great kinship with the awkward, the quiet, the solitary and the shy, so nerds and geeks were very much my people. The story I told myself was that I should always take their side.

Danny Simon's advice to be alive to social movements served me well through the years, but it also made me hyper-vigilant for what might next be coming down the pipe. I picked up on the Gamergate movement early on, through my interest in computer games, which was ostensibly what the movement was about. On Gamergate, there are few facts on which people agree. It properly kicked off when a computer game designer named Zoë Quinn was the subject of an angry blogpost by an ex-boyfriend. Quinn faced accusations of sleeping with reviewers for favourable press, and her outraged friends reacted the way outraged friends will do. Gaming journalists tried to come to her aid with a number of angry think-pieces that fired up a lot of young men who had nothing to do with Quinn's harassment. The alt-right – represented in the popular imagination by the provocateur Milo Yiannopoulos – used the opportunity of this heightened sense of grievance among young men as a recruitment tool. To a good little lefty like me, this made him, and those like him, public enemy number one. How DARE he use the SACRED NERD PASTIME OF GAMING to RECRUIT for the FAR RIGHT? During a calm in the media storm I was helping to create, he replied to me on Twitter. He actually said (maybe not this exact wording but certainly along these lines): 'Just you wait until they come for you.'

Outrageous! Ludicrous! Why would they come for me? I was Team Nerd, Team Geek, a good little progressive, a true believer, and on the right side of history, because my side had the artists, the coders, the gaming designers, the cool podcasters, and everyone else that formed part of an entirely new social, business and cultural framework that had sprung up overnight. What Yiannopoulos was hinting about in his reply was something I was not yet able to hear. Those gentle nerds whose cause I took up, whose corner I fought, were just like any other group of people, with sadists and psychopaths and misogynists (ooooh, so many misogynists) among them too. They'd just never had the chance to show it before the internet gave them the upper hand. This was the real Revenge of the Nerds.

So I did my bit in the Gamergate wars because I was convinced the Far Right was using the issue to recruit and mobilise against my tribe. But while there certainly was recruitment going on, and virulent misogyny abroad, not all of it was coming from the Right. Gamergate was a loosely connected confluence of forces and motives, and certainly the pro-Gamergate side contained many who found common cause in bullying and harassing women from online spaces. But that wasn't the full story, despite my zealot's certainty that it was. Only later did I realise that the same accounts who were shouting that the Nazis were coming were also shouting

'Nazi!' at lifelong left-wing feminist activists, journalists and academics.

The extreme, polarising language used by the online left created a picture of the opposing side that I now suspect was only partially in focus. There certainly were some villains at that time, but I'm no longer confident I always knew who they were, especially as I discovered that more and more accounts with female names actually belonged to blokes. I was slightly friendly with one account called some variation or other on 'SuperGamerGirl' – again, I thought, *Yeah! Why shouldn't girls play games!?* – but the owner turned out to be the kind of dude who looked like he'd correct you if you called Gandalf a sorcerer rather than a wizard.

Another narrative to which I had unconsciously signed up was that the Right were evil and that they were using dog whistles to advance their cause, injecting anti-Semitism, racism and other -isms back into the discourse in the form of comedy. It was in this fertile and febrile atmosphere that I heard about a Scottish YouTuber named Mark Meechan, or 'Count Dankula', who had filmed a video of his girlfriend's dog which he trained to give a small Nazi salute every time he said phrases like 'gas the Jews' and '*Sieg Heil!*'. He was arrested and charged, which I thought was an overreaction to a distasteful joke. But I had little sympathy for his plight, as I thought he was a literally a Nazi, rather than someone trying to make an audience of internet 'edgelords' chuckle. Photographs of Meechan with Tommy Robinson provided the circumstantial evidence I needed to add texture and depth to the story I was telling myself.

In my evidence-gathering, I relied on the same sources that would later come after me. Many times, Meechan attempted to reach out to me, to take the conversation past the ludicrously hostile manner in which I was conducting it, but it was to no avail. I had made my mind up: Count Dankula was a fascist using comedy to advance his fascist aims. To my eternal shame, I even tried to hobble a crowdfunder that he had started to raise money for his defence. The story I had told myself was more powerful even than the hundreds of messages I was receiving, telling me that there was no meaningful connection to Robinson, that Meechan wasn't a Nazi, and I had got this one terribly wrong. Some time later I sent a video apology to Meechan which was screened at a comedy event staged to help his defence fund, and he was gracious enough to applaud the video and accept the apology. I repeat it unreservedly here.

From the outset, the same online activists were using cancellation, protests and shaming to achieve their aims. Unlike me, some quickly recognised the Left's lurch to authoritarianism. Mark Fisher, a Marxist academic at Goldsmiths in London, wrote an essay critical of identity politics called 'Exiting the Vampire Castle'. In it, he pleaded for the Left to return to a class-based analysis and reject the aggressive tactics that increasingly accompanied 'woke' politics. 'We need to learn, or re-learn, how to build comradeship and solidarity instead of doing capital's work for it by condemning and abusing each other,' he wrote. 'This doesn't mean, of course, that we must always agree – on the contrary, we must create conditions where disagreement can take place without fear of exclusion and excommunication.'

He was cancelled for writing it, and killed himself in 2017.

INTERLUDE

I WANT TO ASK YOU a question before we launch into the second part of this book, a question that should be easy enough to answer. You may have noticed a lot of people asking the question 'What is a woman?' recently. You may also be wondering why even top political figures have been unable to come up with a response, or worse yet, have decided to provide absurd quotes that will haunt them to their graves, such as Labour leader Keir Starmer's claim that it was 'incorrect' to say that only women have a cervix.

But there's another question, equally important, that for some reason we never hear asked, let alone answered.

Quite simply, what does 'trans' mean?

Seriously. What does it mean? Does anyone know? I certainly have never heard the same definition twice. I used to think it meant transsexual. To me, there was a clear difference between those who had suffered enough dysphoria that it sent them to the operating table, and Eddie Izzard, a cross-dressing man who was once asked why he wore women's clothes and answered, 'They're not women's clothes, they're my clothes.'

Transsexuals suffered terribly because of a disconnect between how they saw themselves and how the world saw them and it was impossible not to sympathise. Your heart goes out to anyone who suffers from so debilitating a condition that they take drastic steps – often life-shortening, always irreversible – by means of surgery and pharmaceuticals, to bring reality into line with a vision of themselves they can't shake off.

Society treated them with a fair degree of respect. The Gender Recognition Act of 2004 encoded their vision of themselves into law and the Equality Act 2010 protected them from discrimination by including gender reassignment in its list of protected characteristics. All this seemed admirable, society doing its best to help troubled people. And crucially, it was only a tiny subset that these laws were serving. Who could object to that?

But one day, early in this fight, I noticed on Twitter a comedian friend deploying the word 'Terfs'. I knew this stood for 'trans exclusionary radical feminist', which is a misnomer, because feminists do not exclude women who want to be men; they support all women, whether trans or not. More importantly, it's a slur that left-wing men throw at women instead of more traditional gender-based slurs like 'bitch' or 'witch'. If you do a search for 'Terf', you'll find it's almost always used in a pejorative context, and rape and death threats won't be far away. So I asked my friend why she was happy to use a term that, even then, I knew was being used to tag women as acceptable targets for violence.

'They hurt my trans friends,' was her reply.

Trans *friends?* I thought. How many had she managed to collect? Unless she was hanging around in hospitals, how was she continuously encountering what we were always told was only a tiny portion of society?

It might have been then that it occurred to me for the first time that maybe 'trans' did not, in fact, refer to transsexuals. This was borne out by a look at the glossary provided by Stonewall, the former lesbian and gay lobby group which has now reinvented itself to focus primarily on 'trans' people. Theirs is a non-definition:

TRANS
An umbrella term to describe people whose gender is not the same as, or does not sit comfortably with, the sex they were assigned at birth.

There are a few problems here. First of all, sex is not 'assigned' at birth; it is observed and recorded, often before birth. And what exactly is 'gender'? Well, let's go back to the glossary.

GENDER
Often expressed in terms of masculinity and femininity, gender is largely culturally determined and is assumed from the sex assigned at birth.

Again, not a definition. You can't not define something and then use it in the non-definition for another thing. After failing to provide clear definitions for its categories, Stonewall's site proceeds to list all the individuals who are supposedly encompassed by those categories:

Transgender
Transsexual
Gender-queer (GQ)
Gender-fluid
Non-binary
Gender-variant
Crossdresser
Genderless
Agender
Nongender
Third gender

Bi-gender
Trans man
Trans woman
Trans masculine
Trans feminine
Neutrois.

Note that transsexual is *second* on the list.

The same Wikipedia which has been smearing me as a bigot for years lists a few more, which I include here mostly for their comic value:

Omnigender
Graygender
Genderfuck
Eunuch
Pangender
Neurogender
Man of trans experience.

I haven't made any of these up. No wonder my Irish comedian friend was suddenly swimming in 'trans' people if literally anyone could call themselves one.

This was around the same time that Stonewall – and its equivalent organisations across the western world – began to push for what is known as self-ID. This policy would mean that, if you were a man who wanted to legally change your sex, all you had to do was declare you were a woman. If this idea were enshrined into law, any chancer could put on some purple lipstick and invade women's spaces, such as changing rooms, toilets and rape-crisis centres. Any male rapist who identified as trans between arrest and sentence could go to a women's prison. Self-ID didn't just unlock the henhouse for any passing predator; it scattered a buffet of treats to lead it to the door.

And still, every argument I heard was predicated on everyone knowing what the word 'trans' meant, and took for granted the existence of a category called 'trans people'. But the more I looked into the issue, the more I found that 'trans people' covered too many different experiences to be a useful phrase. It described both the young women who were succumbing to a new, even more viral form of anorexia – one that caused them to remove their breasts and take drugs that gave them the dubious gift of male-pattern baldness – and the middle-aged men who decided to leave their families in order to live as clownish visions of the women they had fallen in love with online. It covered young men disgusted at what they felt was their own toxic masculinity, and young men who enjoyed nothing better than indulging in it. These groups had little in common with each other. 'Trans' was not a stable category.

There were two other things I discovered in quick succession. While there's no precise data on the 'transgender' population in the UK, estimates suggest it is around one percent, which means roughly 670,000 people. The information also suggested that the *majority of trans-identified males retained their penis*. These weren't transsexuals. These were just men, acting under a variety of motives, some benevolent, some far less so. But crucially, under self-ID, there was no way for women to tell the difference.

Most astonishing of all, I also discovered that within this community of what we might call ultra-low-commitment gender voyagers, the position of transsexuals had been so thoroughly undermined that there was even a derogatory word for them amongst trans rights activists.

They were called 'Tru scum'.

Not only did 'trans' suddenly *not* mean transsexual, it now referred to people who were sending actual transsexuals abuse.

The first scandal, for me, was the death and rape threats being sent to feminists online. This led me to investigate some of the people who were being protected by this uniquely violent form of discourse. Over the years digging into this issue, I've highlighted the cases of quite a few dangerous people but, for the sake of brevity, I'll give just one example. One example, but a significant one. Aimee Challenor.

When Ashton Challenor began dressing in girls' clothes and calling himself 'Aimee', he immediately gained a crucial upgrade in his social status by suddenly qualifying as a 'transgender teen'. In his home town of Coventry, he caught the attention of local LGBT groups and progressive political organisations eager to champion a fashionable cause. Over the next few years, Aimee's political career and online profile could not have been hotter: he joined the Green Party of England and Wales and, within less than two years, became its national spokesperson for equality. By the age of twenty, he was running for deputy leader of the party, and was celebrated with a fawning profile in *The Guardian*. All of this took place under the close supervision of his father David, who followed Aimee into the Green Party and acted as his representative and photographer.

Footage of Aimee at an Oxford Union debate reveals an awkward young man with long hair and acne, an unexceptional talker and thinker plainly out of his depth, repeating trans-activist talking points to yet another docile audience too cowed to ask questions. Not the first time it has happened in politics by any means, but there was something off about the swift rise of this political mover with no charisma, ability or insight, and that something was his father.

David Challenor is a paedophile. In 2016, he was arrested and charged with twenty-two serious criminal offences. He had tied a ten-year-old girl to a joist in the attic of the family home, where Aimee also lived, and proceeded to rape and torture her with electric shocks. At least one very senior Green Party official knew about these charges but didn't speak out, even when David Challenor was officially listed as Aimee's election agent in Coventry South at the 2017 general election and at the local elections the following year. When the Coventry Pride committee got word of the charges, all they could muster was a meek request that Aimee stop bringing his father to their events.

It wasn't until David was sentenced to prison – he's now serving a twenty-two-year sentence – that word finally got out and the Green Party launched an inquiry. Long before the inquiry reported back, Aimee cried 'transphobia' and ran into the welcoming arms of a bigger party, just as eager to climb aboard the trans bandwagon: the Lib Dems. They dumped him less than a year later when it emerged that he was engaged to marry an American 'furry' fetishist named Nathaniel Knight, who openly bragged on social media that he had written pornographic stories about molesting children.

Having crossed the pond, Aimee tried his hand at US politics, where once again his trans identity opened doors and he quickly became a fundraiser for Elizabeth Warren's campaign for the Democratic presidential nomination. When Warren dropped out of the race, Challenor turned his focus towards online media influence. He teamed up with one of his childhood coterie of much older crossdressing/diaper-wearing/furry fetishist friends, Peter 'Katrina' Swales, and they became influential moderators at the social media behemoth Reddit. They gained total or partial control of about eighty 'subreddits' (topical forums) including r/JoeBiden, r/LGBT, r/trans, r/transgenderteens, r/ask_transgender, r/gayrights, r/LGBTstudies, r/LGBT_KidsZone. They used their grip over LGBT social media to silence critics who brought up safeguarding issues around trans activism, such as vulnerable minors being targeted and groomed by adult men with fetishes. Aimee became so powerful at Reddit that the corporation brought him onto its payroll, but he was then dropped when Reddit users started asking questions. It's widely believed that Challenor continues to moderate a swathe of Reddit's forums.

I do have some sympathy for Challenor, who is highly likely to have been the victim of abuse himself. One day, he may come to realise it and remove himself from those who have manipulated him for so long. On the other hand, I have nothing but contempt for the politicians, charity bosses and journalists who thrust him into a spotlight for which he was entirely unsuited, abandoning all critical thinking on hearing the word 'trans' and silencing whistleblowers who tried to raise the alarm. (A member of the Green Party, Andy Healey, lost his membership for doing just that. He still hasn't received an apology.)

The point is, there is no way Aimee Challenor should have been advising on safeguarding in institutions like Girlguiding, MI5 and the NHS. But that was exactly what he was doing because, while his father was facing charges for one of the worst crimes imaginable, Challenor was a member of Stonewall's Trans Advisory Group at the very time that organisation was working to introduce self-ID across the UK.

Challenor is just one example of what I called a 'central outlier', someone supposedly unrepresentative of the 'trans community' yet who was lauded and promoted within it until his behaviour and associations made him too toxic even for the organisations that had enabled them. There were others: Jess Bradley, the first trans officer of the NUS, who was suspended and never reinstated after he posted pictures online that seemed to show him flashing his penis at work; Beth Douglas, cited by Scottish politicians as an inspiration while they were pushing through their own recent version of self-ID, who was suspended by the Scottish Greens after posing with weapons in tweets inciting violence against women; Sam Brinton, a 'non-binary' deputy assistant secretary in the Office of Nuclear Energy under President Biden, arrested three times in one year on suspicion of stealing women's clothes from airport carousels, and convicted twice.

The muddiness of the word 'trans' empowered these

opportunistic men, even as it disempowered children and women. A whole new form of 'health care' has popped up, devoted to an unclear, ill-defined condition while enriching plastic surgeons and drug companies. Young girls began demanding 'top surgery', the cutesy term that hides the horror of elective double mastectomies, and taking testosterone, which has irrevocable effects on the body after only a few weeks of use. The children most at risk from these procedures are those who do not conform to sexist stereotypes, such as girls who like to climb trees and play football. And if you're a boy unlucky enough to have been born into a family of closet homophobes, an early affinity for princess dresses or *My Little Pony* playsets could be enough to convince your parents that they have found a 'solution' to the 'problem' of having a son who may grow up to be gay.

A fact that most people didn't realise until recently, and even now must make them feel like someone has slipped something into their drink, is that while the rest of the world was going about its day, feminists and trans rights activists were engaged in a furious battle around a belief in magic.

Thanks to an effective embargo on reporting of this issue, many more simply didn't know that this battle was happening at all. Like a war between werewolves and vampires in a novel for teenagers, the fight took place in parallel with real life, its victims hidden from view by a complicit media working with activists who were following what has since become known as 'the Dentons playbook'.

In 2019, the law firm Dentons, which bills itself as the largest in the world, collaborated pro bono with the Thomson Reuters Foundation and an international LGBTQ+ youth and student network called IGLYO to prepare and publish a 65-page document called *Only Adults? Good Practices in Legal Gender Recognition For Youth*. While both Dentons and the Thomson Reuters Foundation insisted this document neither constituted legal advice nor necessarily reflected their views, it essentially outlined a strategy to advance gender identity ideology in the shadows, sneaking its key ideas into law bit by bit while hiding behind more popular (read: lesbian and gay) causes.

One of its main preoccupations is the worldwide enactment of laws that would allow children to change their legal sex without adult approval – not even (or, rather, especially not) parental consent. It describes in great detail the strategies it recommends to trans lobby groups and activists to achieve this goal, such as avoiding coverage in the press, limiting public discussion of the issue, courting young politicians, and misleading the public by using the rhetoric of gay rights as a 'veil of protection'. It's quite extraordinary. Have you ever heard of a civil rights movement that avoids the media?

And yet it makes perfect sense. This is a form of activism which depends on the uncertainty and confusion that has formed around the word 'trans'. In the absence of stable meaning, politicians flounder, columnists falter, celebrities repeat mantras that keep them out of trouble. But the fact remains, we still don't have an answer to the question.

What does 'trans' mean?

16

CANCER BECOMES THE LEAST OF MY PROBLEMS

SOME TIME AFTER THE period of intense, unrelenting, grinding stress that was my attempt to write an American *IT Crowd*, with my involvement in the fight against the rise of gender ideology beginning to bubble in the background, and Trump in the White House, I was having a shower. The back of my hand glanced against my 'boys', to use one of Seinfeld's many exquisite euphemisms. Men are supposed to check their testicles regularly for anomalies, but even that tiny contact with the lads told me that something had, overnight, gone terribly, terribly wrong at what I like to call 'headquarters'. A chill went through me that, for a moment, negated the effect of the shower; one of my 'boys' suddenly appeared to be wearing a thick, woollen scarf.

A very short time later I was speaking to a testicle ultrasound specialist who had recognised my name.

'Gaww, loved *Father Ted*.'

'Oh, thank you!'

'Shame about yer man.'

'It was, it really was.'

These exchanges never bother me but they usually don't end with me getting the gang out. But he maintained his professionalism throughout and soon left the room to collect the results. When he came back, all the happiness at recognising me had vanished from his face. I guess it's a nice measure of how much people love my show that he looked positively distraught.

'Good news?' I said.

'No...no, I'm sorry. I'm sorry; it's not.'

I offer this conversation as more evidence, along with the various stories that bobbed up during #*MeToo*, that you should never have fans look at your testicles.

The doctor who then came into the room was not a tall man, and very young, which frightened me as a combination, because young, short people often turn out to be children, who should not be performing complicated medical procedures. But he put me at ease by walking to the gurney, which was raised quite high, turned around, and then leaped backwards onto it to sit. Even the attempt would have impressed me, but the fact that he carried it off with such élan immediately endeared me to him and make me think yes, I can place my squad in the hands of this man.

'Yep, you do have a problem.' He said. 'It's just one testicle. You only need one. We'll just chuck the other one away.'

It's interesting, isn't it? A few weeks earlier, I would have taken the removal of a testicle as bad news. But now? Why, I could have danced a little jig.

Told the family, tears, more blood tests, much love from friends and public.

A beloved comedy writer in the fight of his life!

Like my first sitcom *Paris*, this narrative ran for six weeks, and then was never seen again.

Waking up from the operation, I felt good, which I took to be normal because I was supposed to be back home within the day. After taking a moment to prod the thick padded bandage now affixed across my left side, I hopped to my feet and began wriggling into my jeans. A nurse came in, nearly yelled in fright and asked me what I thought I was doing. I was instructed to get undressed again and placed back on the gurney to wait for a doctor. I did so and lazily opened Twitter, still feeling pretty all right with the world.

At this point I had not quite nailed my colours to the gender-critical mast. I had defended the women being smeared with the slur 'Terf', and was being monitored by Irish trans activists as a result. But I had not yet entered the field with banner flying. As I looked at Twitter that day from my hospital gurney, I thought: what am I so scared of? Why am I nervous about getting involved in this debate? I knew my positions were sound, and I was sure that once people saw that I was arguing in good faith, they'd see the problems with gender ideology and we could have a sensible, grown-up conversation about it. So I sent a few tweets carefully explaining my position. Job done!

Meanwhile, the wound under my bandage was beginning to communicate urgently to me. I tried to stand up, and pain travelled through my body at broadband speeds. I had to lie as flat as a board in order to unfeel it. At some stage I think I saw my doctor and thanked him – it's all a blur really – but when I was finally told I could go, I couldn't stand up. Lying down was only marginally better. The gurney was as comfortable as a kitchen counter, but they didn't have any beds so, in desperation, they asked me to try to walk one last time. The nurse and my wife bought me to my feet like the Amish raising a barn and after a moment steeling myself, I was able to waddle a few steps and gently, slowly turn to face them again. Helen saw my face and burst into tears. Apparently, I was bone white. Finally convinced I wasn't faking it for whatever reason, the staff found a bed. I was taken there using one of those boards you've seen in every hospital drama, except usually when people have been in a massive car accident.

I could write a Proustian passage about the sensation of hitting that bed after lying on that gurney all day. It defied space and time, extending what should have a moment of fleeting relief into infinity. I lay there feeling like an Arabian prince until at last I raised my head over the clouds and saw that the people around me were very, very ill. Now that I had a bit of peace, and the pain was subsiding, I started to take stock of things and piece together what had happened in the intervening five or six hours.

The morphine, which had allowed me to: a) hop into my jeans after the operation; and b) enter the most toxic cultural debate of the twenty-first century, had definitely worn off. Standing up to go to the toilet was a Jack London adventure. I was still doing my penguin walk to get there, as the pain was excruciating, but however bad it got, I wouldn't have switched places with the patient I saw earlier in the day who had a curtain drawn around him and then screeched with pain in a way that normally would have made me snap to my feet in alarm. As I couldn't move, I just absorbed it instead. It made my bones hum with terror like an orchestra of struck tuning-forks.

I tried to stay very still between trips to the toilet, which I had to plan using a series of moves and hacks I'd picked up from previous visits. I thought of my dad and his golf tips again. 'Harvey Penick's Little Red Book of Going to the Toilet.' There was a moment during peeing, the shiver I'm sure you all know so well (wait, do women get it?), and when I could feel it coming I knew the pain was going to put on another commanding performance. Lying in bed again, I got cramp in my leg and similarly had to let it have its way with me because stretching out my toe to relieve it would have reactivated the wound and finished me off.

Soon, the drugs began to work their magic again and the intensity of the pain began to fade. From the soft cloud of my bed, I could see the evening light through the windows. The visitors had gone and all was quiet. I still couldn't move, but I was so comfortable in comparison to being on the gurney that, for the first time in hours, I finally began to relax.

I decided to have a look at Twitter to see how things were going.

Holding my breath so as not to anger the scar, I saw that my careful explanation of my position had certainly had an impact. An American trans activist and journalist called Parker Molloy, who worked at the influential American left-wing website *Media Matters*, had sent me a number of increasingly frenzied direct messages. After the third or fourth time telling Molloy of my hospital situation, I eventually had to end the conversation more robustly. Meanwhile, another tweeter hopped into my replies to say, 'I wish the cancer had won.' That was when I discovered a Twitter setting that turned off notifications from people who didn't follow me. I knew the cancer comment was the first of many, so I turned the setting on and haven't turned it off since.

I later learned that, when I refused to be browbeaten into submission, Molloy went around to people in his real-life, actual physical offices, and stood over them until they unfollowed me on Twitter. That reminded me of a story I was told by Damian Corless – the man who got me into journalism – and which he captured in his enormously enjoyable book *Party Nation*, a history of the dirty tricks employed by Ireland's 'gombeen' politicians. On the morning of Ireland's 1982 general election, the solicitor Pat O'Connor, a close friend of the sitting Taoiseach (prime minister) Charles Haughey, was charged with attempting to vote at two polling stations in the extremely tight constituency of Dublin North. O'Connor had been allocated ballot papers at two polling stations and had opted to use 'his full allocation', as Damian dryly put it. By lunchtime, the damaging news was splashed across the front of the *Evening Herald*. Activists from Haughey's Fianna Fáil party mobilised, driving around the district's newsagents trying to snap up every copy in bulk. After the polling booths shut that night, a car pulled up outside the opposition Fine Gael headquarters and one of the occupants hurled a bundle of *Herald*s through the front door.

The low-rent audacity of it never failed to astonish me. They bought all the newspapers! And then dumped them like corpses outside opposition headquarters when they had outlived their potential for harm. Now we have the digital, American version of O'Connor – Parker Molloy and his brand of entitled, catastrophising, Worst Best Friends occupying workplaces all over the Western world. All of them demanding the 'correct' pronouns and standing over work colleagues as they delete people from their phones.

It certainly enrages Molloy that some people refuse to see him in the way he demands to be seen: as a woman. The obeisance they require of us is dubbed 'kindness' by trans activists, a quality often in short supply when it comes to their dealings with others. One of Molloy's claims to fame is that he told another trans-identified person to 'DRINK BLEACH' in an exchange of private messages. There's a heavy irony that many people blocked or unfollowed me and my reputation nosedived because I fell foul of someone who told a trans-identified person to kill themselves.

The first of many betrayals came from Amnesty Ireland. When Ireland voted to overturn the abortion ban – thanks in very small part to the efforts of my English-born wife and me – Amnesty tweeted that the vote was a victory for 'pregnant people'. I don't remember when I saw it – it might even have been from my hospital bed – but I found it enraging. My wife wasn't a 'pregnant person'. She was a woman, and a mother. After a century of Irish women's suffering, Amnesty Ireland had decided to spit in their faces by removing them from the scene of their greatest victory over the Catholic Church.

Having finally taken the plunge online and identified myself as a 'Terf' ally, I was subjected to a number of 'waves' of activists on Twitter. First came the faceless anime accounts, which looked exactly like the same accounts that had been sending abuse to women during Gamergate, and indulged in the same kind of violent threats. They blinked out of existence after I fiddled with my settings, but hot on their tail came the 'trans ally' celebrities who didn't understand the issue beyond the opportunity it gave them to broadcast their virtue and harass me. I was astonished when one of the cast of Hat Trick's *Derry Girls* started campaigning for my removal from Twitter. And a US comedian I otherwise admired, Michael Ian Black, who just a few weeks earlier had been angling in a good-humoured way for a job from me, said something so bizarre that I'm not sure I was able to come up with a reply. I'd been alerting him to the practice of young teenage girls wearing breast binders to flatten their breasts, a part of 'trans healthcare' that, like many other terms with the word 'trans' affixed, meant precisely its opposite.

A year earlier, a major US study* had found that almost ninety-seven percent of women who bind their breasts experience a negative physical effect from the practice. Back, chest, shoulder and abdominal pain are par for the course. The study reads like the description of a Biblical plague. Almost half of the women consulted had experienced musculo-skeletal problems due to binders' unnatural reconfiguration of the bones and muscles in the upper body: from bad posture to spinal and rib changes, shoulders 'popping' in their joints, overall muscle-wasting and even fractured ribs. Half of binder-users experience shortness of breath, and a small number end up with respiratory infections. Forty per cent experience neurological problems: dizziness, lightheadedness, headache and numbness are all common. And three-quarters

* *Chest Binding and Care Seeking Among Transmasculine Adults: A Cross-Sectional Study* by B.A. Jarrett, A.L. Corbet, I.H. Gardner, J.D. Weinand & S.M. Peitzmeier.

experience skin and tissue problems: itching, swelling, tenderness, and sometimes permanent scarring. The Victorian corset had been reinvented for an even more misogynist era.

I didn't tell Michael all of this; I didn't think I'd have to. I thought he would jump out of his shoes in his haste to help stop such clear brutality. But then he said, to my eternal astonishment: 'Graham, the kids are working something out.'

What was that now? They're *what*?

I have a daughter. My first responsibility is to keep her safe. It is simply not possible for young women to be safe in a world where cosmetic self-harm is being normalised. How could my American showbiz friend treat these horrors so flippantly? Was it a consequence of living among so many plastic surgeons? It was 2018, and I hadn't yet realised that the children of the privileged were feeding their parents a line of gobbledegook, cut-and-pasted from websites like Tumblr and Reddit, which had in turn trickled down from the craziest corners of American academia. Most extraordinary of all, the adults, many of whom worked in industries normally associated with liberalism or progressivism, like the media, the theatre, publishing and the art world, were helping to amplify and spread these same crackpot ideas. Non-binary identities, fluid genders, 'born in the wrong body'… Nonsense, in other words. There remains not a shred of scientific evidence for the existence of a mysterious essence called gender that people are somehow born with, and yet these middle-class industries had fallen to an ideological coup, with women in each one relating near-identical stories of harassment and threats to their livelihood if they dared dissent. Within both the art world and publishing, lists of 'Terfs' were circulated, with the aim of terrorising and isolating those named.

An early sign that all was not going to go well in my awareness-of-the-issue/stop-calling-me-a-bigot campaign came when I started meeting the parents of that American invention, the 'trans kid'. A cartoonist who drew a caricature of me for my 'Why That's

Delightful' website complained when I began to object to the misogyny of the movement.

'Graham, I have a trans child,' he said.

'I have a daughter,' I replied.

The more I've learned about the kind of parents who greet the discovery that their kids are 'trans' with anything other than the words 'uh, oh', the more I've come to understand the hostility with which they greet any kind of scrutiny. The US podcaster Jesse Thorn, on whose show I appeared when was I not yet radioactive to the tastemakers of Los Angeles, decided his child was trans under the following circumstances. 'When she started kindergarten,' he tweeted, 'my wife was bathing her. An adult friend of ours had just come out as trans, and my wife mentioned that not all girls have vaginas and not all boys have penises. Our daughter asked, "Some girls have penises?" My wife said yes. Whether you were a boy or a girl wasn't about your private parts. "I'm a girl with a penis," my daughter said.'

When my son was four years old, we hardly ever consulted him on the matter of whether he was a boy or a girl, but apparently in Jesse's family – and those of many more of what we might call the podcasting middle classes – the four-year-old holds the veto. More recently, Thorn wrote: 'Our kid is nine. Puberty is on the horizon. This year for the first time she saw a doctor who specialises in adolescent medicine for trans kids. We're so grateful we live in LA and have access to caring medical pros who are up on the latest research and standards of care.'

Only in a place like Los Angeles could plastic surgery and pharmaceuticals be elevated to the level of 'standards of care'. I hope Jesse's kid – and his whole family, for that matter – get out of it OK.

'Why do you care so much?'

That would be thrown at me a lot by people trying to shame

me into silence. The implication is that a concern for women's rights (normal, explicable) is actually an obsession with trans rights (bigoted, deranged). But trans rights only become an issue when they negatively affect women's rights. It's that simple, and there aren't too many areas where these conflicts come into play. However, when they do, it's devastating. All over the world, male prisoners are being admitted to women's jails if they announce they're trans some time between arrest and sentence, and female prisoners run the risk of receiving extra time on their sentences for 'misgendering' these opportunists. Female athletes are starting to leave their sports, unwilling to accept the humiliation of being beaten by men with the inbuilt advantage of male puberty who now claim to be women. I personally have been contacted by two rape survivors in Scotland who are self-excluding from rape crisis centres because of the comments made and ethos represented by the trans-identified male CEO of Rape Crisis Scotland, Mridul Wadhwa, who once said that 'bigoted' rape victims would be in danger of not recovering fully unless they addressed their 'unacceptable beliefs' (namely that men are not women).

In the early days, I did my best not to 'misgender' anyone, because even I was half-hypnotised by the powerful narrative spell woven by the cult of gender and believed it a mysteriously terrible sin. But in this book, you'll have already noticed I use sex-based pronouns. 'Misgendering' became taboo practice because of the combined efforts of trans activists and the privileged members of the laptop classes enforcing the new orthodoxies, but it's a taboo that has been imposed without debate or consent, and I believe it leads to dangerous confusion and obfuscation. If a celebrity comes out as trans or non-binary, the media fall over themselves to use his or her new pronouns. When this involves the use of 'they' for a single individual, it tends to make an article unreadable. It's even worse with news reporting involving those who identify as trans – notably on the crime pages. The ideological capture of the media was well underway when the more-captured-than-most *Independent* ran a story headlined, '"Armed and Dangerous" woman sought for allegedly killing boyfriend and brother'. You had to do some puzzled digging before you discovered that the 'woman' was a man and the 'boyfriend' a woman. Through a gentle tweak by an unseen hand, the meaning of essential words had been changed without our consent, and journalists used this planted evidence to pin the blame for a horrific episode of male violence on women.

If we comply with the demand to call the male-bodied swimmer Lia Thomas 'she', that makes it easier for Thomas to compete in women's races, which he naturally tends to win because he's so much stronger than his female competitors. The pernicious idea that even mentioning Lia Thomas' birth-name (William) is hateful has helped create a looking-glass world which robs everyone of their ability to think or describe what they see with their own eyes. Grave punishments await those guilty of 'dead-naming'. According to our new ethical overlords, the Oscar-nominated actress Ellen Page no longer exists, having now announced that she is a man called Elliot, and activists and 'progressives' consider it a hate crime even to mention her former name, even though doing so is neither criminal nor hateful.

These taboos, supposedly driven by 'kindness', empower the most dangerous men in society. If we manage to successfully rewire our brains to such an extent that we see Eddie Izzard as a woman and Page as a man, it will be easier for opportunistic predators like Adam Graham – the double rapist almost admitted to a Scottish women's prison by Nicola Sturgeon's government – to access single-sex spaces across society, not just in prison.

No matter how many times I explained all this, the same question kept coming, over and over. 'Why do you care so much?'

'Why do you not?' was all I could say.

As the harassment continued, I began having nightmares about imprisonment. In the dreams, I had a memory of having been in prison already, as if this was my third or fourth visit. I'd never had a similar feeling of persistence in dreams before, but there was a period where I would go to sleep wondering if I'd learn more about this parallel biography of mine. In other dreams, I was working on a show, surrounded by old friends and collaborators. I preferred the prison dreams because waking up from them was a relief.

While awake, the anti-anxiety meditation on which I was now dependent left me unconcerned at the attacks I was continuing to receive online. Someone said, 'Jesus, Graham, have you seen your replies?'

'No, I turned the notifications off.'

'You should look at them.'

Why would I look at them? It didn't matter if people hated me. It was an inevitable consequence of my activism. If I'd known I'd be putting up with it for six years, I might have felt differently. As I mentioned, I thought my old mates would be along to help any second. I didn't think they'd be sitting in the audience shouting, 'He's in the attic!'

I spoke to various old colleagues, who always found a way to escape making any public sign of fellowship or comradeship. The hate just kept coming, despite my proving time and time again that the arguments we were making, my feminist friends and I, were perfectly valid. Without any big names placing their flag with mine, the ideology remained fashionable. Couldn't my friends see what I was sharing? The testimonies from lesbians, from detransitioners, rape victims, therapists and athletes? The damage to children?

The academic and environmentalist Derrick Jensen asked to interview me for his Resistance Radio podcast, which seemed like the perfect opportunity to clarify my views. It was a good conversation, and at one point we addressed the fact that I'd taken an unpopular position and everyone was shouting at me to reverse course. I said:

Since I made the decision to start talking about this, I knew there would be pushback. But what I didn't quite realise was how it goes from people who are ideologically opposed to what you're saying, telling you to stop, but then it leaks, it starts to kind of bleed into people who agree with you, also saying 'you need to stop'. I mean, most people online have been very happy to have me on their side and speaking up. But you do have people who do get very nervous, you know…because the opposition is so extreme and so frightening. Eventually everyone is asking you to stop. But, you know, my feeling is that I can't. I can't because it's too important.

It's too important to the women in my life and it's too important to me. How can I ignore something like that? I'm now in a position where I can answer the question, honestly: if you were around at the time of something terrible happening, like Nazism or whatever it happened to be, would you be one of the people who said no, this is wrong? And you know, I feel happy in myself that I, I've been one of the people standing up and saying, no, this is wrong. Despite everyone telling me not to.

Barely hours after the podcast appeared, *Pink News* ran a story about the interview with the headline 'GRAHAM LINEHAN COMPARES TRANS ACTIVISM TO NAZISM'.

17

MY CAREER COMES
TO A SCREECHING HALT

A LITTLE BIT AFTER MY BRUSH with cancer, I brushed with something almost worse. A man who had been going under many different names: Tony Halliday, Steven Hayden and now 'Stephanie' Hayden.

Halliday/Hayden is a former prisoner who now presents himself as a lawyer (although he is not in fact qualified either as a solicitor or a barrister). He has a very thin skin, and seemed to make it his mission to try to wreck the life of anyone who offended him. When one member of Mumsnet posted on Facebook – in admittedly colourful language – that Hayden was a convicted criminal and vexatious litigant, he lobbied the police to arrest her, and she was charged and convicted of 'persistently using a public communications network to cause annoyance and anxiety'; this was quashed on appeal. Another woman was arrested at home in front of her two young children and put in a prison cell for seven hours after she referred to Hayden on Twitter as a man.

I first encountered him as a member of a group of transsexuals who had organised on Twitter under the name @TSVoices to oppose self-ID. Concerned that the rights they had already won would be undermined by the move towards self-declaration, which was already broadening the definition of 'trans' so widely it was rapidly losing all meaning, they asked me to give them a mention in a tweet, which I did.

But I believe Hayden had joined the group with the intention of destroying it from within – I still have no idea whether he's actually transsexual or merely a crossdresser, although I suspect the latter – and, overnight, the group dissolved in acrimony. Hayden even sued one of the transsexuals in the group.

Then I received a tip-off about him, concerning alleged financial irregularities. I publicised this accusation, but Hayden didn't challenge it when he came after me. Instead, he complained that I had publicised confidential information by referring to his former male identities. He also said that several of my tweets were defamatory, including one where I wrote: 'I don't respect the pronouns of misogynists, stalkers or harassers, and Tony is all three.'

Hayden served papers to my home and reported me to the police on the same weekend. *The Guardian*, whose editors seemed to have given up any pretence of being even-handed on this issue*, published an article headlined 'Graham Linehan given police warning after complaint by transgender activist', in which it claimed I had been given a 'verbal harassment warning' by police acting on Hayden's complaint.

What had actually happened was that I received a phone call from a policeman in West Yorkshire who seemed confused when I

---

* Two female-gender critical journalists, Suzanne Moore and Hadley Freeman, eventually had to leave the the title after being sidelined and harassed by staff at the paper.

told him that I'd blocked Hayden on Twitter months ago, so could hardly be accused of harassing the guy. The policeman then said something like 'stay away from her, *awright*?' and rang off. For a national newspaper to headline this as a 'harassment warning' – a formal document that needs to be delivered in writing – was disgraceful but, I would come to learn, typical of how many journalists liked to frame things that involved feminists and their allies. I couldn't afford to fight *The Guardian* in court, but after seven months of wrangling, the paper eventually removed the word 'harassment' from the first paragraph, which was too little, too late. By then, the 'police warning' of the headline had morphed on social media into 'police caution' – which is issued where a crime has been committed and requires an admission of guilt, neither of which had happened here. *The Guardian*'s sensationalised headline and introduction – for a story you might more truthfully headline 'Confused copper menaces *Father Ted* writer on behalf of aggressive ex-con' – enabled that to happen.

I found it grimly funny that the UK police and media were acting as reputation managers for a cartoon character like Hayden, but my wife was terrified. Then, Hayden posted on his Twitter the Companies House number for our production company, which revealed our home address.

While Hayden undoubtedly takes offence very easily, I'm convinced that he undertook the entire project in order to terrorise us. We Hayden victims tend to stick together, and I found out from other members of this unlucky club that he makes sure to serve papers at the same time as he makes a police report. Then he waits a few days before asking for money, to be paid within a tight deadline, to drop the legal case. He usually asks for £500, but in my case he bumped it up to £4,500 because he thought I was rich.

He and his friend Adrian Harrop, a Liverpool-based GP who was temporarily suspended from practising medicine as punishment for his aggression towards women on Twitter, were among the trolls who targeted a Catholic journalist called Caroline Farrow, live-tweeting a visit to her home in a way that seemed designed to frighten and intimidate her. When Caroline's visa to visit the USA was withdrawn just before she was about to travel, Harrop tweeted that he'd just visited the US embassy in London. 'As always, consular staff very efficient at dealing with my...important diplomatic business,' he gloated, with a wink emoji.

Those dot-dot-dots, with their heavy hints at the unsaid, are a calling card for this particular type of bully. Another example is the Scottish soap actor David Paisley, who managed to bring the iconic gay magazine *Boyz* to its knees. When the thirty-year-old publication's managing editor, David Bridle, wrote a single non-committal tweet to publicise a webinar by the newly founded LGB Alliance – declared a hate group by trans activists, despite being run by two left-wing lesbian veterans of countless gay rights battles – Paisley organised an advertiser boycott, crippling the publication within twenty-four hours. The business never fully recovered.

I count this form of activism as low-level terrorism aimed at women, gay people, trans-identified people, and little old me. But, like low-rent versions of Kevin Spacey's opportunistic serial killer in *Seven*, Hayden, Harrop and Paisley could not have had such success without accomplices in the police and the press. The ideologically captured *Attitude* magazine rewarded Paisley's behaviour by putting him on its front cover and giving him an award, while *The Guardian*'s mendacious reporting of the Hayden incident has followed me around ever since it happened. The false claim that I received a police caution for transphobia is constantly repeated to friends and colleagues to justify my cancellation. It was even presented to my publisher as a reason not to publish this book.

There are only a handful of activists doing most of the damage here. The police could cut a good deal of the toxicity out of this debate if they knocked on a few of their doors, instead of knocking on doors on their behalf. These activists – both the countless faceless ones and those unwise enough to pin their names to this movement – specialise in bespoke harassment: either combing through your Twitter feed to prepare the dossier that will condemn you, or targeting those close to you when they come up with nothing. Since I was a virtuous leftie, they couldn't pin anything on me, so they created their own little doorstep dramas in which the police and the press were happy to play their part. It was surreal how swiftly these internet lowlifes gained such power over society. I began to feel like I was in one of my own sitcoms. It was so ludicrous. Surely some of my old friends would dash to my side – if not for me, then for their own daughters, or mothers, or girlfriends, or wives, or sisters.

One day, thinking of Harrop's harassment of Caroline Farrow, I called him 'Doctor Do-Much-Harm' in a tweet. The next morning, the police turned up at my family's door. I told them I wouldn't be changing my online behaviour one iota, and that Harrop was a danger to women and a sadistic bully to them online. The policeman nodded, said something about free speech, and left. I was delighted that this time I was prepared for such a visit, but it wore heavily on Helen, which is what it was meant to do.

'Don't worry,' I kept saying, 'Someone will step in soon, someone will say something.'

Five years ago.

Around this time, I received a letter from Sonia Friedman, one of the biggest theatre producers in London's West End.

> We have been in discussion with the Peter Shaffer estate about commissioning a new companion piece for the classic one-act farce *Black Comedy*. Traditionally it has been paired with Shaffer's *White Lies* and also at times Tom Stoppard's *The Real Inspector Hound*. However, we all agree that in order to produce *Black Comedy* again in the West End, we need to find a new and exciting response to

the play that gives it a new vitality and a real sense of purpose and event… Graham Linehan is, of course, right at the top of our dream list as someone who we might be able to attract to this idea. I'm attaching a short briefing document which gives some more background along with a sense of what we are hoping to achieve. Might you have time to take a look and then I hope we could we find a time to discuss on the phone soon?

Peter Shaffer's *Black Comedy* is possibly the most ingenious farce ever written. It's about a young sculptor whose plan to impress his fiancée's father by borrowing expensive furniture from his wealthy neighbour goes awry because of a power cut. When the lights go out, bedlam ensues as the sculptor tries to return the borrowed items before his neighbour returns early from a trip, all while dealing with various high-stakes visitors. What sets the play apart is its use of 'reversed lighting': when the stage is dark, the characters behave as though the lights are on; when the lights come up, the actors, suddenly visible, pretend they're experiencing a full blackout. It's a genius concept and a production I'd seen years before with David Tennant in the lead had left me giddy and envious.

Due to *Black Comedy*'s high concept and the physical demands it puts on its cast, it can't sustain a whole evening at the theatre, so it's short, and an additional play usually accompanies it. I had actually seen the production mentioned in the letter, the one packaged with *The Real Inspector Hound*. So the letter was heady stuff that grew even headier when I met Sonia Friedman and learned from her that whatever I wrote was to be paired with the show permanently. No more cycling through short plays to find a suitable beau; whatever I wrote was going to go arm-in-arm with its majestic suitor forever.

Going from lowly sitcom writer to being considered worthy of pairing with Schaffer and Stoppard had me floating home, my mind already shuffling excitedly through possibilities. It had to be something which emulated *Black Comedy*'s daring use of the form, and my first vague thought was a stage split horizontally in the middle, representing two apartments. In the bottom one, a rich couple getting ready to leave for dinner; above, a gang of thieves waiting for them to leave so they can execute a robbery, as in the old French thriller *Rififi*. I just needed to figure out what the people in the flat were arguing about, and how that argument might affect the robbery, and vice versa.

That was as far as I got with it. I was taken off the project only a few days later because Peter Shaffer's estate decided on the late playwright's behalf that they 'didn't want to get involved' by 'taking one side or the other'.

In fact, my career was over before the stitches from my operation had healed. Almost immediately, more jobs began to fall away. A tour to Australia to teach comedy was cancelled by the touring company Frontier because they 'wouldn't be able to afford the security'. I discovered later this was a standard excuse given to those of us declared unclean by the new sacred class. I'm also the person who worked with Steve Martin and Martin Short for the shortest period of time. Five minutes, I think it was. A producer offered me the chance to develop the comedy-drama TV series *Only Murders in the Building*, in which both starred. I had a flat-out offer, and then within minutes I got an email from the same producer, rescinding it. Someone else with a prior claim had suddenly materialised, I suspect around the same time a Twitter user in the producer's office told him I was a bigot.

Before the gender hoopla, I only knew people in the media. Now, virtually no one in the media would return my calls but I began to count as friends social workers, police officers, solicitors, barristers, doctors, nurses, academics and one central figure at the original Stonewall Riots in New York, Fred Sargeant. While the last few years have been in many ways a rerun of the loneliest period of my life – my childhood, the last time I felt so utterly excluded and alienated from society – they've been invaluable for me as a writer. Boy, have I suddenly got a lot of grist for my mill. It's almost too much grist. Maybe take it easy with all the grist!

One of the charges against a social worker, Rachel Meade, which resulted in her being disciplined by her professional regulator and suspended by her employer, was cited in a public-facing report on the case. She had, it seemed, reposted material 'regarding and by Graham Linehan... [who] has been cautioned by the police because of [his] behaviour'. The framing provided by Tony Halliday/Steven Hayden/Stephanie Hayden as a means of harassment against me, was now being used to target and harass other people. I find it astonishing that Robin Moira White, the trans-activist barrister who took the case on behalf of Social Work England, seems not to have known about Hayden's history.

Two years after her ordeal began, Rachel rang me with some good news: Social Work England had finally dropped the case against her. 'Because they had to take out the bit about you, we got a chance to challenge them on various other things as well,' she told me. 'It was fundamental. Without that, I don't think they would ever have given in.' It seems that rumours and smears are not acceptable forms of evidence in a legal process, not yet anyway.

At the time of writing, Rachel is still suing both Social Work England and her employer, Westminster City Council, for damages, because the whole episode was devastating for her.

Often, these punishment courts are an end in themselves. According to the author Naomi Klein, Latin American dictators don't always murder their political enemies: goons in President Victor Paz Estenssoro's Bolivia often just snatched difficult opponents from the street and took them for short, stressful holidays in the wild so they'd miss key votes. In the UK, work tribunals and disciplinary investigations take the place of the Amazon rainforest, and a whole generation of progressive women have been silenced and sidelined as they're forced to defend themselves against trumped-up charges of bigotry, brought by the enforcers of gender ideology whom they were unfortunate enough to have as colleagues.

The process is the punishment. Trans activists have learned that a baseless accusation of transphobia is enough to take aggravating women out of the picture for significant periods of time. The Green Party, after decades of being considered eccentric and unserious by a doubtful public, decided to woo that same public by calling its female members 'non-men', and expelling or barring from internal elected office women who failed to bow to the new ideology. Emma Bateman has been elected three times as co-chair of Green Party Women. After her second two elections, she was suspended twice from the party on spurious grounds. At the time of writing, there's still no date given for the hearing for the first offence.

One of the few people I do still know in the creative arts is the choreographer Rosie Kay. Her attempted cancellation began in the garden of her home in Birmingham in the summer of 2021. Covid-conscious, she had arranged a party with her company of young dancers; by inviting them to her home, there was less danger of them deciding to celebrate the end of rehearsals elsewhere and come down with an infection that could derail the show. Towards the end of the party, the discussion turned to Rosie's plans for a follow-up, an adaptation of Virgina Woolf's gender-bending knockabout, *Orlando*. In the course of a suddenly heated discussion, she explained to the young dancers – some of whom went by 'preferred' pronouns – that she strongly believed in the reality of sex because she and her son had both almost died while she was in labour. During that ordeal, her womanhood was literally a matter of life and death for her. Her husband would never know that experience, and that difference between them meant something.

To the little sparrows of the Church of Gender, this was all high heresy, and could not be tolerated. The dancers harangued Rosie to such an extent that she soon found herself hiding in her own bathroom.

When they subsequently brought formal complaints to her company, she was subjected to two investigations. 'They cancelled *Orlando* and then were making efforts to re-educate me, to stop me from centring women's rights in my future work,' Rosie told me when I visited her home shortly after all this stuff hit the newspapers. 'It was existential to me. I had to resign from the company I founded, citing constructive dismissal. I no longer had any trust that the charity trustees or management were fulfilling their part of my contract or the charitable objectives of Rosie Kay Dance Company.'

I asked her what those charitable objectives were.

'Supporting the artistic work of Rosie Kay to tackle and explore controversial and taboo subject matter through her dance works.'

I thought I'd misheard for a second. 'That's actually what your company was supposed to do?'

'Yep.'

Rosie refused to follow the script. Instead of crawling away to lick her wounds, she went public, turning the tables on her accusers and the organisation that still bore her name. Her former colleagues then folded the company, which meant she couldn't sue them. In other words, she saw a business she had built up for years spirited from beneath her on spurious charges of transphobia. I couldn't help thinking of Thomas Putnam in Arthur Miller's *The Crucible*, who accuses his neighbours of witchcraft in order to snatch their land.

Then there's the children's author Rachel Rooney. Working with illustrator Jessica Ahlberg, Rachel wrote a picture book called *My Body Is Me*. Its message was that children should be happy with their body. That's it. That's all it said.

Unfortunately, trans rights activists dislike any mention of being happy with your body as it undermines the message that being trans is a thrilling and transformative lifestyle choice that prevents you from becoming anything as drab as a gay teenager or, God forbid, a lesbian. Rachel, on the other hand wanted kids to be grateful for their bodies, and comfortable within them, because why on earth would you want anything else?

Here is the complete text from the short, colourful book:

My Body is Me!
I am my body. My body is me.
It's a wonderful thing, I'm sure you'll agree.
My body has feelings and thoughts that I own.
It's working right now and it will when I'm grown.
It eats and it drinks. It poops and it wees.
And if it gets flu, it is likely to sneeze.
I am my body. My body is me.
It's a wonderful thing, I'm sure you'll agree.
My body can mend from a bruise or a break.
Sometimes it sleeps but it's often awake.
It itches and tickles. It slowly grows hair.
Mostly it's dressed. In the bath it is bare.
I am my body. My body is me.
It's a wonderful thing, I'm sure you'll agree.
My body can act like a low-flying plane.
A mermaid. A dragon. One part of a train.
It climbs and it swings like a real chimpanzee.
But always gets down and comes home for its tea.
I am my body. My body is me.
It's a wonderful thing, I'm sure you'll agree.
Bodies are different… Children are too.
Some prefer pink things… Some prefer blue.
Some love to get muddy… Others do not.
Some like cold weather… Some like it hot.
Sometimes we're gentle. Sometimes we're tough.
Yes, EVERY body can do all this stuff.
I am my body. My body is me.

It's a wonderful thing, I'm sure you'll agree.
Wherever you travel, your body goes too.
You're never without it, whatever you do.
You're born in your body. You don't have a spare.
So love it. Hug it. Treat it with care.
Bodies are great! They fit perfectly.
I am my body. My body is...ME.

Tweets calling the book terrorist propaganda and likening Rachel to a white supremacist were amplified by many prominent people within the publishing industry. Clara Vulliamy, an established writer and illustrator, and daughter of the children's author Shirley Hughes, wrote a long thread that condemned the book without having read it. Vulliamy implied the book would be used to undermine 'trans children'. She publicly warned an agency that employed Rachel to present her work in schools: 'You need to be aware of this with author Rachel Rooney who is on your books; ideologically driven school visits could see us all in deep water.'

The author's 'trade union', the Society of Authors, declined to offer support to Rachel, which may come as less of a surprise if you've seen the output of its chair, the novelist Joanne Harris, on Twitter. Harris is another 'trans ally' who declined to condemn death threats against J.K. Rowling. So devastating was the experience that Rachel stopped writing books for children and has now taken on a part-time care job.

This is what I'm talking about when I say that trans rights activists will target you whatever the scale or nature of your sin. I'm a big, stubborn Irish straight white male who doesn't suffer fools gladly, and a lot of you think I brought all this on myself. But what did Rachel do to deserve cancellation? Nothing. She wrote a beautiful, kind, responsible book for children, and she got the same treatment I received: they tried to destroy her life. If there's any justice, people will be reading Rachel's books to their children for decades, whereas names like Clara Vulliamy and Joanne Harris will be remembered only as a warning to future generations of the terrible danger of fads in an online world.

As I've mentioned, transsexuals are treated roughly by trans rights activists if they dare dissent from the official activist line or acknowledge the reality of their own biology. When transsexual teacher Debbie Hayton started writing informed pieces in the national press that were critical of reality-denying gender ideology, trans activists in Debbie's workplace embarked on a bullying campaign that rivalled anything being doled out to actual women. Other transsexuals, such as Aaron Kimberley of the Gender Dysphoria Alliance and US podcaster Corinna Cohn, have endured terrible harassment at the hands of so-called 'trans allies'.

That should tell you that this is an ideological battle, not an ethical one. I know more trans people than some of the people calling me transphobic. They're just not the right kind of trans person, in that they're not wedded to an ideology that believes women don't exist as their own sex-class.

Many of the women whose side I've taken have told me their boyfriends/husbands don't get it. To many of those men, it's as if women fighting for their rights is something like hosting a bridge evening: 'She's off doing her woman's night.' Then she starts losing opportunities, losing friends; she starts getting controversial – maybe the police swing by, or the lawyers get in touch on the orders of the various high-profile 'trans allies' who enjoy victimising heretical women. That's usually when hubby looks over and says, 'You've got to cut this out right now. It's not important enough to go through all this.'

Trans activists target women and trans people most of all, but I'm by no means the only man to have suffered because of them. Some thirty years after we'd worked together on *Paris*, I crossed paths once more with James Dreyfus.

After our sitcom, he'd made his name in a string of comedy shows including *Gimme Gimme Gimme* and *The Thin Blue Line*, a police comedy where he put in a winning performance as that production's Trigger (or 'Dougal' if you like). I persuaded him to sign a letter asking Stonewall, the former lesbian and gay rights charity which has altered its remit and done more than any other institution in the UK to promote extreme gender ideology, to reconsider its stance on the issue. James agreed without hesitation and was a valuable person to have alongside such feminist luminaries as environmentalist and whistleblower Helen Steel and academic Linda Bellos, both of whom were suddenly being labelled as something close to vermin for expressing opinions that every rational person simply took for granted.

Drafted by Jonathan Best, the former director of the international arts festival Queer Up North, the letter argued that Stonewall was 'seeking to prevent public debate of these issues by branding as transphobic anyone who questions [its] current trans policies'. Among other entirely reasonable requests, it asked the charity to 'commit to fostering an atmosphere of respectful debate'. Since it appeared online in 2018, the letter has been signed by more than eleven thousand people. But within a day of its being published, Stonewall gave their answer: a flat no. Even asking the question was painted as a moral failing. So it came to nothing, but I was still pleased that James had shown such bravery and I felt sure others would follow his example.

Again, I didn't count on this being a wholesale failure of the celebrity class. Five years later, James is still being hounded by trans rights activists because he signed the letter, and he has had difficulty finding work. In 2021, the company Big Finish released *Masterful*, a celebration of fifty years of The Doctor's arch-enemy, The Master. James had played this part on their *Doctor Who* audio productions. The credits featured every living actor who had taken the iconic role…except James. They left him out. Because he asked for a respectful conversation, the cowards at that company decided he had somehow acted shamefully, and they shamefully removed him from the list.

When the history of these years is written, it's not only the extremist activists who will be recalled with revulsion, but also the spineless corporate figures who never even made an attempt to resist them. Their inaction contributed to the ruin of James Dreyfus' livelihood, all for the sake of preserving their own comfort. Worse yet is the betrayal he endured from his colleagues. A brilliant comic actor, a gay man, abandoned by the very people who should have had his back, because the celebrity class is more interested in looking like they're doing the right thing than actually doing it.

Meanwhile, my wife was watching me lose jobs and opportunities. I couldn't ask her to stop asking me to stop, because she was protecting our family too, so a chasm opened up between us. It didn't help that my experience on *Motherland*, the BBC sitcom about competitive middle-class parents, was not ideal. My marriage broke down soon after the first series, and since my wife was one of my three co-creators, you'll forgive me if I don't dwell on the minutiae. But I'm proud of the pilot episode, the only one I really worked on, and I hope you'll carry on watching the show, not least because it's one of the few things that may yet keep me off the breadline.

Helen was also looking for normality. Birthdays came and went, and they weren't fun occasions; they were overshadowed and fraught. On the day I threw a rare birthday party for her, the magazine *Vogue* published an article by its trans columnist, Paris Lees, attacking me directly. This was the glossiest publication to denounce me to date, so it lay somewhat heavy on my mind throughout the evening.

Helen was perfectly within her rights to ask me to cease operations. But I couldn't do so for another reason, which is – and this is something that everyone who's in this fight knows – the Gender Stasi never forgive. The singer Macy Gray was asked by Piers Morgan about trans-identified males competing in women's sports. She said: 'I will say this, and everyone's going to hate me, but as a woman, just because you go change your parts, doesn't make you a woman. Sorry.' Blurted out as if not saying it had been burning her up, that sentiment, shared by the vast majority of people around the world, was enough to make the sky fall in on her. After three days of bullying, she made a cowed, on-air apology. I imagine she had to, so that the woke activist staff at her record company wouldn't bury her new album, so the activist staff who book guests for BBC music programmes wouldn't lose her manager's number, so the activists moderating music forums and the activists working in every part of the business she was a part of wouldn't declare her an unperson. Macy Gray yanked the record company's leash simply by standing up for herself as a woman and they yanked back hard enough to bring her to her knees. She just about made it through to the other side by virtue of delivering that humiliating apology, a strong woman humbled by forces she hadn't realised she'd taken on. But the activists will only remember her for her original sin, not the apology, however many stations of the cross she observes to absolve herself.

The same was true for me. Even if I had been prepared to recant or keep my mouth shut, it wouldn't do any good because my heresy was out there and would never be forgiven. I was fighting for women and children, sure, but also for my reputation and my ability to make a living. Helen didn't understand that I would never be confident of a having a job again until the entire gender ideology movement, which has caused so much misery, was burnt to ashes.

People would sometimes ask 'what's your endgame?' and that was it. I wanted to reveal the havoc gender identity had wrought on society, expose those who had enabled it and help bring about its end.

18

THE RESISTANCE

In the UK, the main charity devoted to children who think they're born in the wrong body is called Mermaids. The woman who served as its CEO for six years until 2022, Susie Green, is open about the fact that her son started being 'trans' after his father disapproved of his gender non-conforming behaviour – specifically playing with 'girls' toys'. She took this child at sixteen years old to Thailand for phallectomy surgery – ie to remove his penis. She admitted all this in a TED talk which received not gasps of horror, but warm applause from an audience of nerds. For years the video was widely available, until it was suddenly deleted in 2023 without explanation.

One of the doctors recommended by Mermaids was Helen Webberley, who was convicted in 2018 of running an unregistered medical agency and would later be suspended from the medical register for putting patients at 'unwarranted risk of harm'. It's shocking that any registered charity would endorse such a person. When I learned that Mermaids received National Lottery funding, I could barely believe it.

I was fairly sure the women of the parenting forum Mumsnet would be as outraged as I was that these dangerous jokers were receiving public money, and few forums were better at organising around this issue, so I told them about it and they managed to get the National Lottery to pause funding.

A British YouTuber called Harry Brewis, who broadcasts videos of himself playing video games under the moniker Hbomberguy, saw we'd had this success and launched a fundraiser for Mermaids in response. He announced he would live-stream himself playing the game *Donkey Kong 64* from beginning to end, encouraging viewers to donate. His sizeable following mobilised and turned the stunt into a viral sensation.

Soon celebrities were joining him live on the stream. The newly elected US congresswoman Alexandria Ocasio-Cortez, just a couple of weeks into office and at the height of the media's adoration, phoned in and offered some anodyne chit-chat about nineties Nintendo consoles in between delivering political talking points about transgender adults, seemingly oblivious that she was on a fundraiser for a charity that endorses medical sex-reassignment for children. Other guests who joined the livecast included the Iraq war whistleblower turned trans activist Chelsea Manning; John Romero, the creator of the classic video game *Doom*; and Donkey Kong himself, or rather, the guy who played the voice of the digital gorilla, Grant Kirkhope.

The broadcast lasted for almost fifty-eight hours and raised over $340,000. A legacy of this stunt was that I was bombarded with Donkey Kong memes, while Harry Brewis was given a Pride Award by the gay magazine *Attitude* for helping to fund the mass-sterilisation of a generation of gay youth.

My voice was hoarse from repeating the same things: they're mutilating gay and autistic children; they're destroying the careers of anyone standing up to them; they're erasing female language. At around this time I was invited to go on *Newsnight*, where I thought we would be taking about all these issues. Like so many others, and like an ass, I was tricked by the statue of George Orwell outside the BBC and the quote on the wall behind it with his words: 'If liberty means anything at all, it means the right to tell people what they do not want to hear.' I cringe to think I might even have shared a photo of that quote in the run-up to the broadcast.

Instead, presenter Sarah Smith and her team made the segment entirely about my involvement in this argument and threw a stream of accusations at me, including that I expressed myself in a toxic way. I asked for examples of this toxicity.

'What about comparing people in the trans debate to speaking out against Nazis?' she said. 'I mean, that's pretty extreme.'

I realised then that it was an ambush. The BBC was continuing the job that *Pink News* had begun. I had been thinking about the Nazi comparison a lot since that headline had appeared, and decided to steer into it. My experience of trans rights activists had widened considerably since they had started targeting me, and I was beginning to realise there were more parallels than I first realised. As Father Ted once said, 'Nazis go around in black telling people what to do', and so did trans activists. They broke up political meetings, used violence and intimidation to achieve their aims and, most strikingly familiar of all, they supported experiments on gay, autistic and gender nonconforming children.

'Well, there's a couple of parallels,' I said. 'One is that at the moment, children are basically being experimented on with puberty blockers...'

I saw a flash of panic in Smith's eyes. She immediately interrupted me.

'Oh come on. You're not seriously trying to say that children going to the doctor and saying that they're worried about their gender is akin to children being experimented on in Nazi concentration camps?'

221

'I'm afraid I am, because Lupron, which is a drug that's supposed to be for end-stage prostate cancer treatment, is being given to young girls. It has never been tested on girls. It has never been tested on women.'

'There's a couple of issues here,' retorted Smith. 'One of them is that these are doctors who are doing this and you don't have any medical training to know about this, but the other is that they are doing it by choice. It is *deeply* offensive to compare this to Nazi concentration camps.'

By now, she had used the word 'Nazi' three times. I tried to get her back to what I thought was the whole point of the discussion, namely the disaster of what was happening to children at the Tavistock gender identity clinic.

'Essentially, if you look at the Tavistock, thirty-five psychologists have quit in three years. Do you think that sounds like a healthy environment for children?'

'I have no idea why people might be leaving,' she replied. 'But I know that children being able to come forward and talk about issues that they feel... It's entirely up to them whether or not they want to do that. Nobody's forcing anybody into anything here.'

For once I was able to interrupt her.

'No, no, I'm sorry. You don't tell children that they were born in the wrong body because they're *children* and they will *believe you*. There are reports from the Tavistock that children as young as four were brought in. These are children, you know, children are still believing in Santa when they're ten. You know, it's ridiculous. It's absurd.'

Smith returned to the attack, more aggressive than ever. 'What evidence do you have that young children are being told they're born into the wrong body? Just because we're having a debate about self identification doesn't mean that young children who still believe in Santa are being told that they have to change their gender. That's ridiculous exaggeration.'

I attempted to introduce some of the facts that were already in the public domain and that I had naively imagined a senior political journalist of Smith's background and stature – she is the daughter of the former Labour leader John Smith – might have at her fingertips.

'Well, one of the other things that Tavistock whistleblowers reported was that homophobic parents were bringing in their gender non-conforming kids and telling them to fix them. You know? There was a dark joke that went around the Tavistock where they said that in a couple of years, there'd be no gay people left. That's why I compare it to eugenics programmes and things like that. It is extremely serious. And all I'm asking for is that people like me and the women that I support are not attacked, that their meetings aren't protested, they aren't abused on Twitter. I've been sued. I've been reported to the police. My wife's address has been published online…'

'Talking about eugenics, and comparing trans activists to Nazis is not going to make this debate less toxic. What you're doing is fanning the flames.'

'Trans activists threaten the feminists I support with rape and death threats. So the idea that there's an equivalence between these two… I am absolutely happy to step out of this conversation completely…'

I tried to mention some prominent and highly articulate feminists who never seemed to be invited on programmes like this, and said I would happily give up my chair for them.

'Quite a lot of women think that they can speak for themselves thank you,' Smith spat back, 'and they don't necessarily need Graham Linehan to come in and talk for us.'

The interview lasted seven minutes in total. Smith brought up the subject of Nazis and went on to mention them six times, while calling my attempt to amplify whistleblower testimony from the Tavistock 'ridiculous exaggeration'.

What I didn't know at the time was that a *Newsnight* journalist, Hannah Barnes, was working on a story that proved absolutely everything I was saying. Sarah Smith and her team had decided to further smear my name for saying the exact same things that one of their journalists would eventually receive widespread praise for uncovering.

To date, I have received no apology from *Newsnight* for my treatment that night.

The intercession of the most famous children's writer in the world was another time in the fight when I thought, 'Well, that's it, it's all over.' So beloved were the *Harry Potter* books that I thought we would see a shift in the conversation. J.K. Rowling's socialist credentials were impeccable, her backstory compelling, and she topped it all by writing a beautiful, compassionate essay on sex and gender that should have left no one in any doubt of the purity of her motives.

But no, not a bit of it. *HMS Rowling* – which had piped on board generations of children, and taught them to read for their pleasure and then for their children's pleasure, and in so doing kept bookshops large and small in business for longer than made any sense in the internet age – was deserted faster than a plague ship. So taboo were the author's perfectly commonplace views on women's rights that the young actors from the *Harry Potter* series instantly betrayed her with a series of statements I would not have made if there were a gun to my head, and I don't even know her. If I were a star who had never shown any ability to act past the pre-pubescent level that got me into the business, I'd be keeping my head down, not signing statements insinuating that my old mentor was a bigot.

Those actors – Daniel Radcliffe, Emma Watson and Rupert Grint – deserve to be remembered as symbols of the most remarkable arrogance, cowardice and ingratitude. Come to think of it, 'Radcliffe, Watson and Grint' sound like the baddies in a story by Roald Dahl, another children's author who fell victim to today's privileged and bored middle-class kids, vandals who went through his books with a chainsaw, displaying the same corrosive, twisted enthusiasm we recognise in religious zealots who find meaning in the destruction of ancient cultural treasures. Suddenly, we're faced with this nannying, nannied generation, itching to delete our childhoods and our achievements from the record because they're jealous of both.

Asking one of these internet witchfinders what Rowling actually said that was so terrible produces nothing. Nothing except countless YouTube videos from countless mediocre men who discovered that a coat of Max Factor covered up the fact that they were talking bollocks. You've never seen a transphobic statement from J.K. Rowling because none exists. So why, then, was a poster with her name on it deemed 'hate speech' and removed from Edinburgh train station? The station's official response said it was because of 'complaints' they'd received, but a freedom of information request revealed they'd not had a single one.

What was so hateful that her name was left out of the BBC's Big Jubilee Read book list in 2022, an absurd, mean-spirited, disgraceful omission? What motivated fan sites to release statements distancing themselves from her? Why did high-profile female comedians sign letters and write disappointed think-pieces condemning her? Even her mildest remarks, unfailingly presented with charm and a touch of humour, could not be endured, and a worldwide denunciation campaign began.

And it is all built on nothing.

There may be no greater example of mass brainwashing than the fact that a great many people under thirty-five believe that J.K. Rowling is a bigot, despite the complete absence of any evidence to that effect. Rowling's real crime was similar to mine – she came to the defence of a 'Terf', in this case Maya Forstater, a woman who was sacked from her job at a think tank because she couldn't ignore the reality of our sexed bodies and still do her job.

Punishment was swift and brutal. *Pink News* were first on the scene. Owned by Benjamin Cohen, whose doctor husband is a former trustee of Mermaids, the title has been successfully sued by two big-name UK lesbians, Joanna Cherry MP and Julie Bindel. Officially an 'LGBTQ+' website, it reports few gay issues and even fewer lesbian ones, existing primarily to pump out trans propaganda. When Rowling tweeted her support for Maya, Cohen and his goons wrote forty-two hit pieces about her in a single week. That's six a day for seven days!

In this atmosphere of intense hostility, the menacing hashtag *#RIPJKRowling* became a trending topic on Twitter. The author then wrote the essay clarifying her views. It was sober and carefully worded. She described 'a climate of fear' that served 'nobody – least of all trans youth – well'. She also wrote at length about her own personal history of domestic abuse and sexual assault. Because of this, she said, she had 'solidarity with the huge numbers of women who have histories like mine, who've been slurred as bigots for having concerns around single-sex spaces'.

Trans activists responded by slurring her as a bigot again. This was immediately parroted by much of the media and what passes for the liberal intelligentsia.

At this point, I began working on a letter to send to all my showbiz friends. In it, I echoed Rowling's observation that 'we're living through the most misogynistic period I've experienced' and I added: 'When the Berlin Wall fell in 1989, it turned out that the vast majority didn't agree with the Stasi – it was only as a result of pluralistic ignorance that everyone thought everyone else agreed with it. A similar scenario is at play here, where the vast majority of people agree with J.K. Rowling but believe that it is dangerous to say so. Yet, as the German theologian Dietrich Bonhoeffer pointed out before the Nazis strung him up, "Not to speak is to speak. Not to act is to act."'

I asked them to consider signing the following letter, which I had drafted with my friend Stella O'Malley:

We are a group of writers, actors, directors, musicians, producers, comedians and artists who wish to speak in support of J.K. Rowling. She has been subjected to an onslaught of abuse that highlights an insidious authoritarian and misogynistic trend in social media. Rowling has consistently shown herself to be an honourable and compassionate person and the appalling hashtag *#RIPJKRowling* is just the latest example of hate speech directed against her and other women that Twitter and other platforms enable and implicitly endorse.

We are signing this letter in the hope that if more people stand up against the targeting of women online, we might at least make it less acceptable to engage in it or profit from it.

We wish J.K. Rowling well and stand in solidarity with her.

Stella and I had written the letter out of sheer frustration at seeing no one stand up for Rowling. We felt there were plenty out there who would; they just didn't have any means of doing so. It turned out to be an easy sell to everyone except the people in my address book. We used Twitter to track down some of the bigger names. John Cleese had to be persuaded that the story of Laurel Hubbard, the mediocre male weightlifter from New Zealand who 'transitioned' to become an Olympian in the woman's category, was actually true. 'But this is what the Pythons were saying!' he spluttered. Many others didn't need this context. Ian McEwan instantly agreed to sign, as did Tom Stoppard, Andrew Davies, Frances Welch, Lionel Shriver, Ben Miller, Frances Barber, Anthony Horowitz and Matthew d'Ancona.

By contrast, many of my old buddies – the gunslingers, the iconoclasts – were nowhere to be seen. One former colleague refused and didn't even bother to explain why.

'I'm not signing that letter,' was all he said.

'Why not?'

'I'm not signing that letter.'

I couldn't believe it. I assumed my performer friends were all aware that once you take the stage, you have a certain responsibility. People look up to you, they like you and trust you, and yet, at a time when the right side of history was glaringly apparent, these same performers allowed writers like J.K. Rowling and friends like me to be set upon by the mob. Almost all of them were silent, and some even took part in the assault.

After Club Z, Stewart Lee went on to make a comfortable living attacking more successful comedians while pretending to be in character. Normally I'd be more polite about a fellow comedy practitioner but Lee is someone who decided to get a few public digs in without ever phoning me to explain where he thought I was getting things wrong. One thing I've discovered about this fight: the people who dismiss and deride you never have the courage to say why. As my good friend Helen Staniland says, 'Trans activists cannot reveal their aims for fear of incriminating themselves.' The same is true of their clueless, careerist, celebrity enablers.

In stark contrast to Lee, there's Griff Rhys Jones. As soon as I asked him, Griff signed the letter – a letter defending not only Rowling, but all feminists, from rape and death threats. It didn't so much as occur to him why you would not sign such a letter.

Another time I thought it was all over was when Martina Navratilova, one of the greatest tennis players of all time, started publicly addressing the problem of male cheats in women's sports. I thought, well, Martina is golden; she's a lesbian icon, she even had a trans coach, so they had nothing on her.

I reckoned without figures such as Anthony Watson, a gay British businessman who is on the board of the US LGBT group GLAAD, who told Martina on Twitter that she should be ashamed of herself for making those same points. Watson, for reasons best known to himself, lobbies for this, the most homophobic movement in history, which tells children who would otherwise likely grow up to be lesbian or gay that they're born in the wrong body and need lifelong medicalisation. He's scarcely a public person, whereas it's hard to think of a more iconic gay figure than Navratilova. That was a big shock to me: that such an inconsequential character could talk to a lesbian hero like that.

One day, I received an email casually telling me that what's generally regarded as one of the best episodes of *The IT Crowd*, 'The Speech', was going to be removed from all future broadcasts of the show on Channel 4. The episode featured what had become a classic moment among fans – a scene in which Moss and Roy successfully convince Jen that they own the internet, which is contained in a small black box with a light on it. But there was also that subplot of Matt Berry falling in love with a transwoman, which of course is what got it banned.

The email from Channel 4 seemed to assume I was fully on board with Stonewall's deceitful messaging. As well as lobbying for changes to existing laws, Stonewall positions itself as a knowledgeable consultant, helping corporations and institutions navigate the minefield of Diversity & Inclusion. This is a minefield created by Stonewall itself, along with its like-minded clutch of fellow charities, each promoting their own distorted interpretation of the law, rather than, you know, the actual law.

The letter said: 'It is fair to say that transphobia has grown in public awareness since this episode was made in 2008, attacks on trans men and women are rising and their place in society is vulnerable and some way from being legitimised...'

None of this is true. Statistics actually show that men who present as women are one of the safest demographics in the UK. Unbeknown to me, however, Channel 4 had a new boss, Alex Mahon, who I later discovered had done the equivalent of raising a flag to stupidity and misogyny by putting her pronouns in her Twitter bio, which effectively meant that Stonewall Law was now in place.

Still unaware of this, I replied that, in my view, the reasons for banning the episode were religious/ideological in nature, adding: 'If you start bowing to the demands of extremists, you will never stop. This is a bigger fight than you realise and you don't have to enter it in this way.'

I assumed that since I had written three successful, beloved and respected sitcoms for Channel 4, all of which were hugely profitable for them, they might give some consideration to my opinion. They're probably still making millions from shows for which I stopped receiving royalties within the third or fourth repeat, but they ignored the points I made, offering only a publicist to help minimise the damage on my reputation they themselves had decided to inflict.

19

THE BEST MATADOR IN ALL MADRID

MY DAD DIED AS HE LIVED; getting a cup of tea for my mum. One night, he walked into the kitchen and didn't walk out. Covid put paid to any thoughts of a wake, but when we arrived at the church, the drive outside was circled by dozens of people who loved him. My dad collected friends like I lose them. We stuck around for a while outside, unsure of what to do. It was, after all, the first time our dad had died. Finally, we realised we had to go in.

Many in Ireland are under the impression that I'm the son of the Irish actress Rosaleen Linehan, but Dad was the only actor in our family. Somewhere I have a Lantern Theatre playbill for a musical comedy called *Sweethearts* with the credit 'Colonel Slingsby: Vincent Linehan'. It seemed to be some sort of Gilbert and Sullivan-style romp. My mum said she and a friend were the only ones in the audience the night they went and she saw my dad peeking out at her through the stage curtain. I wondered if he was disappointed by the small turnout but she replied that no, he was just delighted to see them.

Dad would give up the theatre because he had a young family and he felt it was unfair to be working whenever he wasn't rehearsing or performing at the Lantern. He spent the rest of his career working for a shipping company, ending up as general manager. But that night, when only my mum, her friend and some stagehands were there to see it, he threw himself into the part and delivered the speech he would deploy at gatherings of family and friends until the end of his life:

> You may have noticed I'm reserved and rather shy,
> and by nature not the kind of man to boast.
> I go hither I go thither,
> but come back with a bigger
> wad upon me than when I went,
> I'm amazing, quite amazing,
> Clearly an incomparable man,
> Very gallant, lots of talent,
> When I say that I can do a thing I can.
> When I was in Spain, I did as I was bid.
> Went to see a bullfight like all Spaniards did,
> Thought if only I had a cloak, I'd be the best matador in all
>   Madrid.
> A matador, then a toreador, they replied 'Si si señor!'
> There never was a meaner bull to enter the arena.
> He saw me and knew he'd met his Waterloo.
> So a hoof he tendered, as a sign that he'd surrendered.
> I just don't know how I do it but I do.

My dad believed in chivalry. That's what he meant when he told me not to be like James Bond. 'Always respect women. Always.' Dad's chivalry was in his bones and he never had to explain it any further, whereas I have had to come up with supporting

Mum and Dad

arguments because I've been challenged by feminists on it. Like most things, chivalry as a code has sexist roots. But at least it's a code. I think men need a code. Call it something else if you like, but I see chivalry as just a basic level of respect for every woman that every man should hold. Our greater physical strength provides enough reason on its own, but if merely belonging to a group signs someone up to enduring intense pain for a week every month, then I think it's fair enough to have a tradition where we open doors for them.

I tried to follow Dad's warning regarding James Bond, but 'always' is a long time. There were occasions where I was thoughtless and cruel. If it's any consolation to those I hurt, I carry those moments around with me, and they occasionally make me catch my breath with the force of the self-loathing. The anti-anxiety medication made those moments go away too, but I know they're still waiting for me on the other side, should I ever summon the courage to go cold turkey.

I understand the wider anger many women feel towards men. Men used to be risking their lives, running around after mammoths, and now even those of us who talk of chivalry sit on our arses in front of our game consoles, trying to recapture some of the thrill of the hunt. But women have much the same amount of work that they've always had. Dad felt that disparity keenly, I think – more than I did during my marriage, to my shame. On weekends, after working all week at a job for which he gave up his dream of being an actor, he would make my mum breakfast in bed. On his birthday, at Christmas, he never wanted a present. 'Sure, what do I need? I have everything,' he'd say, hugging her at the cooker as she swatted him away.

When you get to a certain age, you become one of two types. You are either driven to the hospital, or driving others to the hospital. My dad was in the latter group. When he wasn't ferrying the poorly, he was bowing his head in church. He went every day, which used to break my heart because his lower back gave him constant pain, and Catholic churches don't mollycoddle their flock with comfortable seating. Aside from my mum, golf was the thing that brought him joy, but his swing of many parts made demands on his spine that toted up to a steep cost in the form of sleepless agony unless he spent the day sitting bolt upright in a kitchen chair.

A bit of a holy Joe. In the fifties. He was one of Christ's good soldiers, if anyone could be described as such. He went and he worshipped, but he didn't leave it at the church. He carried it with him everywhere he went and he walked in a certain way because of that. He never slouched into a room the way I do. He was upright, because he was proud. Not just of his faith, but of his luck. He married the most beautiful woman in Dublin. All these things put him on high definition. That's what carried him into the kitchen, over to the teapot, every time until the last.

You'll often hear it said that Ireland has self-ID and there haven't been any problems. This is only true if you don't see the female prisoners in Limerick jail as fully human.

'Barbie Kardashian' is a deeply disturbed young man who, despite having violently assaulted and threatened to kill multiple women, currently resides in Limerick women's prison. His childhood was a horror story: after witnessing his father physically, emotionally and sexually abuse his mother, he became conditioned to join in the abuse. By the age of ten he was ordered to be placed in foster care. In the years that followed, he had to be relocated to a series of care homes due to escalating acts of carefully planned, premeditated, violent physical and sexual aggression against female staff, culminating in an attempt to kill a social worker. During the attack he ripped off clumps of her scalp and tore her eyelids while attempting to gouge out her eyes. He told the Gardaí that the woman's screams were 'music to my ears'.

As his eighteenth birthday approached, Irish authorities found themselves in a race against time to prevent him becoming legally free to leave state care, despite his telling a social worker that his 'continuing wish to murder and to rape' women was 'a source of pleasure' to him. On the day he was released, the Gardaí issued a nationwide alert about a homicidal teenager on the loose. Before long, the police arrested him on charges of threatening to kill his mother. He had threatened to go to her house and put a 'knife into her body and into her genitalia [and] prolong my mum's suffering for as long as possible'. She had to relocate to an undisclosed location and go into hiding.

By the time of her son's arrest he had legally declared himself a woman, because in Ireland, as in Norway and Denmark, becoming a woman is as simple as filling out a form. This allowed him to be remanded to a women's prison following his arrest. Having been found guilty of threatening to rape, torture and murder his mother, he was sentenced to five and a half years in prison. As I write this, he continues to serve that sentence in a women's prison.

Those women in Limerick Prison are at the very margins of society. They will never bump into fashionable female comics at Soho House, or fashionable female politicians in Westminster, Dáil Éireann and Holyrood, where gender-neutral toilets are nothing more than a cocaine-dusted lark, the very embodiment of their luxury beliefs. Marginalised, vulnerable women – victims of poverty, of rape, or war, or all of the above – are invisible to these children of privilege as they tell us breathlessly about their mate Shon who wears eyeliner and thinks he's a new kind of human.

Unfortunately, these children are the ones who will tell you that self-ID carries no danger for women, and they're the ones with the massive online reach. Instagram, Twitter, *The Graham Norton Show*, *The Guardian*… In contrast, if the women of Limerick Prison have an issue with the psychotically violent misogynist placed among them, they can only share their concerns with the uniformed men who escorted him in.

If American movies have taught me anything, it's that we Irish don't shy away from a fight, unless you count the massive world war against Nazism which, for reasons that seemed valid at the time, our government thought it would be wiser to sit out. For my part, I flew into battle full of beans but, to my astonishment, no one turned up to lend a hand. All the connections I'd made throughout a life in showbusiness suddenly meant nothing. I begged friends to step in and say something. Not about me, necessarily, but about women and children. About how they had a right to single-sex spaces, about how children shouldn't be undergoing experimental treatments with no evidence base, about the crime against humanity that is telling gay and autistic young women that if they only removed their breasts then they would be happy. Most of them stayed silent.

My Twitter account began to act strangely just after lockdown began. From the women who had been banned before me – in numbers I gave up trying to track because Twitter was banning virtually every woman who said 'if you have a uterus, you must be female' and 'only women get pregnant' – I learned that this meant I probably didn't have long left on the platform. And so it was.

The reasons for my final expulsion from Twitter, when it came, were left vague. I was 'misusing the platform' in some way that was never explained. That meant journalists could sniff around the non-scene of the non-crime and pronounce me Probably Guilty of Something. Being kicked off was a massive blow, which may be hard to understand if you've never used the site. But consider this: at the peak, I'd had nearly 900,000 followers. Speaking out about gender ideology had already cost me about a third of that following. Now, at a stroke, I'd lost all my remaining reach. I no longer had any means of answering back when trans activists spread rumours about me, and my ban helped convince a wider audience, on Twitter and far beyond, that I'd done something wrong.

With my marriage now over – I finally left the family home just before the start of the first Covid lockdown – this was a very lonely and frightening time. I lost my last remaining connections to my old life when a number of journalists who I thought were on my side decided to unite in something of a prison stabbing. I found out later that one of them was merely playing the role of a gender-critical feminist in the UK while telling her American readers a completely different story; another was too cowardly to enter the fight yet regularly attacked those of us who *were* doing something. Meanwhile, I had agreed to do an interview on a new DVD of the original film of *The Ladykillers*, because of my stage adaptation, but a few days after I was chucked off Twitter this was cancelled, adding to the sense that I was losing everything. I got a nice little lecture from someone at Studio Canal too: 'It's a very sensitive time and one which sees our industry working to be better and most certainly inclusive.' Not sensitive or inclusive to women or their supporters, as always.

Unlike my dad, I don't tend friendships. I lost touch with Geoffrey Perkins because I'm an idiot. Although I was annoyed with a few decisions he made, and he was surely frustrated that I didn't do *Hippies* or a second series of *Big Train*, whenever we met it was always warm between us. But I didn't keep in touch. I have that thing where I just assume people won't want to hear from me. My wife was always great at assembling birthday parties where she ensured I'd see the people I love, even if only on a yearly basis, and I'm sure I eventually would have bumped into him at one eventually, but Geoffrey died out of nowhere, just walking down the street – something I still find hard to believe. I mention him because it was only at his and my father's funeral that I observed the phenomenon of mourners applauding the departed. Geoffrey's friends did it before they walked away from the grave. In my father's case, the people who gathered at the circular drive outside the church, kept out there by Covid fears, started clapping as our car drove away from the church after the service.

When we got back to the small house out of which I once thought I'd be able to move my mother, she told us another of her insane stories. At one point, apparently, she considered sprouting a green thumb by trying to grow carrots at home. But they turned out very small. So she went to the library, because the people who made Google were still toddlers, and she asked the woman behind the counter, 'Do you have any books on gardening?' And the woman said, 'Oh yes, what kind of gardening?' And my mum said 'Oh, you know, I'm trying to grow carrots. I grew some already, but they were so small, they'd only be fit for dwarves.'

And she said that they both looked to their right, and 'wasn't there a dwarf standing there?'

Sometimes the only thing about these stories is you do have to ask her to repeat the punchlines because they're so odd.

'There was a what? What?'

'There was a dwarf, a small man. Standing on my side of the counter. A dwarf though, not just a small man. An actual dwarf. Standing right beside us. In the library. I just hadn't noticed him. And I was talking about carrots fit for dwarves. What are the chances of that? I never in my life saw a dwarf in Castleknock.'

We shared memories of Dad. My dad, who would switch off any film in which a baby cried as he knew the child's distress had somehow been elicited for the sake of the cameras; who used to chase us when he was angry but never seemed to catch us; who poked his head out of a theatre curtain and saw the only audience that ever meant anything to him – my mum, a woman he loved so much she was treated within our home as a sort of celebrity. I told Mum how Ireland's referendum on same-sex marriage had provided one of my final happy memories of him, of how the event proved that we had reached a point in our relationship where one of us could be persuaded by the other. Together, we overcame any differences of opinion that we had in the past, and voted to remove, we thought, the last few remaining chains of ignorance and bigotry still wrapped around our suddenly secular island.

But I did not know that the Bill was a form of cover. Because around the same time, self-ID was slipped into Irish law, quietly, silently, without debate, without Irish women ever being able to discuss what it meant for their privacy, their safety and their dignity, without any of us ever knowing that the deeply disturbed, violently misogynistic Barbie Kardashian now had access to the women he had promised to harm. Maybe Ireland hadn't changed as much as we thought. The happiness of gay people was the subject of discussion and debate and a final understanding between us. But the happiness of yet another sacred class was a foregone conclusion.

20

THE ASSASSINATION OF
'FATHER TED THE MUSICAL'

To WRITE THIS BOOK, I use the US-made software Grammarly, which tells me I've made a mistake whenever I type words like 'colour' and 'paediatrician'. There's a paid version which I imagine allows you to switch to UK English. I have a feeling that most people will stay on the free model and the American spelling of most words will become standard. In the same way, the belief system of a corrupted American academia gradually permeated our own outlook, with little awareness of how the change came about. The same software that insists I've got 'colour' wrong also tells me that the word 'detransitioner' – which describes the growing number of people who have taken physical steps to become 'trans' and then changed their mind – does not exist. If you ask ChatGPT about anything related to women's rights, you get an impromptu lecture on trans rights. With this finessing from Silicon Valley tech firms, society soon found itself nodding along to a 'civil rights movement' that promoted body disassociation, along with its surgical remedies, while empowering the always-online class of male who wrote the code for the same platforms.

My Beatles theory sadly failed during testing. I now have a new theory, and the results are already in.

We now know it is possible for a group such as trans rights activists to poison the internet's nervous system, to use it to overwhelm society with so much misinformation that reality itself warps and woofs. The most extreme voices are finding it too easy to steer others who have less certainty about their opinions, who have a desire to be told what the right thing to do is so they can go and do it. Not bad people. Busy people, who are nevertheless well-meaning. But when we trust to the cat's cradle of gossamer-thin connections we've made online, fail to check primary sources and even find that our primary sources are suddenly unreliable, then we leave ourselves open to having our society hacked by a loose conspiracy of online weirdos who know exactly what buttons to press to make life's vending machine give them what they want.

And if you don't believe such a thing is possible, ask yourself why so many otherwise sane human beings believe that a bunch of lesbians and feminists turned into Nazis overnight. And what happens when a better-informed minority decides to go against the suddenly sizzlingly fashionable takes? Like 'transwomen are women', a take of such volcanic heat that it created a looking-glass world where, to return to an example I've mentioned before, the winner of two women's weightlifting gold medals at the Pacific Games in 2019 was a man named Laurel Hubbard, leaving two indigenous women half his age to be content with silver and bronze.

Turning on a comments section under our lives was a surveillance system we installed ourselves, ensuring we could never get too far out of line, never push too hard against what was suddenly the 'majority' opinion. I pushed back and I lost everything. But I knew from day one that it was too important a fight to turn down. I sleep like a baby, and not only because of the anti-anxiety meds. I was protecting my family, I was standing up for women and children, people would surely come around eventually. Best of all, I had insurance in the form of an idea. Something so big, I didn't think there was a hope in hell they could take it away from me.

The rise of Trump had put a thought in my head. America's new Prez had come from nowhere and ended up, *Curb Your Enthusiasm*-style, in hilarious predicaments with the highest of stakes. Jeremy Corbyn, Labour's perennial backbench pain in the arse, had also been goosed into late-career activation and wound up on a similar trajectory. One example of this *Being There* phenomenon of unsuitable people being promoted way outside their comfort zone was wild enough, but two? It seemed to me that it was becoming A Thing. It started me thinking... If people with no experience, and entirely the wrong temperament for a job, could rise to such positions of power, why not Father Ted Crilly?

Writing movies stopped appealing to me because I was always more comfortable in the playpen provided by a half-hour sitcom. The stakes in my stories were never too high, which meant that thirty minutes, or the Channel 4 twenty-four, suited me perfectly. But if Ted became a cardinal, he'd be in the running to become pope, and then the stakes would begin to get very high indeed. A film with different actors playing our characters wouldn't work; it would be too literal, and somehow disrespectful to the TV cast. Besides, if you were bringing back these beloved characters, you had to begin thinking about how you start to dig deeper into them, they would need depth, big moments of their own...

I realised I had a musical.

Amateur dramatic groups are always writing to ask for permission to stage episodes of *Father Ted*. I don't always turn them down, but I've always felt slightly uncomfortable with such requests, because those episodes were designed for the screen, not the theatre. I wanted to give these groups something written for the stage, something that each of them could interpret how they wished. Something joyously theatrical with singable songs and a great story. I used Jack Viertel's book *The Secret Life of the American Musical* to structure it, thinking of the as-yet-unwritten songs as pearls on a thread that could help us find our way through the plot. I knew the ending already – I wouldn't have started without it – and Arthur and I wrote the 'book' (the fancy-pants word used for scripts in musicals) using the comforting and familiar rhythms of our characters. After a painfully protracted contract negotiation, songs from Neil Hannon began to arrive, all up to Neil's usual standard: witty and sharp, with a touch of melancholy even in the catchiest or funniest of numbers. Paul Woodfull, our old mate from the Joshua Trio, also came on board to write additional music and lyrics. Surrounded by some of my oldest and dearest friends, I felt safe.

We found our Parochial House gang again, a process made easier by the standard set by the TV cast, their performances acting as a base camp rather than a destination, and led by a brilliant, roguish Ted played by Risteárd Cooper of RTÉ's satire *Après Match*. We put it on its feet twice, first a read-through and then later a second one with properly rehearsed if unambitious dance routines for the songs. It rocketed along, despite the odd and fashionable decision to have black characters doing the parts of well-known Irish characters, something that embarrassed the actors as much as it did us.

If you haven't heard a black Londoner trying to do the 'I hear you're a racist now, Father' character in a West of Ireland accent, be grateful. Also it was somewhat insulting, as we had structured the show so that there would be a natural diversity to it. Once, when I met Sonia Friedman, she told me she was arguing with Tom Stoppard about a similar attempt to place black Jewish cast members in Vienna for his play *Leopoldstadt*. 'He's having them, whether he likes it or not,' she said. I'd like to see if theatre producers would enforce Jewish actors on a play about Harlem.

But aside from these tiny grains of grit, working on the *Ted* musical was a culmination and distillation of every lesson I learned along my career, how to collaborate, how to structure, when to follow your nose, how to give ideas a fair shake. In the rehearsal room, I was helping to direct it, showing future collaborators how the show should feel. The script could probably have used another pass but then again, what couldn't? We were well on our way.

I thought the *Ted* musical might be my pension – perhaps even make my fortune if I could get it right. The movies weren't a tight fit and sitcoms had suddenly became an uncertain source to rely on for my family's security. Coming up with an idea for the *Ted* musical was like striking gold that I had buried myself. I knew it would be funny, I knew the songs would be great, I knew it would be a huge hit. What I didn't know was how resolute the forces against me actually were, and how quiet my colleagues would be in the face of their onslaught.

The waters started getting choppy when I was first given what I like to call 'the talk' by Sonia. The talk is always the same and it's basically 'stop talking', which always sounds reasonable until you remember that children are being hurt, and women are being harassed, threatened with violence and having their livelihoods attacked. I didn't understand how anyone could be silent in the face of all this. It was, in fact, a moral and ethical imperative for *everyone* to speak up about it. The meeting proceeded amicably enough under the gaze of Sonia's many Olivier awards until she said the only words absolutely guaranteed to make a cartoon hat pop off my head and steam come out of my ears.

'You're on the wrong side of history,' she said.

The red mist descended and I suddenly found myself in a raging argument with this powerful woman who held my musical in her hands. Hearing one of these copy-and-pasted, thought-terminating clichés from the mouth of a colleague was more than I could bear. The phrase was at that point heavily deployed to suggest that those of us standing up for women and gender-non-conforming children were going to be even more reviled than we were at that moment

– which was plenty reviled, to the point where family and friends were turning their backs on us. Personally I don't want to live in a world where little boys playing with dolls and little girls who don't like wearing pink are subjected to lifelong medical intervention because lunatics think these kids are in the wrong body. If that's the right side of history, then history can go fuck itself.

The meeting ended with both of us trying not to catch the other's eye in case it kicked off again.

When J.K. Rowling, a close friend of Sonia's, expressed her complete support in her moving and compassionate letter for the feminists fighting this war on women and children, Friedman's tone completely changed. We had a second meeting where she was upbeat. I presumed, because I still stupidly always thought the best of people, that she would now start fighting back against the woke activists in her company. I thought Rowling's move had given Sonia permission to examine the issue properly, to see the homophobia, the misogyny and the danger to children, to know that a brave stance from someone of her stature could turn the tide not just for me, but for her friend Joanne. Once again, I thought the musical was safe.

But I realise now I should have used that moment to insist on an apology from Sonia. It turned out that neither she nor Hat Trick had been moved by J.K. Rowling's essay at all.

I thought at least that Jimmy Mulville of Hat Trick was on my side. Having been generous to me while my career stalled, and as the original producer of *Father Ted*, the company had a big stake in this new venture, but now the Hat Trick people began to go the other way. A familiar trajectory. They are all for your freedom of speech as long as you're not being heard. When the Ted musical started becoming more of a reality, the producers became more insistent I stop talking. But again, erasing an entire sex class, endangering children, destroying the livelihoods of those objecting... I didn't see how I could ignore these issues, and I began to get increasingly angry that I was being asked to do so.

Not long after the disastrous clash with Sonia, I had another meeting, this time with Arthur and Jimmy, around the supposed problem of my defending women and girls, in which, as always, no one could locate the flaw in my analysis because no one could be bothered to state what it was. I had explained over and over again: 'Children are being hurt. Women are being harassed and hounded, losing their livelihoods. Women are losing their sports, their language, their privacy.' An endless list of evidence, backing up everything I was saying. Finally, I fell on a subject that I thought could not be denied, the violent, terroristic nature of trans rights activism, which both Arthur and Jimmy had seen destroy my life; for which, in fact, they both had ringside seats. Of course, they could hardly deny that.

But then Jimmy said something that made my stomach sink.

Casually, off-handedly: 'Well, there's bad behaviour on both sides.'

I should have known right there that the musical was doomed.

Over the previous five years, I'd been documenting the terroristic nature of trans rights activism. My friend JL and I have even got a page on my website entirely dedicated to recording such incidents, because supposedly progressive newspapers certainly don't record them. For example, if you look at *The Guardian*'s output in those five years, you won't read about the trans rights activists who nailed a dead rat to the door of Vancouver Rape Relief, or the trans rights activists in Paris who defaced a memorial to infants killed by shaken baby syndrome because they deemed its creators to be 'Terfs', or the trans rights activists surrounding the meetings of feminists, bashing the windows and doors to intimidate and frighten anyone within. But we've got it, we've got all of it, or certainly most of it, on our website.

There is no equivalence between these incidents and the activism that has arisen to resist them. Women have never surrounded a meeting of trans-identified people, they have never sent violent death and rape threats to trans-identified people. Women write essays and make arguments. Women gather to speak to other women. Women place stickers reading 'ADULT HUMAN FEMALE' on lampposts; they don't nail dead rats to doors, or post death and rape threats to the authors of children's books.

I suspect I know the kind of person who fed Jimmy this line, which I had heard a million times before, repeated ad infinitum by the connected children acting as the propaganda arm of trans activism. It would have been someone who happily announces their pronouns at meetings, giddy on the power afforded them by this simple religious observance, one which allows mediocre people to exercise outsize power in a workplace; someone who can threaten their boss with the same thing meted out to me, or to the lesbian barrister Allison Bailey, whose colleagues at Garden Court Chambers turned into Stasi operatives, monitoring her phone calls and reducing her case work to almost nothing.

'Both sides' is a poisonous smear. No one on my side of the argument insists that people should be shunned by polite society, be banned from speaking and have their livelihood destroyed. No one on our side wears T-shirts with slogans like 'Kill all Terfs', 'Punch Terfs' and 'Die Terf Scum'. Instead, women wear comedy dinosaur costumes (a poke at senior politician David Lammy, who said feminists were like dinosaurs hoarding their rights), wield Suffragette banners and read poetry. We disagree with trans rights activists. That's it. We disagree that we all have some mysterious essence called a 'gender', something that can be 'born into the wrong body'. I disagree, just as I disagree that terminating a pregnancy is a sin, or that the really quite gross wafers I consumed throughout my childhood were the body of Christ.

When Rowling tweeted for children, asking them to draw scenes from her online fairytale *The Ickabog*, trans activists posted pornography under her messages. On our side, writers like the lesbian journalist Jo Bartosch catalogue the daily developments in this battle for a wide variety of publications; on their side, the trans activist journalist for the *Independent*, Gemma Stone, has tweeted

With one of David Lammy's 'rights-hoarding dinosaurs' at a picket of *The Lancet*. The medical journal had beclowned itself by emblazoning its front page with the words 'bodies with vaginas', to avoid saying 'women'

multiple times about his desire to spray his urine on women's toilet seats. To my ears, 'bad behaviour on both sides' meant Jimmy was reading from a script, coached by the activist or activists who had his ear.

Similarly, later, when I phoned Neil Hannon to garner support, he said, 'Some of the things you've done have been questionable.'

'Give me an example.' I replied. 'Give me one example.'

Long pause.

'All right, well maybe not.'

Even those close to me thought I had done something wrong; they're just never sure what, and the truth of it – that I'm the victim of village gossip on a global scale – is simply too much for them to take on. I'm not a billionaire, I'm not even a millionaire. I wasn't only being punished for my beliefs, I was being punished for not having enough money to safely hold them.

I wrote a letter to Jimmy, Sonia, Arthur, Neil and Paul. I told them that far from being on the wrong side of history, I had been proved right again and again. I reiterated that gender ideology was destroying lives and that 'both sides' were not to blame for the toxicity of the debate. Finally, I wrote:

> My daughter is not a 'cervix-haver'. She is a woman and she is my daughter. Don't anyone dare use *Ted* as leverage to make me abandon my daughter, or I will simply take it elsewhere. I'm sorry to have to put it in such strong terms but these people are monsters and everyone needs to start standing up to them. I can't force you to be brave but I can ask you to stop adding to the pressure that is currently on me. I will not abandon my daughter.

The final scene in the terrible downwards-spiralling drama that was the end of the musical was a meeting with Jimmy in the Hat Trick offices. He made me travel from Norwich to London, so, like a sap, I presumed it would be good news, a plan on how we were to move forward while I carried on raising my voice on a crucially important issue. But no, there were dirty looks from Hat Trick employees I had known and worked with for years and when we finally sat across from each other – Jimmy and a lawyer from Hat Trick on one side, and my agent and I on the other – Jimmy told me I was to remove my name from *Father Ted the Musical* or he would not make the show.

The show I had tended for the best part of half a decade, rewriting, refining, every draft leaping ahead in quality and giving us a new set piece, a new character, a new song, every time. It was a bonsai tree, delicate and almost perfect. It just needed a snip here and there. It was the culmination of almost everything I had learned over thirty years of working in comedy. And now, just as Rosie Kay lost the dance company that bore her name, I was losing my creation.

I'd never experienced anything like the coldness and contempt with which I was treated at that meeting. Once again, I asked what I was being accused of. Jimmy rolled his eyes, as if it was self-evident. It wasn't evident at all. In six years, none of the people who shot me nasty looks, or gave the press a juicy quote about me, or refused to share a stage with me, has ever been able to tell me where my analysis is wrong. Most of them can't even summarise my position. No-one has ever been able to tell me why I shouldn't be defending my daughter.

Once again, at this final meeting, desperately, I tried to explain what was happening to women's rights, and to the young girls mutilating themselves because of—

'I DON'T CARE!' Jimmy shouted.

I was so astonished, I couldn't speak. I scraped the chair back and left the office without hearing the offer with which they were about to insult me. Head spinning, I found a nearby hotel to land in a chair and ordered a drink. Soon my agent, who I had, in my anger, disgracefully left behind at the meeting, arrived to tell me that for the right of declaring me an unperson, Hat Trick were suggesting an up-front payment of £200,000 as an advance on my royalties – on the presumption, I'm guessing, that I was too broke to refuse. I said I was prepared to minimise my involvement, just coming along to the odd rehearsal to see how it was going.

No, I was told; they wanted a 'clean break'.

Initially, I agreed to go along with it, because they were right about one thing at least. I was broke and I needed the money. I started drafting a statement with Jimmy. If I was going to be framed out of the picture by whatever cult member was dripping poison in Jimmy's ear, I wouldn't do it pretending I'd done anything wrong.

Because I hadn't done anything wrong. I wanted something in the statement that made that clear. That way, no matter how deranged my colleagues were making me feel, I would have something in writing that at least acknowledged in some homeopathically minute way that I was a victim of harassment.

And the money… Two hundred grand would have solved a lot of problems. It still would.

But then, at some point during this process, I happened upon an interview with the mother of one of 'Lia' Thomas' competitors. Lia, you'll remember, is the trans-identified swimmer who had decided not only that he was a woman, not only that he would begin stealing women's medals and prize money in the female category, but that he would do it while also breaking women's boundaries in their changing rooms as well. The mother had to remain anonymous because if anyone knew who she or her child was, trans activists would attempt to destroy their lives.

Here's part of what she said, between gulps of air as she tried not to sob, about her daughter's experience:

> She worked through how to shake hands at the end of the race and how to make sure that she wouldn't cry, something I'm apparently not doing… She also worked through how many towels to take in her bag into the locker room in case she needed to cover herself completely as she changed. All the girls knew Lia was still physically intact and had been using the locker rooms… I asked my daughter what she would do if Lia was changing in there. And she said resignedly, I'm not sure I'd have a choice. I still can't believe I had to tell my adult-age daughter that you always have a choice about whether you undress in front of a man. What messages have these girls been receiving? How many of the other girls were feeling this? My heart was ripped apart.

Maybe it's because she was talking about her daughter. But reading that testimony closed the door forever on me making any kind of deal with Hat Trick.

If you're in this debate on the gender critical side, you're called a bigot so regularly that even when you've proved to your own satisfaction over a thousand times that your positions are sound, a certain doubt can linger. 'Maybe I have this wrong,' you think. 'Maybe my colleagues all know something I don't about the medical scandal, about the safeguarding scandal, about the sports scandal.' But then someone like that swimmer's mother comes along. A mother in tears because, like me, she had discovered that the well-being of our female children was no longer a priority for society.

I rejected the deal. I was prepared to betray myself for £200,000, but I couldn't abandon my daughter.

21
GREEN SHOOTS

From the moment I started standing up for women's rights, a series of harassment campaigns began, a steady assault on my sanity that I have withstood for almost six years:

- My family's home address is released online.
- The police come to my door no fewer than three times on behalf of the man who released my home address and his associates.
- A children's TV show that Helen and I created together is targeted by Irish activists at the Dingle animation festival. A statement by the producers has to be released distancing me from the show.
- An Irish comedian who we had in our home, and who didn't have the courage to confront me himself, takes his feelings out on Helen when she calls him to offer help on

a script.

- When our marriage collapses under the strain, I move out. One day, I come home to a note in the internal, shared postbox of my building. 'TRANS RIGHTS ARE HUMAN RIGHTS. FUCK YOU, GLINNER,' and realise that an activist knows my new home address.
- Stephanie Hayden sues me twice. The first case results in a drop-hands agreement. The second is thrown out of court.
- At the time of writing, I'm being sued by David Paisley.
- Someone ejaculates on a photo of me, takes a picture of it and posts it on Twitter.
- Someone takes a photo of me sitting outside a café, posts it on Christmas Day and tells people I'm there at Christmas because I've lost my family.
- Trans activists tweet about dancing and pissing on my grave, adding that my ex-wife and children will piss on my grave too.
- A medical professional mocks up a fake prescription under my name and posts it online to suggest I have gone insane.
- A private detective is sent to my ex-wife's home. No one should know her address.
- Someone writes a fake obituary of me. It reads, 'Graham Lineham [sic] Dead at 57: Disgraced TV writer spent the last several years of his life unemployed, divorced, and as a prolific Twitter troll. The once-beloved television writer, Linehan, suffered a stroke during a livestream where he was wearing a wig and shouting about the "trans agenda". He is survived by an estranged child who asked to not be associated with her father for the purposes of this article.'
- Ryan Butcher, 'head of news' at *Pink News*, the website that has run so many hit pieces on me that I keep having to rewrite the number as I work on this book, tweets: 'There is a Father Ted Musical that is make or break for him. Let's

get it banned from theatres, lads!!!!!'

- I am regularly called a Nazi sympathiser, Holocaust denier, Covid denier and climate-change denier.
- *Pink News* runs a story accusing me and my therapist friend Stella O'Malley of assembling a 'horrifying database' of therapists 'willing to abuse young people'. We threaten legal action. The story is immediately taken down.
- When the feminist YouTuber Magdalen Berns is dying of a brain tumour at the age of just thirty-six, my visit to her is surrounded by so much vicious gossip that I have to interrupt the family's grieving to ask them to release a statement refuting it.
- Someone tweets I want to have sex with Magdalen Berns' corpse.
- Someone else tweets that I should be tried and convicted for sex crimes, chemically castrated, and have 'rapist' tattooed on my shaved head to warn others about me.
- Fake posts on Mumsnet in which I 'confess' to sending women photos of my penis are widely circulated, along with a faked screenshot in which I am supposed to have said: 'I had to send my daughter's friend home today. I couldn't stand looking at the state she was dressed in. A child dressed up like a whore is distracting aside from the obvious moral implications.'
- Day after day, the same trans activists who destroyed my marriage mock me for being divorced.

Do something I would never do. Do a search on my name. Do an image search on my name, or any kind of search of my name. My reputation has been completely destroyed by the same kind of coordinated, always-online men who went after Posie Parker, Holly Lawford-Smith, Abigail Shrier, Mark Fisher, Michael Bailey, Kathleen Stock, Magdalen Berns, Maya Forstater, Allison Bailey, Katherine Deves, Sall Grover, Ceri Black and countless other people, mainly women, whose names and bravery in the face of this insult, this onslaught, this all-out war, would fill another book.

I thought Jimmy, Arthur, Neil and Paul could see what was happening from their ringside seats: that my opponent had a horseshoe in his glove and the referee was in on it. I thought they had some sympathy for what I was enduring, but now I realise that I was just being managed.

During Covid, I had written a sitcom for Jimmy called 'Cancelled' that tried to laugh off what happens to artists who step out of line. I should have realised that it would never get made the moment I got back notes from a sensitivity reader, something I was only vaguely aware existed until that point. Jimmy, in a panic, quickly told me that I could ignore the notes. But the fact that Hat Trick uses a sensitivity reader at all provides some clue as to why comedy is in such a grim state at the moment.

I think there was one note that said something like 'people might think you're making fun of diversity and inclusion measures'. Too fucking right I was. They are a tool for elites, not the marginalised. Women were living in fear of these measures which made everyday resistance to males in their spaces taboo.

Whenever you see an anonymous Twitter account belonging to a 'Terf', check their timeline. You won't find any abuse, you'll hardly find any bad language. It's not how women tend to communicate with each other. The reason they're anonymous is that in 2023 it is simply unsafe for your career and your family's safety to be a feminist. The 'diversity and inclusion measures' hanging over every workplace don't cover fifty-one percent of the population.

Arthur, Neil and Paul properly broke my heart, though. I had known all of them for the better part of my life, in every meaning of the phrase. Paul's humour and sense of showmanship had always been inspirational. I still count Neil as one of the greatest songwriters of all time. I can't forget the achievement I shared with Arthur of *Father Ted*; together, we had broken the ice that had formed over Ireland's religious past, and played some part in allowing the country to start moving forward. But soon after the meeting where Jimmy tried to remove me from the show, I realised with a plunging sensation of dread, one that even cut through the anxiety medication and made my heart fall into my stomach, that they all must have given their consent for what he'd done.

Each betrayal sits in my memory like crows dotted along a telephone wire. And I'm far from alone. Once, on my website, I asked people to talk about those they had lost because of their involvement in this debate. Here's a selection of the replies:

I had a friend/penpal I met through a fandom we shared. We used to text and share cards but they blocked me and called me disgusting when I shared my view that biological males shouldn't be allowed to compete on women's sports teams.

One of my longest friendships. We had been mates for almost two decades. She never said anything, just ghosted me entirely. It hurt.

My younger brother and his husband. Two gay men who thought it completely all right that if you say how you identify then that's what you are. I told them I thought they were missing the point. They unfriended me about a year ago. No contact since. I suppose this means 'no debate'.

I volunteered at the local hospital. Was close to a girl that called me Auntie, I called her niece. She went to college bisexual, came back pansexual, calling me a hateful bigot for being a lesbian. I had not changed at all. But suddenly in her eyes, I became a hateful bigot.

I lost a lifelong friend (35+ years) over it.

I'm literally being kicked out of my home for my gender critical views at this time and also lost a close friend for this reason.

I lost a twenty-two-year friendship because of who I'm friends with and my activism. More concerned about being 'tainted by association'. She slowly shut me out until I confronted her and she admitted it. Now that whole friend circle, people I've known for up to twenty years, have all distanced themselves. They were my closest friends.

When my friend of more than twenty years, the journalist and broadcaster Jon Ronson, got back in touch after publicly criticising my support for fairness in women's sports and my opposition to men being placed in women's prisons, I thought the penny had finally dropped for him and he had found his next big subject. As the author of *So You've Been Publicly Shamed*, his 2015 book which contained sympathetic portrayals of other victims of online mobs, I presumed he had suddenly realised how the internet was industrialising the practice of public shaming. I believed he wanted to make amends for not stepping in to help me when it was most needed.

Not a bit of it. Jon wriggled and thrashed every time I asked him a straight question. By email, I sent him some examples of the men invading lesbian dating apps such as Her (which I too joined, to prove the point that any man could). These men often made absolutely no effort to look like a woman, let alone 'live like a woman', whatever that is supposed to mean. I asked Jon if he thought they were male or female. He refused to answer. Men invading lesbian dating apps was the clearest evidence of homophobia and rape culture that I could present. Not only was Jon not covering it, not only was he unconcerned about it, I couldn't even get him to acknowledge it.

One day last summer, Baroness Emma Nicolson asked me to be her date for a Booker Prize party. Emma, a former Conservative MP who is now, in her ninth decade, a tireless member of the House of Lords, has taken up the fight for women with the same tenacity and poise that has characterised her long career in public life. One of her particular interests is single-sex provision in the NHS. She told me that, years ago, attacks on patients by other patients would happen quite frequently – especially male-on-female violence. This situation only changed thanks to a determined, thirty-year-long drive for single-sex wards by health ministers and MPs from both the UK's main parties. This drive had achieved ninety percent success by 2009 when, according to Emma, *something* happened and the NHS began to transform itself into what it is today: another institution dangerously giddy on gender identity.

'There was a simple document called Annex B,' she told me in an email, 'which declared that – contrary to official policy to date – women's wards became inclusive of males claiming womanhood.' Those male patients claiming to be women were to be recorded as female. Nearby women patients weren't to be told there was a male-bodied person on their ward. If any of them simply used their eyes and complained at what they saw, they were to be assured that 'transwomen are women'.

'If they questioned the nurses, they were told the man was a woman. Thus, the assaults by male on female could not happen. Yet, since the male of the species is innately wishful of intimacy with females, of course it did happen.'

'Wishful of intimacy with females' is why I love Emma. She's as classy as I am not, but her dry language hides deep concern. She added: 'Annex B lies contrary to good practice, as the Acts of Parliament declare that personal dignity and privacy are paramount. A male in the bed of a female destroys that legal obligation of the hospital to provide care and protection for their patients.' This is only good news for one particular group. The internet didn't just give rise to an online Stasi, it also provided every Jimmy Savile with a global constituency of Jimmy Saviles, suddenly able to coordinate and organise politically, eliminating entirely the need to be slipped a set of hospital keys.

Emma's late husband was Sir Michael Caine – not the actor, but the head of the food wholesaler, Booker. It was he who set up the UK's most prestigious literary prize and, after his death, Emma became a trustee of the Booker Foundation, and later an honorary vice-president. When she began speaking out in defence of women's sex-based rights, a group of well-known writers denounced her and she was promptly sacked from that honorary role.

One of the pretexts was a tweet about the trans model, Munroe Bergdorf, for which Emma publicly apologised, even inviting Bergdorf for a meal. It then emerged that her main accuser, the Scottish writer Damian Barr, had posted a string of derogatory tweets about 'trannies' in the days before the trans cause became fashionable. As poacher turned witch-hunter, he was immediately forgiven by his trans activist friends and remains a cosy member of the literary establishment. Emma, by contrast, was condemned.

By last year, she had been cautiously allowed back into the Booker Prize tent, with an invitation to the party for the shortlist announcement. As her date, I felt a bit like John Merrick at the opera. Publishing, as I've previously highlighted with stories like that of Rachel Rooney, is a highly captured industry.

That said, the evening produced a few green shoots of hope. I met someone from the Society of Authors who whispered to me, 'Sorry about Joanne.' That was a reference to Joanne Harris, the Society's snarky chair, who has made no attempt not to take sides in the industry's culture wars. 'And sorry about everything you've gone through.'

I was grateful, but even at its worst, I was beginning to see that it hadn't all been bad. I've experienced moments of great kindness. The women at the American feminist organisation WoLF sent a letter of condolence when my father died, and expressed gratitude that he passed on his values to me. Two entirely different women who I've still never met each gave me £8,000 when I was being sued, because they thought it might help keep my marriage together; another gave me £16,000, and has not seemed overly concerned about ever getting it back (although she may read that sentence with alarm). Jonathan Ross showed me great kindness and was perhaps the only one of our friends who tried to help my wife and me keep our family together. A therapist who specialised in trauma gave me free sessions for the best part of a year. When I try to pay contributors to my website, they refuse to accept the money.

Father Ted's exact words, in a sentence he decided to leave unfinished, were: 'Nazis go around in black, telling people what to do, whereas priests...' No one minded that Nazi comparison, funnily enough. Still, these days I'm more careful with my wording. Having given the matter careful thought, it's clear to me that trans rights activists are more like nascent Nazis, before they were able to bureaucratise and normalise and make more efficient acts of unimaginable evil, and put the thugs carrying them out into natty uniforms.

Like National Socialism, gender ideology is a movement that attracts the worst of people. Time and time again, central figures in the trans rights movement are revealed as grifters, thugs, paedophiles or perverts, a loose conglomeration of the kind of people who in the past would have been drawn to a career in strike-breaking, or the Magdalene Laundries, or the tobacco industry, or private military contracting. From the crazed mothers of 'trans' kids to flat-out con-men using a trans identity to escape pesky creditors, many of them have significant followings on social media. This lends them an authority they do not merit, similar to the credibility bestowed on the rantings of lunatics by the normalising magic of spellcheck.

One year after Emma Nicholson emailed me about the disintegration of basic safeguarding principles at the NHS, a freedom of information request by Heather Binning of the Women's Rights Network revealed that 6,500 sexual attacks had occurred in

UK hospitals within three years.

That's forty-one attacks every week, for three years .

Despite her attendance at the shortlist party, Emma was, for the fourth year running, excluded from the main event: the award ceremony for the prize that was her late husband's legacy.

22

CHARGE!!!

A New Zealand playwright named Arthur Warring, a man I'd never met, got in touch to tell me about a blogging website called Substack which was hoping to hoover up all the people who were being silenced on social media, of whom I was just one. I'm not sure what I would have done if I hadn't fallen straight into the arms of this great service. With my Substack, 'The Glinner Update', I could begin earning a living again, now as a journalist. I give my articles away free because I think the material I'm uncovering – daily dispatches of mind-blowing stuff carried out in the service of extreme gender ideology – is too important to hide behind a paywall, but around ten percent of my subscribers are kind enough to donate. That's enough to keep me going, as long as I don't think too hard about the eye-watering tax bill that acts as the only reminder that I once had a television career.

The other thing I realised was that I had to get comfortable on

With my fellow YouTuber and close friend Helen Staniland (centre) and Karen Varley from Conservatives for Women

another platform. I quickly learned how to edit YouTube videos, but I learned even more quickly that I didn't want to edit YouTube videos, so I made friends with people who did. I also befriended Photoshop artists, journalists and humorists, many of whom had to stay anonymous because any association with me would lead trans rights activists to try to destroy their lives.

Soon my website was firing out emails several times a day because I was one of the few people reporting on the insanity of the gender movement, and the insanity continued to roll in, all day, every day. On my YouTube channel I also launched a talk show called *The Mess We're In*, which I co-host with Helen Staniland, the passionate Welsh feminist who has thrown herself into this battle on Twitter, and Arty Morty, a gay activist and writer based in Canada. We started to meet online once a week to broadcast an hour-long chat about the latest developments in what we all saw as an all-out war on women, keeping it funny and light as we explained to people what was going on.

In its two-year run (so far), we've produced over a hundred episodes, with our guests including politicians from across the political spectrum, such as Labour's Rosie Duffield and the Australian Liberal candidate Katherine Deves; respected scientists in the study of transsexualism (such as the sexologist Ray Blanchard); public figures who've been cancelled, among them Maya Forstater and the artist Jess De Wahls, whose work was briefly removed from the Royal Academy shop at the insistence of a single trans activist; journalists like Suzanne Moore and Helen Joyce; authors, publishers, activists, educators; trans-identified people such as Debbie Hayton, Fionne Orlander and Scott Newgent; and detransitioners including Ritchie Herron and Sinead Watson, whose bravery in speaking out about their situation has encouraged many others. Viewership continues to climb steadily, with an average of more than 11,000 viewers per episode. It's not Joe Rogan figures, but it'll do.

Many of us in this fight have had the same trajectory, in that trans activists told us to educate ourselves – and that's what we did. We went away and did the reading.

In 2022 I summoned up the courage to visit the Edinburgh Fringe. Stand-up comedy is another microclimate heavily patrolled by the enforcers of gender identity orthodoxy. There's a whole subset of trolls whom I know as the League of Terrible Comedians, and the online comedy news source *Chortle* is captured by activists. But my friend Elaine Miller was doing a show in the belly of the beast, and if she had the guts to mingle every night with people who hated her, then I figured the least I could do was buy a ticket and support her.

Elaine's show was called *Viva Your Vulva* and, as the title suggests, it was partly a biology lesson. A few days before my arrival, she received the much sought-after five-star-review from

The Scotsman, but she had also been targeted throughout the previous month by the usual suspects. Trans rights activists find any mention of female anatomy highly offensive, to the extent they have targeted for abuse Hibo Wardere, the Somali-born author and activist who has spent her life campaigning against female genital mutilation. After all, if female genital mutilation is real, then so are females, and that's currently one of the Forbidden Things That You Must Not Say. If you think that's an exaggeration, try asking a few left-wing politicians – or the editor of *The Guardian*, or Jon Ronson – what a woman is.

While walking to Elaine's show, I noticed a poster for another act, with a guy dressed as Jesus gurning at the camera, and it occurred to me that, in this particular moment, there were few safer targets for humour than organised religion. The Catholic Church was still a force to be reckoned with when we created *Father Ted*, so making fun of it had a point. The point also gave it an edge, more keenly felt in Ireland than in the UK, but there nonetheless. But the New God is the God of Gender, who has an American accent and more money than the Catholic Church during the Renaissance.

When Moses went up Mount Sinai to get the Ten Commandments, he had only been gone five minutes when his followers started worshipping a statue of a cow. In the same way, we installed this new god just where God used to be, in the cavernous hole left by his departure. Corporations rather than churches led the call to prayer, their articles of faith as mysterious and arcane as the Virgin Birth and the Holy Spirit. Instead of those science-defying miracles, we now had children who had been born in the wrong body, their true selves only blossoming into existence over the jagged lines of a fresh double mastectomy. With its remembrance months and awareness weeks and international days of action, the gender movement has more holy days than a medieval calendar, and many, many men 'dressing up and telling us what to do', to paraphrase Ted. An ideology imported wholesale from the high priests of America's broken academia, heavily funded by big business and enforced by a left-wing online class who resemble a religious police, gender now holds a position in society roughly equivalent to the one the Catholic Church held in Ireland when I was still chucking ten pence pieces into arcade cabinets and the Boomtown Rats released 'Banana Republic' with its refrain *Everywhere I go/ Everywhere I see/ The black and blue uniforms/ Police and priests*.

Elaine's show was aimed at all women, including those who identify as male. This was another charge added to her rap sheet. One of the orthodoxies of the new god is that you must on no account remind these women (confusingly called 'transmen') that they are actually female, even if that means their understanding of their own health is limited or non-existent. Elaine knew that this made her cheerful and empowering show a highly political event in a Fringe that had somehow come to represent stifling artistic conformity and intellectual dishonesty.

The same year, the other victim of the religious police who now run the Fringe was the comedian Jerry Sadowitz. Sadowitz's graveyard misanthropy had been a staple in Edinburgh for decades, but now he was cancelled after a single show at the Pleasance Theatre. The activists working there had done what they had set out to do, just as the activists at the Old Vic robbed London of a production of Stephen Sondheim's *Into the Woods* because of ex-Python Terry Gilliam's involvement. (Gilliam's crime was to have made a joke about being a 'black lesbian in transition'.)

One of the things I always liked about Sadowitz is how he himself looks like something that jumped from a deck of cards. Vulpine smile under a top hat and Jewish curls, a joker and a jester in the classic sense, one who wears the king's nerves to a dangerous extent. In a time of rampant conformity, the jester should be a protected species. We should be breeding them like pandas, not pushing them towards extinction.

In Beatrice Otto's history of court jesters, *Fools Are Everywhere*, she writes: 'I cannot think of one instance of jesters being documented with incomprehension. People do not seem to write along the lines of "the Emperor revived an ancient custom and brought a thing called a *jester* into his court".' What we have in the jester is a tradition stretching across history, across cultures. It may now have met its match in a group of privileged, authoritarian, middle-class theatre kids telling us what we can and cannot think.

Today, the emperor's throne is occupied by these children, traumatised after being raised by iPads, scanning the court for opportunities to be offended. For this task, they have the acuity of hawks; in everything else, they are as docile and trusting as cows. They would march into a slaughterhouse as long as someone gave them the WiFi password.

Sadowitz's show was summarily shut down with barely any acknowledgement from the UK comedy establishment that something momentous was happening. By this time I was accustomed to the cowardice of my old colleagues, but I still couldn't believe the silence that met the news. If there was anyone to rally around, it was him. Well, in fact it was Elaine, but Sadowitz would have been safer. In defending a fellow jester, they could have defended free speech and comedy without even mentioning women's rights. But even this is beyond the group of comedians I used to know, who used to challenge their audiences and now just caper for them. The ticket punchers at the Pleasance had worked Sadowitz over, and when they should have been on the scene, the comedy community became aware of something remarkable, something that had eluded their notice until then, happening down the street, and out of earshot of the sound of thumps and jangling bells.

It's because of Elaine that I know that everyone who starts cross-sex hormones – an established pathway for teenage girls who decide they want to be boys – will go into early menopause. Sometimes, that means thirty years too early. The same women will also be at far greater risk of osteoporosis. Oestrogen is known to have a protective effect on the female heart, so suddenly heart failure comes into the picture. There is sufficient evidence for medical organisations specialising in multiple sclerosis to write articles on how to meet the needs of the growing numbers of young, transitioned women seeking treatment. These are just the health catastrophes we know about, and they are lurking around the corner for young people whom no one thought to warn of the risks of medical transition. It's another scandal in plain view, just lying around, with few journalists and even fewer politicians interested in picking it up, because their kids might shout at them.

'We can guess what will happen to female bodies who start cross-sex hormones at a young age,' Elaine had told me, 'because we have the example of female athletes who were doped with anabolic steroids by Eastern Bloc countries in the seventies and eighties. These women were masculinised by the steroids and a disproportionate number of them seem to have passed away prematurely. I doubt that a human could get fitter than an Olympian, yet it appears that a number of them died suddenly of cardiac issues. I think only MI5 will know the full story.'

No data is being collected on transmen – women who want to be men – who die prematurely. In fact, if a woman has a gender recognition certificate, then her death will be officially registered as that of a male. Elaine added: 'I do see on social media cases of sudden unexplained deaths of people in their thirties who transitioned ten or more years earlier. What's behind that? Is anyone looking into it? Does anyone care?'

Viva Your Vulva was described by one theatre critic as 'heading to be the most loathed show on the Fringe'. Elaine's audience was treated with cold hostility by many of the staff at the Gilded Balloon. When I met her for a drink beforehand, she told me that the night before, a male comedian spat at her on the street. Even something as clearly benevolent as this show must be destroyed, its creator demoralised, because women may no longer assemble to discuss anything that doesn't involve men, and because gender identity is the new religion that you must not mock.

At Elaine's venue, the staff guided me straight to the show and away from the bar as if I were an unexploded bomb. If the staff didn't like Elaine's audience, they certainly weren't going to make an exception for me. Luckily, my escorts appeared to be fans and were perfectly genial. I certainly received better treatment than those who attended her show only the day before – a staff member had to be relocated when he began hassling women he saw waiting to go into the theatre, complaining that they were giving off 'Terf vibes'. The open hostility and aggression displayed by these young men towards women never fails to astonish me.

After the show, I went for some drinks in a distant bar with Elaine and some of her friends and supporters. I had a feeling I was still being shepherded away from anywhere that might excite gossip. The stress of an Edinburgh run is bad enough without making even more enemies among the staff working on your show. God knows how much worse I would make the situation if some drunk decided to concoct a drama with me in the Gilded Ballon. When lending support to friends, I have to consider that I can sometimes attract more hostility their way, notorious as I am. It doesn't help that I'm six foot three and as inconspicuous as an ostrich. I've often watched in anguish as my assistance turns into its opposite.

I never know the reaction I am going to get from people, so, as I passed two hipsters on the way back from Elaine's gig, I was relieved to get the same friendly nod I remembered from the days before I became infamous. In fact, the more I move about in meatspace, the better I feel about things.

It struck me that night that in the real world, even at the Edinburgh Fringe, most people do not really believe in gender ideology. Outside of these online hothouses where mediocre bullies flourish like triffids, words like 'cis' struggle for breath and traction. I've only ever had a handful of people looking for trouble. The rest of the time, it's those who want to thank me for *Father Ted* or for my activism. I get free coffees, free drinks in bars, even if I can never fully relax; a gunslinger at last, I do tend to sit with my back to the wall.

There's a theory that a successful ending to a story is one that works on three levels: technical, emotional and philosophical. Technical just means the workings of the plot are satisfied: the microfilm that must be delivered is delivered, or it is not. The emotional ending relates to whether the central character finally learns to love, or hope, or look after abandoned puppies, or what have you. If the main character doesn't sort out his shit, it's not a happy ending, even if the technical ending turned out OK. In *Jaws*, the technical ending is when Roy Scheider shoots the canister in the shark's mouth; the emotional one is when he paddles back to shore with Richard Dreyfus. When I saw that ending as a child, I almost shouted at the screen, 'HE'S NOT SCARED OF THE WATER NOW!'

This running negotiation between character and plot gives us a story, but great stories require a third aspect: the philosophical. A truly great story is one that asks a single question again and again, and finally, in the closing moments, provides some manner of answer, and that's what reverberates with us as we leave the cinema. 'People are basically good' may seem trite, but if a film makes a strong case for it, after a couple of painful hours where the matter was genuinely in question, the results can be profound.

What kind of ending will this one be, the one that comes just after I finally realised that even those closest to me were never coming to help? In one episode of *The IT Crowd*, I gave Roy the line, 'People – what a bunch of bastards', and I understand his view. I don't think I have words for how disappointing so many people have been. When I broke cover for the line of trees and shouted 'Charge!', there should have been more than one person from my past running alongside me. Only James Dreyfus was there and, because he was so isolated, he's suffered ever since. God knows, both he and I have explained our entirely conventional opinions a thousand times. We didn't just mumble something and run, like Simon Pegg in the sketch.

People – what a bunch of bastards.

And yet, and yet…

I think of my Dad. 'Why would you want to read that, when there are so many *beautiful* things in the world?'

A few months ago, I moved into a new flat, one that overlooks a particularly pretty part of London. I get the same little nods as I got that night from the two hipsters in Edinburgh. I'm on my lowest dose of the anxiety medication yet. My flat is big enough for the kids to stay over, and I've nearly finished this book.

Gender identity has started to unravel. The deeply controversial Tavistock Centre is to close, to be replaced by regional clinics which will take a holistic approach to treating dysphoria, looking at what other factors may be involved when a child says they wish they were the opposite sex. Following Maya Forstater's groundbreaking legal victory, where she established beyond doubt that believing in biology is protected under the Equality Act, two more women treated appallingly by their employers, the ceramicist Claudia Clare and Denise Fahmy of the Arts Council, have won their cases at tribunals. And just today, as I put the finishing touches to this chapter, Mermaids has lost its baleful attempt to strip the LGB Alliance of its charity status. When Mermaids brought this case, attacking the only lesbian and gay charity in the UK which rejects gender ideology, it managed to put not only itself, but the entire gender machine, in the dock. Mermaids itself is now under statutory investigation, and the 'affirmation only' model for treating children who present as trans is at last being properly questioned.

During the case, the LGB Alliance's co-founder Kate Harris, a former fundraiser for Stonewall, burst into tears during questioning as she was forced to spell out the self-evident truth that lesbians don't have penises. Having to refute these ludicrous lies in a British courtroom is a special torment that society has suddenly

With Kate Harris and Bev Jackson, founders of the LGB Alliance, at their first conference. Kate and Bev are two of the bravest women I've ever met, which is saying a lot, because I hang out with a lot of brave women these days

decided lesbians need to experience, even those like Kate and her co-founder Bev Jackson, who fought Section 28 and grieved through the Aids crisis. Like Fred Sargeant, who was present at every night of the original Stonewall riots and lived long enough to see 'queer' revisionists rewrite gay history before his eyes, Kate and Bev are gay elders who have been rewarded for a lifetime of service by being smeared as bigots by figures such as the Good Law Project's Jolyon Maugham, whose ludicrous name I dream of never having to spell again, and the SNP's disgraceful John Nicolson, who wasn't even out of the closet when Kate and Bev were out fighting for his rights.

Kate's a tough cookie. It takes a lot to make her cry, and she'll probably be embarrassed I've included the moment in this book. But it was pivotal. Anyone watching the tribunal on video link or reading the media reports afterwards could see the homophobia encoded into the heart of the gender movement.

One of my new friends, Ritchie Herron, a detransitioner who is now in his mid-thirties, texts me.

'Big news coming.'

These days, there always is.

I heard somewhere that five years is the average length of time it takes for a period of madness to take hold and then burn away. That timescale fits here, and it does feel like we're at the end of one cultural convulsion and the beginning of another. The war for public opinion has been won, the harassment of lesbians like Kathleen Stock and Allison Bailey can no longer be denied, and the thing we've been waiting for, the first legal actions taken against medical bodies involved in the transitioning of children have begun to happen.

Ritchie's big news turns out to be a judicial case, launched by himself and the father of another patient, against NHS England, for failing to provide appropriate treatment for adults with gender dysphoria, especially for patients who (like Ritchie and his co-petitioner's child) are on the autistic spectrum. Trans rights activists hate sunlight, and detransitioners like Ritchie, Sinead Watson and Keira Bell, who sued the Tavistock in another landmark case, are flinging open all the windows. Betrayed by society and abandoned by many of their friends, these brave people are an embarrassment to the activists who showered them with love and lies as they were making the worst decisions of their young lives. They are a living testimony to the madness that the Western world entered into about a decade ago. It's their voices – the children who followed the Pied Piper, but came back – that will lead others out of the trap.

I know that workplaces are filled with men and women who do

With Maya Forstater, Caroline ffiske and Heather Binning at the launch of their Respect My Sex campaign, raising women's rights at the 2022 local elections

not comply with these new religious observations, the pronoun declarations and days of silence for fictional dead trans kids. I had a duty to speak the truth because I didn't have a boss. I still don't, so I can just keep on telling the truth. That's all I can do. Tell the truth, and wait. I do still believe that most people are good and want to do the right thing, and if you're patient, they eventually will. As they say in poker, you just have to grow a leather ass.

My nerves have been shredded, though. For these last six years, I'd found it almost impossible to completely relax. Even when playing a computer game – about the only thing that would take my mind off what was happening – I could feel that the muscles at the root of my tongue were rigid, as if something inside me was continually prevaricating between a fight or flight response; that indecision was all contained in a single muscle in my mouth which I didn't know how to unclench.

In fact the last time I remember being completely at ease was just after my operation, when I still had trouble moving. I was lying in bed, the afternoon sun falling onto the bed through the window, my daughter gripping me tightly around my neck. She couldn't let me go because of the fright of what had just happened to us. She didn't say anything, she just held on. I wasn't complaining. She held on and on.

When I was a teenager, I barely understood stand-up comedy when I tried to give it a go. But now jokes have started occurring to me again, so, perhaps inspired by Elaine Miller's bravery in Edinburgh, I decide to have another crack at it. Why the hell not? After all, it's only been thirty-six years.

Comedy Unleashed, a club in Bethnal Green, is one of the few places on the comedy circuit that the new religious police don't bother patrolling. Devoted to free speech, it hosts comics who have at one point or another faced the wrath of the mob. When there, I often find myself shaking hands and apologising to people at whom I once shook a pitchfork myself. It never gets easier, but it's good for the soul.

Stand-up is a craft that you learn through doing, so I don't expect to kill on my first gig. If people recognise me, which is by no means certain, I know I can coast for a while on good will. Jerry Seinfeld said you have a grace period of ten minutes before the audience expect you to actually start being a comedian, even if you're a beloved celebrity. I figure I should ask for five minutes.

At the club, a comedian tells me: 'The circuit is rough at the moment. Half the night is spent reminding the audience they're allowed to laugh. You have to follow all these acts who are there because of an endless box-ticking exercise and they sort of police the laughs themselves, endlessly correcting themselves and apologising and admonishing. "As a white cis woman...", "as an Asian straight man..." None of them think they're allowed to make fun of anything beyond the range of their own experience.'

I wonder how that bodes for my trans material. I have a routine about solving the sports problem by allowing transwomen to be referees: 'I would imagine there is a shortage of women referees. Women don't give a fuck about rules. They're savages, they're barely human! Have you ever tried to teach one the rules of a board game?'

I have asked the promoter not to advertise the fact that I'm on. I want to start testing myself in front of audiences who perhaps don't know about the last six years of my life, but there is a miscommunication and the audience is heavily populated with feminists. Women who, like me, have been misrepresented, mocked, vilified, dragged through courts and employment tribunals, approached by police and told that if they insisted on having opinions then there was going to be trouble. And it all happened to them, to us, in plain view, on a stage, you might say. Yet journalists lost their pens, celebrities studied the ceiling, politicians made fools of themselves. Meanwhile, Emma Nicholson was robbed of a trace of her husband, Rachel Rooney was robbed of her career, Rosie Kay was robbed of her dance company.

As for myself, I was robbed of my marriage, of a musical that took me years to write, and of friendships I'd made over a working lifetime.

But now, in a small club in Bethnal Green, I'm surrounded again by friends, mostly women who saw each blow land and never left my corner. My plan to see how I go down cold is in the bin, but it doesn't matter. If I'm going to keep doing this, I need to give myself a few breaks.

I realise that this is a perfect way to kick things off, a comedy gig in front of what many would consider the toughest crowd of them all – feminists. Defamed throughout history as humourless, and not likely to be in the best of moods right now.

I'm drenched in sweat. Often, while moving my hands I take the microphone too far from my face and people miss crucial parts of the set-up or punchline. A couple of times, the lights dazzle me and I unconsciously try to move out of their glare. Stand-up is a craft, one I never even considered trying to learn until my career shrank to the size of this small, spotlit stage.

I get my first laugh, a sound like birds taking off, and finally, something within me begins to relax.

ACKNOWLEDGEMENTS

One of the best things about my strange new life is where I've ended up. Appropriately enough for my new, ghostlike existence, South London feels like a place out of time. The walk along the river makes me feel like I imagine Peter Ackroyd, the literary chronicler of London, must feel every day, deeply connected to the history of an extraordinary place, not just travelling over a bridge on the way to make a small slice of it. The future sweeps by too, or the heavily futurist present, in the form of the ferries that travel the river, hunt-class catamarans with 'Uber' written on the side, painted black and white like X-wings, the spaceships in *Star Wars* that first made me look at the credits at the end of a movie and set me on the road that has reached some sort of ending here.

I realise that along the way to this destination I made friends who have in common one particular trait. My circle now consists almost entirely of brave people. Brave men, but even braver women, because the punishments meted out to them are often far worse. The punishments have, in fact, been designed to hurt women more – shaming, threats of violence and social ostracisation – and were then easily transposed to the gay men and disobedient trans-identified people who joined the fight. Some of those people have helped me with this book, and many more have been inspirational. I am filled with horror at the idea that I will forget any of them. But here goes anyway.

My most immediate thanks go to my long-suffering editor Simon Edge, whom I have brought close to madness through my cluelessness as to what goes into the making of a book. I dread to think what this one would have been without his scrutiny and advice, but I know it would have been a thin shadow of what you now hold in your hands. I'm just as grateful to Dan Hiscocks for having the courage to commission it in 2020, at a time when the tide had not even come close to turning. Thanks for your courage and your foresight, Dan.

I am not my favourite subject matter, and the idea of writing a memoir was so abhorrent to me that it was especially difficult to get a first draft done. Luckily, I had another great friend in Arty Morty, who made that process far less painful by interviewing me and providing me with a solid starting point to write each chapter. He might be amazed to see how far the book has come, but it would not have made the journey at all had we not set off on it together. Thank you, Arty.

My eternal gratitude also goes to Jane Harris for the care she showed not just to *Tough Crowd* but to me, and the gift she gave me in providing an introduction to Polly Clark, my dear friend who kept me and the book going in the final crucial months. When we met, we both took it as a good sign that she shared a name with *Father Ted*'s romantic novelist crush, and our instincts were solid. Polly, you not only saved a book but probably saved my life. I'll never forget your kindness.

I'm slightly horrified that her name comes so far down the page, as Stella O'Malley was such a constant, reassuring presence that I have no doubt she also saved my life multiple times by putting each fresh disaster into emotional and historical perspective. She knew I was caught up in the gears of something huge and unprecedented, a victim of those 'interesting times' that the Chinese curse warns us about, and she gave me the tools I needed to survive them. It's a debt I'll never be able to repay.

Thank you also to Rosie Kay for agreeing to be interviewed for this book; to Rachel Rooney for giving me permission to quote the full text of her lovely, 'heretical' *My Body is Me!*, and to Bev Jackson, who provided my initial introduction to Eye Books.

Thanks to Christine for entrusting me with her amazing collection of production photos.

I've been blessed with the friendship of Alasdair Gunn and Saoirse Connolly, and my love goes out to them, to Joe Burgo, and to all others working at Genspect. The same goes for my colleagues on *The Mess We're In*, Arty, Helen Staniland and our producer, Jen Gill. We created something truly special in it, but even more valuable is the privilege of calling you all my friends. My thanks also go to all those guests who appeared on the show and helped us document an extraordinary time in history.

In addition I want to thank those who allowed me to publish their words on my Substack, some of whom I've never met in person, and others whom I only know through usernames that read like characters in fantastic fiction: ripx4nutmeg, Genevieve Gluck, Mole at the Counter, Girl Afraid, Robert Jessel, Patricia Naughton, James Roberts, Victoria Smith, Eliza Mondegreen, Bill Moon, Alan Henness, Innocent Bystander, Bryndís Blackadder, Rebekah Wershbale, Colette Colfer, Tom James, Julia Williams, Emma Bateman, Nev Wilkinson, Róisín Michaux, Rev Stuart Campbell, Chet Festive, 'Irish Woman', Clean City Bird, Neil Dorin, Laura Becker, but above all JL, who has tirelessly tracked the march of gender identity in her weekly 'War On Women' updates on my Substack. The constant onslaught of outrages would have been far too much for me to cover on my own, but they had to be covered. She caught everything that fell through the cracks and always refused payment for it, another small but significant act of kindness that convinced me to keep going in the very darkest days. Thank you, JL.

I would like to extend my deep gratitude to the countless individuals who contributed their talent, dedication and sweat to the various productions in which I had the privilege of being involved. I would name them, but I have to be mindful that a mention might be detrimental to their careers in a heavily captured entertainment industry. Hurting their prospects is the last thing I want to do.

My thanks also go to:

Those who took out a paid subscription to my Substack and kept me from bankruptcy while writing this book.

Kate Harris, Kate Barker, Malcolm Clark, Eileen Gallagher and everyone else at LGB Alliance.

Fred Sargeant, a legend from the Stonewall riots who fought for the truth even as history was being rewritten before his eyes. We'll never let them get away with it, Fred, don't worry about that.

Derrick Jensen, for his friendship, kindness and wisdom.

Kellie Jay-Keen, whose bravery has been a constant inspiration, Venice Allan, Aja the Empress and all I met at the various Let Women Speak events I've attended in London, Northern Ireland, Scotland and Wales, especially the stewards and speakers.

Jane Goldman and Jonathan Ross for their kindness.

Harry Miller, Sarah Phillimore and all at Fair Cop.

Everyone at the Free Speech Union. (Join the Free Speech Union!)

Dennis Kavanagh and all at the Gay Men's Network.

Everyone in The Room Where It Happens and my various secret WhatsApp groups. I'm particularly proud of helping to form the Norwich one, which is always a hive of activity. *Vive la résistance!*

Emma Nicholson, Maya Forstater, Lily Maynard, Allison Bailey, Heather Brunskell-Evans, Helen Joyce, Stephanie Davies-Arai,

Helen Saxby, Sharron Davies, Barry Wall, Martina Navratilova, Birdy Rose and Doozer, James Dreyfus, James Chiavarini, Dr Az Hakeem, James Esses, Lisa Marciano, Raquel Rosario Sánchez, Lisa Keogh, Milli Hill, Andy Lewis, Tonje Gjevjon, Sall Grover, Katherine Deves, Holly Lawford-Smith, David Bridle, Rachel Meade, Jess de Wahls, Ceri and Lauren Black, Rosie Duffield, Miriam Cates, Beth Grossman, Lissa Evans, Anna Loutfi, Rose Anderson, Jo Bartosch, Elaine Miller, Andrew Doyle, Benjamin Boyce, Ella, Michael Biggs, Susan Evans, Paul Bowen, Ally McCormack, Amparo, Andrew Thorne, Bernard Lane, Paul Bowen, Arthur Warring, Joanna Cherry, Sarah Campbell, Nina Paley, Caroline ffiske, Sarah Kingwell, Sherena, Stella Weller, Elle, Michael Foran, Kate Coleman, Damian Corless, Stephen Wilson, Kara Dansky, Homunculus, Billy Bragg in a Billion, Dave Baxter, Kaz, Hatpinwoman, Emma Hilton, Eldur Isidór Deville, Rebecca Johnson, Christian Henson, Mark Meechan, Kathryn Jones, Josh Howie, Ed Frew, Sarah Holmes, KFP, Queen Meabh, Gareth Roberts, Keith Jordan, Chris Elston, Glenn Rickwood and Robin Gibson, Sinéad Watson, Keira Bell and Ritchie Herron.

The women who were publicly fighting this fight before most of us were aware something dark was happening. They provided me with insight, theory and paved the way for others to follow. Joan Smith, Germaine Greer, Julie Bindel, Kathleen Stock, Suzanne Moore, Jane Clare Jones and Hadley Freeman are some of the best-known examples, but there are many more.

The women of the Women's Rights Network, Labour Women's Declaration, Conservatives for Women, Liberal Voice for Women, the SEEN Network, Women's Liberation Front, Sex Matters, Fair Play For Women, For Women Scotland, Get the L Out, the Independent Council on Women's Sports (ICONS) and Woman's Place UK.

The friends I made among the trans community, among them Miranda Yardley, Seven Hex, Fionne Orlander, Debbie Hayton, Dr María Inés de la Cruz, Aaron Kimberley, Aaron Terrell and Corinna

Cohn.

Liz Berns and all who knew and loved Magdalen Berns, a woman who will be remembered in the same breath as those who fought at Stonewall. A lesbian who fought bravely against heterosexual oppression and orthodoxy when it was deeply unfashionable to do so. This book is dedicated to my daughter but I offer it also in memory of Mags. There should be a blue plaque outside any building she inhabited.

My sister Christine and my brothers Gavin and John.

My mum and dad, who never lost faith.

My kids, the best thing that ever happened to me.

PICTURE CREDITS

Author's family collection:
p23, 26, 97, 138, 233

Additional sources:
p80, 83, 94, 99, 101, 104, 113, 139, 140, 143, 145: Christine Cant
p264, 273: Karen Varley
p248, 275: anonymous contributors
p279: Polly Clark